ADVANCE PRAISE FOR

Dangerous Dames

"*Dangerous Dames* is a thoughtful and richly descriptive continuation of the critical conversation begun in *Bad Girls*. As definitions and understandings of feminism continue to evolve, we remain tasked with attending to the interaction between media representations and both new and older generations of cultural audiences. The book identifies the material conditions which necessitate critique, explains the significance of popular representations of women's lives, and offers a clearly articulated justification for selection of the films and other media examined in the book. *Dangerous Dames* demonstrates that cultural ambivalence is still in play with representations of women; the female characters can resist—but not dismantle—the structural inequalities in contemporary American culture. The authors' selection of films demonstrates the hunger that exists for narrative empowerment of women in popular culture while carefully walking with the reader through the possibilities for change arising from those depictions. The book convincingly argues that while popular imagination has evolved progressively since *Bad Girls* was published, it still does not fully encompass the burden of inequality on the lives of women and girls."

—A. Susan Owen (University of Puget Sound) and Sarah Stein (North Carolina State University), co-authors of *Bad Girls: Cultural Politics and Media Representations of Transgressive Women*

"*Dangerous Dames* skillfully coordinates critical encounters with contemporary media texts. Through sustained analysis of texts like *Hunger Games*, *Wonder Woman*, *Proud Mary*, *Caprica*, and *Deus Ex*, Hundley, Chevrette, and Jones astutely demonstrate the cultural and political stakes of representing powerful, female-bodied characters. Across their case studies, they investigate the politics of aesthetics, arguing that particular aesthetics shape (but do not determine) political efficacies and asserting a tempered but hopeful relationship between media representations and structural change. Throughout, the authors imply the question—What does feminism want?—to which they respond: To be understood as plural, variegated, contestatory, and dynamic. Compellingly, they mark their own analytic starting point as intersectional, and they model, for beginners and experts alike, how to select and employ specific conceptual resources like performativity, necropolitics, and posthumanism to best unpack and illuminate the case under investigation. Media fans themselves, Hundley, Chevrette, and Jones invite us to struggle with our fandom and to be accountable for the joy or pleasure we take from media consumption as they demonstrate how recent pop culture texts are riddled with cultural and political ambivalence. *Dangerous Dames* helps us to find the words to explain our complicated relationships with media texts that feel—that are, we hope—feminist and progressive."

—Daniel C. Brouwer (Arizona State University)

Dangerous Dames

CULTURAL MEDIA STUDIES

Leandra H. Hernández and Amanda R. Martinez
Series Editors

Vol. 1

The Cultural Media Studies series is part
of the Peter Lang Media and Communication list.
Every volume is peer reviewed and meets
the highest quality standards for content and production.

PETER LANG
New York • Bern • Berlin
Brussels • Vienna • Oxford • Warsaw

Heather L. Hundley, Roberta Chevrette,
and Hillary A. Jones

Dangerous Dames

Representing Female-Bodied
Empowerment in Postfeminist Media

PETER LANG
New York • Bern • Berlin
Brussels • Vienna • Oxford • Warsaw

Library of Congress Cataloging-in-Publication Data

Names: Hundley, Heather L., author. | Chevrette, Roberta, author. |
Jones, Hillary A., author.
Title: Dangerous dames: representing female empowerment in postfeminist
media / Heather L. Hundley, Roberta Chevrette, & Hillary A. Jones.
Description: New York: Peter Lang, 2020.
Series: Cultural media studies; vol. 1
ISSN 2641-1415 (print) | ISSN 2577-6231 (online)
Includes bibliographical references and index.
Identifiers: LCCN 2018055998 | ISBN 978-1-4331-6301-2 (hardback: alk. paper)
ISBN 978-1-4331-6302-9 (paperback: alk. paper) | ISBN 978-1-4331-6303-6 (ebook pdf)
ISBN 978-1-4331-6304-3 (epub) | ISBN 978-1-4331-6305-0 (mobi)
Subjects: LCSH: Women heroes in mass media.
Classification: LCC P94.5.W65 H86 2019 | DDC 302.23082—dc23
LC record available at https://lccn.loc.gov/2018055998
DOI 10.3726/b14812

Bibliographic information published by **Die Deutsche Nationalbibliothek**.
Die Deutsche Nationalbibliothek lists this publication in the "Deutsche
Nationalbibliografie"; detailed bibliographic data are available
on the Internet at http://dnb.d-nb.de/.

The paper in this book meets the guidelines for permanence and durability
of the Committee on Production Guidelines for Book Longevity
of the Council of Library Resources.

To all the dangerous dames: stay dangerous.

CONTENTS

Acknowledgements   ix

Introduction: Paradoxes of Gendered Power Relations
and Representations   1

Chapter 1. Superficial Postfeminist and Postmodern
Portrayals: Hegemonic and Hypermasculine Ideologies in
Kill Bill, Volumes 1 & 2   23

Chapter 2. Appropriating Feminism: The Naturalization of Patriarchal
Power Structures in *The Hunger Games*   43

Chapter 3. Ass-Kicking Women and the Fight for Justice:
Constructing a (White) Feminine/ist Icon in
Wonder Woman   67

Chapter 4. Visualizing Violent Femininity: Race, Sex and Femmes
Fatales in *Atomic Blonde* and *Proud Mary*   89

Chapter 5. Hybridizing and Networking Beyond Boundaries: Cyborgs
           and Cognispheres in the *Bionic Woman* and *Dark Matter*   111

Chapter 6. Transcending Boundaries: Posthumanism and
           Transhumanism in *Caprica* and *Deus Ex*   133

           Conclusion: Envisioning Feminist Futures   153

           Index   169

ACKNOWLEDGEMENTS

In one way, this project began as an office conversation, and yet it extends *Bad Girls: Cultural Politics and Media Representations of Transgressive Women*. Therefore, we express our gratitude to its authors A. Susan Owen, Sarah R. Stein, and Leah R. Vande Berg. Their voices from the Mothership, articulating their care and concern for the future, have been heard loud and clear. Our aim was to augment their insightful brilliance.

Although these foremothers provided a model, our professors introduced us to a foundation of knowledge. Hailing from different academic programs enabled us to strengthen our argument, critique texts, and learn from each other. Therefore, we are grateful to the layers of educators, including our professors, colleagues, mentors, and students who ask questions, challenge us, and afford opportunities for thinking about our culture in a variety of ways.

We extend our thanks to the Peter Lang Cultural Media Studies series editors Leandra H. Hernández and Amanda R. Martinez. Their interest in how political, cultural, and media landscapes help shape our society coalesced with ours and created a home for our work. Furthermore, we appreciate the professionals at Peter Lang who were always supportive and responsive. They not only materialized our thoughts but marketed and distributed these ideas, allowing others access. We are also grateful to the Office of Research at Middle Tennessee State University for assisting with some production costs.

First and foremost, Heather Hundley wants all readers to know that the authors participated equally, despite the listing of names on its cover. She feels fortunate to have met and collaborated with Roberta Chevrette and Hillary A. Jones. For this, she forever thanks them and other dangerous dames in the world for questioning and challenging the status quo as well as considering possibilities for an improved future.

Roberta Chevrette offers gratitude to her coauthors, Daniel Brouwer, Amira de la Garza, Aaron Hess, Karen Leong, Vicky MacLean, Sujatha Moni, and Tom Nakayama for inspiring ways of thinking and being. She thanks the dangerous dames whose friendships carry through the years and over state lines and extends a special thank you to Ashleigh McKinzie for porch writing sessions, Gino Giannini for a chapter title idea that helped issue forth this project, JoAnn Chevrette for her support, and Jordan Knight for keeping Nashville life filled with love, joy, and music. She would also like to thank her Women in the Media Fall 2018 students for fueling her scholarship with their insights, passions, and hope for a better world.

Hillary Jones extends appreciation to her coauthors, for rigorous readings and research, lively exchanges, and careful editing. She would like to thank Amber Davisson for introducing her to Roberta and Heather. She is grateful for an engaging conversation with Josh Korpela that led her to play the *Deus Ex* games. She would like to recognize her colleagues Shane Moreman, Diane Blair, Aimee Rickman, Kathleen Domenig, Carl Burgchardt, and Marnel Niles Goins for their unflagging support. Finally, Hillary thanks Greg Lankenau for sitting through repeated viewings and play sessions, talking through ideas, reading drafts and providing feedback, and exhibiting patience and unwavering encouragement through the birthing of this book.

INTRODUCTION: PARADOXES OF GENDERED POWER RELATIONS AND REPRESENTATIONS

Power relations are gendered, organizing bodies and relationships in significant ways—sometimes with devastating results. According to a report from the United Nations, one in three women worldwide has experienced intimate partner violence or sexual violence ("The World's Women," 2015). An alarming 41 % of transgender youth in the United States have attempted suicide (Haas, Rodgers, & Herman, 2014). Men—especially black men—in the United States are incarcerated at disturbing rates, most frequently for non-violent crimes (Wagner & Sawyer, 2018). Mass shootings continue to increase in the United States, and 98 % of perpetrators are white males (Follman, Aronsen, & Pan, 2018). The United Nations estimates approximately 70 % of the world's poor are women, suggesting patriarchy disproportionately impoverishes female bodies (Abercrombie & Hastings, 2016). Each of these statistics reveals the material consequences of gendering power as cis, white, and hegemonically masculine. Nevertheless, increasing access to power is something we are taught to desire and strive to accomplish.

A ubiquitous concept often associated with physical or economic strength, power aligns with masculinity because men frequently possess stronger physiques. In a patriarchal, heteronormative landscape, economic power is gendered as masculine because men are awarded higher salaries, positioning them as household breadwinners in heterosexual relationships. Furthermore, they have greater access to corporate positions of power. The top 10 wealthiest people in the United States are men, and, according to the Associated Press (2017), "the eight individuals who own as much as half of the rest of the planet are all men" (para. 1). For example, Dwayne "The Rock" Johnson, known for his brute strength, chiseled features, and wealth, models the linking of power and hypermasculinity. Through success partly derived from his size and strength, he became Hollywood's second highest paid actor, earning $65 million in 2017, and he is considering entering politics (Kelsey, 2018). Similarly, older generations witnessed Arnold Schwarzenegger transition from world famous bodybuilder to actor to politician, serving as California's two-term governor from 2003 to 2011 and illustrating the entangled relationships (and stereotypically masculine associations) among physical strength, economic prowess, and political influence.

Although power is marked as masculine in many ways, contemporary society is not void of feminine empowerment. Just over 50 years since the beginning of the major civil rights movements of the 1960s and 1970s, including Civil Rights, Women's Liberation and the second wave of feminism, the American Indian Movement, Chican@ Rights, the Farmworker's Movement, and the launch of environmentalism and ecofeminism, we have witnessed positive strides for women in the United States. Victories such as the Food and Drug Administration's 1960 approval of the oral contraceptive pill and the Supreme Court's decision in Roe v. Wade (1973) have allowed women to control their own reproductive rights, moving towards women's status today. Additionally, though not yet fully actualized, the Equal Pay Act of 1963 and Title VII of the Civil Rights Act of 1964 encouraged more women to enter the workforce.[1] Recognition of sexual harassment and sexual assault has increased dramatically in the past 50 years, leading to contemporary agitation globally. With increased resources and legal protections available, more women attend universities and earn bachelor's degrees, participate in all levels of government, fight in combat, and lead as business tycoons—venues where women were not permitted in the not-too-distant past.

Although women have always been strong and powerful, those who stand out as cultural icons typically have been the exception rather than the rule. For example, although female-bodied aviators abound (Haynsworth, Toomey, & McInerney, 1998), Amelia Earhart is the lone woman in aviation known widely prior to 1970s astronaut Sally Ride. Rosa Parks ironically takes a back seat to her male counterparts, including Malcolm X, Stokely Carmichael, and

Martin Luther King, Jr. Similarly, civil rights activist and labor leader Dolores Huerta is overshadowed by her co-founder of the National Farmworkers Association, César Chávez (Sowards, 2010, 2012). Media mogul Oprah Winfrey, touted by *Forbes* and *Fortune* as one of the world's most powerful women, "is the only person in the world to have appeared in *Time's* list of the most influential people 10 times" (Nearmy, 2016, para. 1). Yet, the ongoing prevalence of gender and race disparities in Hollywood continue to draw scholarly attention (Reign, 2018; Thompson, 2018).

Nevertheless, trailblazing figures have led the way for other strong and powerful women. Since the 1980s, female-bodied aviators and astronauts have become much more commonplace. Female-bodied politicians have increased, as well. For example, 39 women have served as governors in 28 states, 307 women have served in Congress, and 19 of the 100 largest cities in the United States have had female-bodied mayors ("A brief history," 2016). Women's presence has increased in the boardroom too, with 24 women leading Fortune 500 companies as CEOs. In 1981, Sandra Day O'Connor emerged as the first, and only, female-bodied Supreme Court Justice until Ruth Bader Ginsburg joined her in 1993. More headway has been made since 1/3 of the bench are women in 2019: Ruth Bader Ginsburg, Sonia Sotomayor, and Elena Kagan. At the box office, *Wonder Woman*, directed by Patty Jenkins, set a new record for a movie directed by a woman in 2017. Such gains have ushered in, for some, the notion that we are now in a postfeminist era. The concept of postfeminism is "fraught with contradictions" (Genz & Brabon, 2009, p. 1), but it consistently denotes the perception that gender equality has arrived—or at least is well on its way—and therefore feminism is no longer needed.

We reject this depoliticizing, perilous viewpoint. Despite the advances made, much work remains at the forefront of feminist activism. For example, even though 59 different women have been to space, that pales in comparison to the 474 male astronauts who have made the same journey. In terms of politicians, the record number of female-bodied governors at any given time was nine in 2004 and 2007; thus only 5 % of the states in the country were governed by women. Similarly, women head only 5 % of Fortune 500 companies. Although Hollywood too is shifting, Patty Jenkins is only the second woman to be the sole director of any live-action movie with a production budget over $100 million (Domonoske, 2017).

In addition to continued underrepresentation in government, economics, and on screen, the gender wage gap in 2016 was 20 % and even larger for women of color, guaranteed paid maternity leave is not available in the

United States, and the second shift persists, with many women still being expected to maintain household, childcare, and parental care responsibilities irrespective of having paid jobs. Indeed, the second shift has expanded into a third, as digital labor has expanded to fill women's leisure time as well (Chess, 2010; Jarrett, 2016; Jones, 2016). Women are overlooked for career advancement more than their male colleagues. In academia, for example, even though women earn just over 50 % of the U.S.-granted Ph.Ds., only 38 % of faculty members overall are women; 46 % are assistant professors, 38 % are associate professors, and 23 % are full professors (Mason, 2011). Considering the occupation alongside family and parenting responsibilities, "across all disciplines, women with children were 38 percent less likely than men with children to achieve tenure" (Mason, 2011, para. 11). "Among tenured professors, only 44 percent of women are married with children, compared with 77 percent of men" (Mason, 2011, para. 14). Thus, even though women are making advances, constraints abound, as evidenced by the glass ceiling and pay gaps, the good-old-boys club, disparate family obligations, social expectations, and sexual harassment, among other obstacles.

Beyond these ongoing structural challenges, the advances made have sparked a backlash. Rising to fame for refusing to honor students' requests to use their preferred pronouns, Jordan B. Peterson typifies this backlash (Bowles, 2018; Lynskey, 2018; Wilhelm, 2018). Bowles (2018) calls him the "custodian of the patriarchy," noting his view that "order is masculine. Chaos is feminine" (para. 3). Wilhelm (2018) describes him as "best known for offending and outraging large numbers of people on television and the Internet over various fraught topics like transgender pronouns, gender roles, and identity politics" (para. 5). He has attracted a large following (and sparked some backlash of his own), exemplifying how outrage is deployed to try to protect the status quo and nostalgic imagined past. Women's advances are perceived as dangerous, and folks like Peterson are actively trying to maintain patriarchal positions of power.

Despite these structural, material, and rhetorical efforts to retain patriarchal power relations, as a result of the 1960s and 1970s movements and ongoing activism, younger generations are exposed to powerful women in greater numbers than in the past. As roles for women have expanded in government and business, so too have roles expanded for women in mediated representations. Indeed, media companies have been quick to capitalize on feminist gains by casting female-bodied protagonists in roles traditionally reserved for males.

Such representations have ushered in a postfeminist media era in which "perniciously effective," active, and overlapping cultural processes work towards the "undoing of feminism[s]" (McRobbie, 2004, p. 255). A number of scholars have traced postfeminist media's defining characteristics (Gill, 2007, 2016, 2017; McRobbie, 2004; Tasker & Negra, 2007). Gill (2017) summarizes the features she first identified in 2007, including

> the notion of femininity as a bodily property; the shift from objectification to subjec-
> tification; an emphasis upon self-surveillance, monitoring and self-discipline; a focus
> on individualism, choice and empowerment; the dominance of a makeover paradigm;
> and a resurgence of ideas about natural sexual difference. (pp. 615–616)

These characteristics have only intensified as postfeminism has expanded and reified, to the point that Gill suggests postfeminism now acts as a "gendered neoliberalism" (p. 620). This has led to postfeminist representations of women who are sexually liberated, reject feminism, or occupy positions of power in "men's" milieu, including sports and the military.

As feminists, we seek to illuminate the rhetorical work performed by contemporary representations of a specific type of postfeminist hero who has garnered a cache of cultural capital: the contemporary female-bodied action hero who is smart, capable, physically agile and fit, accomplished in her career, and proficient with weaponry and technology. We recognize that gender exists on a continuum, including nonbinary and trans experiences and expressions. Our use of the term "female-bodied" as well as "women" in our analyses is not to privilege a harmful and exclusionary biological definition of gender. Instead, our use of these terms is intended to reflect slippages between sex and gender in the popular imagination, and especially in the media construction of dangerous dames.

Fierce, frequently sexy, often feminine but sometimes androgynous, these heroes take no shit. Not only are their female bodies a focal point for their construction as strong and exceptional action heroes and women, but they are also frequently characterized by presumptions regarding biological "essences." It is precisely this conflation of sex and gender that we seek to illuminate and problematize as we examine constructions of gender routed through sex stereotypes. We note that persons of all genders, sexes, and sexualities are affected by the subject positions proffered by these texts; the gendered exclusions within the rhetorical construction of the "female-bodied" warrior are thus at the heart of our analyses. Examining examples of these representations over the last quarter of a century and across media, we ask: what equipment and constraints emerge from these portrayals of dangerous dames with greater access to power? Do women exhibiting these powerful characteristics provide us with new or unique equipment for living and feminist ways of being? What complications or contradictions arise for meaningful feminist action via these mediated representations?

Why Study Representation?

We have briefly traced some of the challenges and gains made by women in the past 50 years. Why frame a study focused on media representations in this manner? Because representation can have life or death stakes. For example, would you be able to tell if someone were drowning? Retired U.S. Coast Guard Chief Warrant Officer 2 Vittone (2013) wryly notes, "Drowning is almost always a deceptively quiet event. The waving, splashing, and yelling that dramatic conditioning (television) prepares us to look for, is rarely seen in real life" (para. 2). If people only learn to recognize drowning from televisual misrepresentations, as a society we risk placing people in dire danger. Similarly, we do not equip non-experts to recognize the symptoms of a heart attack. Corliss (2017) explains, "People sometimes describe heart attack symptoms as chest discomfort or pressure, while others say they feel an intense, crushing sensation or a deep ache similar to a toothache" (para. 3). Real heart attacks may occur as depicted in fictional narratives—as dramatic pain radiating from the chest down the left arm—but many individuals do not share these symptoms. This limited representation has the potential to cost someone their life. Representations can be very serious indeed.

Representations also affect what people imagine as ideal. Pollan (1998) documents how McDonald's aesthetic demands for picturesque, uniform French fries led them to purchase almost exclusively Russet Burbank potatoes. Unfortunately, these potatoes are prone to net necrosis. Pollan explains that to overcome this purely cosmetic defect, farmers "must spray their fields with some of the most toxic chemicals in use" (para. 51). Farmers avoid their fields for days after spraying and must tent harvested potatoes to off-gas prior to shipment. The desire for a reproduction of the image of a perfect fry, long and golden without lines or spots, superseded concerns about consumers' or suppliers' health, environmental ramifications, or nutritional content (granted, this might be asking a lot of a fast food item). This image created real-world demand and grave effects. Representations of an ideal can supersede what it signifies.

Representations may even be indistinguishable from that which they represent. Magritte's wry, surreal paintings such as "The Treachery of Images" ("*Ceci n'est pas une pipe*") and "Not to be Reproduced" emphasize the futility of reproductions and symbols to capture truth. He critiqued representation almost 100 years ago, but these paintings eerily presage the contemporary world. In digital spaces, for example, representation is the same as the real. How are the words from one's lips more "real" than those one types into a phone? Indeed, sometimes the image or representation might be more "real" than the "real" thing. For example, take Barthes's (1977) discussion of Italianicity. When U.S. American students are asked to depict "Italy," they frequently and consistently draw from marketing imagery of marinara sauce, pasta, and pizza. Students who have travelled to Italy often disclose that they have been disappointed to find it is not "Italian" enough! In this manner, the image supplants the real.

Baudrillard (1994b) saw this implosion coming. Drawing on the ancient Epicureans' concept of the simulacra, he theorized how the copy and the real implode in hyperreality, which typifies our contemporary symbolic landscape. When the sign/signifier are coterminous and inextricably intermingled, the representation and the real become indistinguishable. We recirculate symbols, images, and ideas. Signs do not refer only to signifiers; as Baudrillard (1994a) posits, they gesture, over and over, to other signs until their point of origin ceases to matter. Meaning emerges from the circulation and reproduction of ideas and images, such that the presentation and the representation are the same.

This collapse of the symbol and its referent animates much of our communication in contemporary contexts, and symbols and stories affect our understanding of the world and visions for the future. Rhetoric is energy. It has the capacity to move others, via purposeful persuasion, constitutive creation, or epistemological shifts of how people understand, navigate, and imagine the world. Thus, engaging with fictional and speculative narratives hardly can be divorced from analyzing the "real" world. It *is* the real world, and it helps us to think, to envision, and to act in new ways in fictional, digital, and material contexts. In other words, if symbols constitute reality and make possibilities and ideals legible, then to understand reality, now and for the future, we must study representations.

Our Approaches

Our approaches are grounded in our training as critical/cultural communication scholars specializing in rhetorical criticism and media studies. We view texts as created artifacts manifesting symbols that have consequences for audiences' beliefs, values, imaginations, and actions. Although this may seem obvious, these aspects of media—their symbolic nature and their consequentiality—are unique contributions rhetorical scholars bring to studying media.

We acknowledge a range of reading positions regarding media's rhetorical functions. They include the uncritical view of media as directly representing reality, expressed positions that mediated texts are "mere entertainment," and views of media as potentially perpetuating beliefs for *some* audiences but not for the individual expressing the view. As rhetoricians and teachers, we challenge these claims. We view media as profoundly impactful in their circulation of specific representations. Even though they emerge within particular histories, contexts, and media landscapes, they are malleable. We believe rhetors make symbolic choices—whether deliberately, routinely, or inadvertently—when creating a text in any medium. It is the rhetorical critic's task to investigate these resulting symbols, and it is our task as teachers to help students understand how media and representations function rhetorically.

Rhetorical criticism entails close, methodical analysis of a symbolic artifact. In analyzing representations in film, television shows, and other media, rhetorical scholars might analyze many aspects of a text. For example, in studying characters, the critic might consider what characters say, the narrative functions they play (e.g., protagonist, villain, supporting character), their occupations, their physical bodies (tall, short, fat, thin, attractive, etc.), their capabilities (strong, weak, superhuman, skilled, able-bodied, apprenticing, etc.), their interactions with others, the clothes they wear, the places they appear… and so on. In addition, rhetorical scholars of media attend to details of production, such as cinematography, sound design, sets, lighting, and other elements, depending on the particular medium. Finally, they may consider political economy and reception, attending to ownership, production, circulation, dissemination, and audience.

As McGee (1990/2009) famously articulated, rhetorical scholars do not encounter and critique bounded objects of study; instead, they create their objects through the choices they make with their critical analyses. In this book, we have chosen to construct artifacts including films, television shows, and video games. We read these texts as constituting and circulating ideas about gender, feminine/ist empowerment, and postfeminism that influence the audiences who encounter them.

Theory and method closely intertwine in rhetorical criticism, with different theories providing lenses through which we analyze texts (Jasinski, 2001).

The theories that most centrally inform our project and the stances we take in this book are drawn from critical/cultural studies and feminist approaches. An awareness of theoretical intersections and lived experience undergirds the work of both critical/cultural and feminist scholars. Cultural studies scholars routinely study subjects and the positions available to them in society and in cultural narratives (Hall, 1997). For those of us who opt to study media texts, representations provide a fruitful way to access the cultural imaginary (Rushing & Frentz, 1991). Barthes (1974) delineates how texts can range from readerly (very open to interpretation) to writerly (more constrained by the rhetor's purported intended meaning). The representations in both types of texts help us account for the rhetorical constraints and possibilities present in society.

Critical/cultural approaches further attune critics to the significance of popular culture in perpetuating ideology and hence foreground questions of power as it relates to sociopolitical structures, institutions, and everyday practices. As critical/cultural scholars seeking to advance social justice, we study symbolic representations to illuminate how narratives articulate and how they function rhetorically. Representations produce and govern knowledge, expectations, what we envision as ideal, and even the nature of reality. When we analyze representations, whether identities or other factors that shape culture (e.g., colonialism, displacement, political economy, family structures, etc.), scholars can explore how these mediated visions affect how we see ourselves as individuals and societies. Therefore, our various chapters employ a range of critical theories to inform our readings of specific texts; these include ideological criticism, biopower, necropolitics, critical race theory and whiteness studies, gender performativity, and posthumanism.

Feminist approaches focus our attention on the gendering of representations, identities, and subjectivities. Our analyses take an intersectional approach that understands systems of gender as constructed through and in relation to other interlocking systems of power and oppression including race, nation, class, ability, sexuality, and empire (Carastathis, 2016; Crenshaw, 1989, 1990; Davis, 1983; Hill Collins, 2000; Hill Collins & Bilge, 2016; Moraga & Anzaldúa, 2015). Feminist approaches understand media as located within wider visual economies that produce gendered gazes and the imagistic manipulation of bodies (Dow, 2006; Lotz, 2001; Modleski, 1991; Projansky, 2001). Finally, feminist approaches attend to the ways women's agency frequently manifests through the construction of alternative sources of power *within* systems of subordination.

The rigorous analyses of media's ideological functions we engage in throughout this book might seem to discount the notion that media offer audiences sources of pleasure, relaxation, and escape. We suspect this is why students often initially express reluctance to treat entertainment media as sites where oppressive and exploitative power relations are perpetuated. As bell hooks notes, audiences wish to reserve "a certain sense of magic" for the arena of media (Jhally, 1997). We do not deny media's ability to create, inspire, entertain, and provide audiences with pleasure. In nearly all the cases featured here, we enjoyed viewing (or playing) the artifacts we analyzed. Barthes (1975) differentiates between *plaisir*, pure pleasure more akin to escapism, and *jouissance*, a joy grounded in play more akin to epiphany. Ott (2004, 2007) extends this, detailing the erotics of reading, emphasizing the joy of engaging with media texts. We experienced *plaisir*, and we derived an eroticized *jouissance* from analyzing them critically and deeply in order to render a complex, nuanced reading of each one.

Who We Are

We write as women, feminists, and scholars in the communication discipline. In interrogating representations of fierce feminine empowerment in contemporary mediated texts, we are fueled by our own intergenerational experiences as they relate to feminist activism and theorizing. Through individual encounters with sexism, sexual harassment, and sexual assault, we have witnessed, and felt, the truth of second wave feminists' claim that "the personal is political" and the relevance of the contemporary #MeToo movement. We honor the truths women of color have voiced about second wave feminism's erasures and ignorance of the positionalities of all but middle-class white women.[2] We remain cognizant that, despite women of color repeatedly raising these points, the bias of white feminism is, in many ways, intact.

In our own teaching and writing, we have embraced the shifts in thinking and theorizing enabled by critical race theory, intersectionality, and whiteness studies; transnational, comparative, and postcolonial feminisms; Indigenous feminisms; ecofeminism; and posthumanist feminism, among others. We have witnessed the emergence of postfeminist narratives and have observed the easy alignments between hegemonic masculinity, neoliberalism, and the narrow definition of "feminism" as individual agency and sexual pleasure presented in postfeminist mediated texts. Our interest in writing this book emerges from the collisions of these frames, which are entangled within the media we engage with as well as within our own personal lives.

The embodied histories and present experiences informing our writing extend beyond and intersect with our gendered positions. Heather is white, U.S. American, a full professor and administrator, heterosexual, married, and from a rural, West Coast, middle-class family background. Hillary is white, U.S. American, an advanced assistant professor, married, cisgender, and from a rural, Great Plains, working class family background. Roberta is white, U.S. American, an early assistant professor, bisexual, femme, divorced, and from a rural, West Coast, lower middle-class family background. None of us are raising children. We are all the first person in our families to earn a PhD, and we all left the places we were raised and now live in urban or suburban environments. Although simple to list, these and other demographic aspects of our identities have complex effects on the perspectives we bring to our research, as do dimensions of our pasts that have led us to the study of feminisms, gender, and representation.

Heather's interest in media began at an early age when, as a latchkey child of divorce, television and her brothers kept her company. As an adolescent in the 1970s and a teen in the 1980s, she encountered the emergence of shows featuring working women as their main characters, such as *Police Woman*, *The Mary Tyler Moore Show*, *Alice*, *One Day at a Time* and *The Bionic Woman*, and she saw the movement of white women into mainstream rock music in performers like Heart, Blondie, and Linda Ronstadt. Growing up, she rejected stereotypical notions of being a girl (such as playing with dolls and wearing dresses) and instead enjoyed participating in sports and other outdoor activities considered to be reserved for "boys" at the time. In fact, in high school she was involved in creating her school's first girls' soccer team, noting the lower quality of field compared to the established boys' team regardless of making the playoffs every season. Despite recognizing that boys were treated differently (read: better), she did not come to identify as a feminist until she was in her late 20s, although others told her that she was.

Hillary was an adolescent a decade later, in the late 1980s, a time featuring popular television with strong women such as *Designing Women* and *The Golden Girls* and outspoken musicians expanding the norms of gender expression, like Prince and Madonna. An avid reader, media geek, and gamer, she was always drawn to independent, strong female-bodied protagonists: Charlotte and her web; Anne of Green Gables; Eustacia Vye chafing at the open moors; Clair Huxtable's work/life balance; Murphy Brown's independence; the fierce battles waged by Buffy, Willow, and Cordelia. The experience that most stirred her to feminism was struggling with Chopin's *The Awakening*. Her undergraduate education helped her to move from judging Edna Pontellier for a dereliction of duty to understanding how we, as a society, fail people when we constrain choice structurally and individually. She quickly evolved to a feminism that was intellectual and political.

Roberta's adolescence in the early 1990s was marked by a continued expansion in the types of women's roles on television, but her shows of choice were *90210* and *Days of Our Lives*, both centered around gender-stereotypic representations and heterosexual relationships. As a child, she was enamored with beauty, lipstick, and high heels, and she would even dress the family cat in frilly princess dresses. Following her father's AIDS-related suicide in 1991, she and her sister were raised by her mother, a high school teacher who never remarried. Roberta's identification as a queer feminist began in high school when she first started listening to Ani DiFranco's music, in which lyrical assertions such as "I ain't no damsel in distress" and "I am a one-woman army" illustrate the kinds of claims to power that characterize the media texts we analyze in this book.

For each of us, our feminist awakenings gave voice to experiences of subordination and inequality we had encountered. Despite the decades spanned by our childhood and adolescence and the range of positions we held in relation to femininity and feminism, one interesting commonality emerges from these stories of our early years: we all came to feminism around the same time, within a span of just a few years in the late 1990s. This is the same period during which sexy female-bodied protagonists became normal, displacing the previously male-dominated world of violence and action en masse. As stylized media representations of ass-kicking women in features like *Buffy the Vampire Slayer*, *Xena: Warrior Princess*, *Alias*, *Kill Bill*, and *Tomb Raider* proliferated, seemingly empowered women took to screens, ushering in an era of postfeminist banality. Perhaps it is more than a coincidence that from our varied histories a mutual interest was born. Of course, all of our relationships to and understandings of feminism have changed drastically in the intervening years as we continue to read, engage in discussions with other feminists, and encounter more life experiences. We share these brief narratives of our subject positions to offer a starting point for considering our relationships to the artifacts we construct, drawn from texts in which a particular version of women's strength—as dangerous, sexy, futuristic, and agentic—challenges and reinscribes gender norms, stereotypes, and binaries.

From our feminist perspectives, the standpoints we bring to our analyses, of course, matter. Our experiences as white women understanding and living through second and third wave feminisms is the place from which we begin our inquiry of postfeminist media representations, their possibilities, and their limitations. To that end, however, we note that although we write as "we" throughout the book, given our collaboration on its content, we are cautious of the unifying voice as it relates to the historic and ongoing universalizing second wave aspirations for solidarity, similarity, and global sisterhood. We did not agree on every point initially, and points of disagreement, divergence, and alternative interpretations led to robust conversations that enriched the readings. We believe this layering reflects feminist approaches that honor intersectionality, difference, and multiplicity.

Why We Write

As critical scholars, feminists, and women, we write for many reasons, but primarily we write because we have something to say and we recognize our position of privilege in having a voice. As scholars, we earned our doctoral degrees learning how to formulate questions, inform our inquiries with theories, apply rigorous methods, and critically interrogate texts. We are not so bold to presume that our findings provide *the* answer, the only or definitive reading; rather, our critical, scholarly investigations offer insights into the contemporary cultural imaginary and open conversation, engaging in critical rhetorical pedagogy (Ott & Burgchardt, 2013). We are not employed at Research One institutions that impose intense pressure on scholars to produce research extremely quickly and place it in limited ("accepted") venues; instead, we work at teaching universities that allow for prolonged reflection and expect quality scholarship but afford us a wider variety of publishing venues.[3] Therefore, we do not write this book because we must do so to advance our careers. We write this book out of intellectual curiosity, as a way to enrich our teaching, as a form of feminist activism, as a response to those before us, and to offer thought-provoking perspectives to those after us.

We write this book because we share many second wave feminists' concerns regarding postfeminist representations of empowered women. As women serving as role models for younger generations has slowly become a norm rather than an exception, we fear youth might gain the impression that feminism is no longer needed, that women have finally reached entry into all aspects of life, and that gendered equality exists. Indeed, we sometimes hear such sentiments in our classrooms.

Despite representations of strong women, gendered equality does not yet exist. We write to address the cultural paradox between the mediated portrayal of powerful women and our social reality. We write because the June 29, 1998 cover of *Time* magazine asked, "Is Feminism Dead?" We write because we are concerned that postfeminist constructions of women's sexual agency can still disempower women through their reliance on body management and the male gaze. We write because of slut shaming. We write because discrimination and misogyny are still rampant. We write because legislators seek to roll back hard-won protections that save women's lives. We write because more than half of the women who are murdered in the United States are killed by their intimate partners (Petrosky, Blair et al., 2017).

We write because the United States elected a president who disclosed in 2005, "You know, I'm automatically attracted to beautiful—I just start kissing them. It's like a magnet. Just kiss. I don't even wait. And when you're a star, they let you do it. You can do anything. Grab 'em by the pussy. You can do anything."[4] We write because millions of people, donning pink pussy hats or not, participated in a worldwide protest January 21, 2017 advocating human rights and denouncing President Trump's election.[5] We write because the June 21, 2018 announcement that New Zealand Prime Minister, Jacinda Ardern, who was the first elected world leader to give birth while in office since Pakistan's Prime Minister Benazir Bhutto in 1990, made international news because a woman had chosen to have a family *and* a career.

We write because the 2017 *Time* magazine "Person of the Year" was "The Silence Breakers." We find the celebration of those who stood up "with individual acts of courage" (Felsenthal, 2017, p. 32) risking their livelihoods, personal safety, and reputations to speak out against sexual harassment and assault in the workplace, to be culturally significant. We are encouraged by the fact that "the women and men who have broken their silence span all races, all income classes, all occupations and virtually all corners of the globe" (Felsenthal, 2017, p. 37). As the #MeToo movement gains momentum, it overshadows those who spoke up and opposed sexual harassment and did not gain support prior to social media, and the embodied outcomes that will emerge from this mediated activism are not yet clear. We write because despite frequent media claims that "things are different" in the #MeToo era, Dr. Christine Blasey Ford's testimony regarding her sexual assault by Brett Kavanaugh failed to prevent his Supreme Court confirmation. We write because on the day of Ford's much publicized testimony, calls to the National Suicide Prevention hotline doubled the normal volume (Sacks, 2018). We write because women's voices continue to be silenced, dismissed, and unheard.

We write because feminists have work yet to do. We write because we hear the concerns from the Mothership (Owen, Stein, & Vande Berg, 2007), the voices of our feminist mentors, the critiques from women of color, and our internal dialogue questioning the intersection of second wave, third wave, and postfeminist concepts. We write because we experience the daily paradox between what we see in the media and what we live on the streets.

Finally, we write because representations matter. Symbols create realities and futures, and in a world where image and reality have collapsed into one another, we cannot become that which we cannot imagine. Burke (1973) notes that literature serves as "equipment for living" (p. 293). We can expand that to encompass all narratives, including those in the texts we investigate and the speculative narrative our inquiry itself offers. Exploration yields new scripts, new possibilities, and new ideas. Although we might extrapolate that texts serve as blueprints, based on this, they need not detail every action and outcome. Indeed, Jameson (2005) suggests the rhetorical function of utopian narratives—namely, hope—affords their primary force. The vision, whether its hopeful nature alone or the specifics depicted, provides new equipment, new ways of being and doing. We write because we are hopeful, and because rhetoric expands the boundaries of imagination.

Preview of Chapters

The book contains six content chapters, this introduction, and a conclusion. They proceed from intersectional analyses of ideological production, spectacular power, and gender and race performativity in a set of films to posthuman analyses of cyborgs and the cognisphere in science fiction television and video games. Our analyses focus on female-bodied protagonists and characters who exhibit signs of strength and power.[6] Throughout, we attend to the complexities of these representations of women's empowerment in postfeminist media.

Chapter 1, "Superficial Postfeminist and Postmodern Portrayals: Hegemonic and Hypermasculine Ideologies in Kill Bill, Volumes 1 & 2," analyzes identities among the female-bodied characters in Tarantino's 2003 and 2004 films. We attend to the lead, Beatrix Kiddo, as well as the ensemble of dangerous dames depicted in the films, in order to unpack how they are constructed rhetorically as professionally successful and strong, as women to be feared and revered. Although these messages are potentially empowering, the films' postfeminist messages and postmodern aesthetics mask the hypermasculine and patriarchal messages imbedded within the films' narrative.

Chapter 2, "Appropriating Feminism: The Naturalization of Patriarchal Power Structures in *The Hunger Games*," continues the ideological analysis begun in Chapter 1. The films depict the protagonist Katniss Everdeen as a postfeminist hero connected with the natural environment. The antagonist is a totalitarian government associated with hypercivilization. By juxtaposing the two, with nature prevailing over hypercivilization, patriarchal narratives, including the reaffirmation of traditional gender roles, the espousal of heteronormativity, and promotion of biological determinism, are naturalized. In doing so, the films appropriate feminism, granting credence to these traditional and limiting ideologies.

Building upon the first part of the book, Chapter 3, "Ass-Kicking Women and the Fight for Justice: Constructing a (White) Feminine/ist Icon in *Wonder Woman*," analyzes how Wonder Woman's 2017 big-screen iteration draws from her storied comic-book past and illuminates contradictions inherent in her representation as a feminist icon. Although the movie at times resists the male gaze and offers feminist critiques, Wonder Woman's portrayal repeats many of the elisions that have characterized liberal (white) feminism, including the embrace of Republican Motherhood, heteronormative structures, and gendered rhetorics of heroism that uphold racist, nationalist, and imperialist endeavors.

Chapter 4, "Visualizing Violent Femininity: Race, Sex and Femmes Fatales in *Atomic Blonde* and *Proud Mary*," turns to the sexualization and fetishization of women's strong bodies in the representation of two 21st century fighting femme protagonists. These female heroes embody many "masculine" characteristics in their on-screen enactments of violence, but both are configured within the tradition of the femme fatale popularized by mid-20th century film noir. By interrogating intersections of gender, race, and sexuality in the media construction of dangerous dames, this chapter illustrates how performative scripts combine to construct, and delimit, pop culture portrayals of women's strength.

In the final part of the book, we turn our attention to contemporary science fiction television and video games. Chapter 5, "Hybridizing and Networking Beyond Boundaries: Cyborgs and Cognispheres in the *Bionic Woman* and *Dark Matter*," considers dangerous dames who have had mechanical manipulations imposed upon them without their consent, turning them into cyborgs and intertwining them with the cognisphere. Employing a posthuman approach, the chapter explores how two Enlightenment binaries (mind/body and human/machine) are revivified and revised by the strong women in these two science fiction television series.

Chapter 6, "Transcending Boundaries: Posthumanism and Transhumanism in *Caprica* and *Deus Ex*," continues our examination of cyborgs and women connected with the cognisphere. Women who have chosen transhuman augmentation in the *Battlestar Galactica* prequel *Caprica* and the *Deus Ex* franchise of video games complicate several Enlightenment binaries: mind/body, self/other, us/them, and human/machine. Altogether, the dangerous dames challenge false dichotomies in ways that reveal the promise of the embodied cyborg and the distributed cognisphere for feminisms in posthuman contexts.

The conclusion, "Envisioning Feminist Futures," serves as an epilogue to our exploration. It features a succinct summary, connects themes across chapters, discusses the ramifications and implications of our analysis, and delineates our visions for the future. Throughout, we endeavor to illuminate the complex environments these dangerous dames navigate and the important rhetorical functions they perform across media. We identify equipment for living they provide, and we document the constraints they face. By doing so, we hope to advance the ongoing conversation about postfeminist media and perform some of the ongoing feminist work needed to actualize a more just and equitable future.

Notes

1. This change affected primarily white women; most women of color and low-income women had been working outside the home long before this time.
2. We utilize the wave framework here due to its recognizability while acknowledging critiques of the wave framework leveled by many feminist scholars. Nicholson (2010) argues that the wave framework is reductive, U.S.-centric, and elides the multiplicity and enduring work of feminist activisms not recognized by this framework. Those interested in learning more about some of the feminist activism led by women of color during the 1970s would do well to consult Roth (2004).
3. This is not intended to impose judgment on or assess the value of research conducted at research or teaching institutions. We are merely pointing out that this research is not motivated by external factors relating to our employment positions.
4. *The Washington Post* obtained and released the tape on October 7, 2016, a month prior to the presidential election.

5. The Women's March recurred January 20, 2018, with millions of people participating around the globe.

6. Throughout, we refer to characters by first names because several of the texts include numerous characters with the same last name (e.g., the Everdeens), and others have no last name (e.g., the title character from *Proud Mary*). To avoid differential treatment among the characters, therefore, we refer to all of them by their first names.

References

Abercrombie, S. H., & Hastings, S. L. (2016). Feminization of poverty. *The Wiley Blackwell Encyclopedia of Gender and Sexuality Studies, 1-3*. Wiley Online Library. doi:10.1002/9781118663219.wbegss550

Associated Press. (2017, January 16). Who are the 8 richest people? All men, mostly Americans. *NBC News*. Retrieved from https://www.nbcnews.com/news/us-news/who-are-8-richest-people-all-men-mostly-americans-n707421

Barthes, R. (1974). S/Z (R. Miller, Trans.). New York, NY: Hill & Wang.

Barthes, R. (1975). *The pleasure of the text* (R. Howard, Trans.). New York, NY: Hill & Wang.

Barthes, R. (1977). *Image – music – text* (S. Heath, Trans.). New York, NY: Hill & Wang.

Baudrillard, J. (1994a). *The illusion of the end* (C. Turner, Trans.). Stanford, CA: Stanford University Press.

Baudrillard, J. (1994b). *Simulacra and simulation* (S. F. Glaser, Trans.). Ann Arbor: University of Michigan Press.

A brief history of women in American politics. (2016, June 9). *Washington week*. Retrieved from http://www.pbs.org/weta/washingtonweek/blog-post/brief-history-women-american-politics

Bowles, N. (2018, May 18). Jordan Peterson, custodian of the patriarchy. *The New York Times*. Retrieved from https://www.nytimes.com/2018/05/18/style/jordan-peterson-12-rules-for-life.html

Burke, K. (1973). *The philosophy of literary form*. Berkeley: University of California Press.

Carastathis, A. (2016). *Intersectionality: Origins, contestations, horizons*. Lincoln: University of Nebraska Press.

Chess, S. (2010). How to play a feminist. *thirdspace: A Journal of Feminist Theory & Culture, 9*. Retrieved from http://journals.sfu.ca/thirdspace/index.php/journal/article/view/273

Corliss, J. (2017, April 17). Could you have a heart attack and not know it? *Harvard Health Blog*. Retrieved from https://www.health.harvard.edu/blog/heart-attack-not-know-20170 41711596

Crenshaw, K. (1989). Demarginalizing the intersection of race and sex: A black feminist critique of antidiscrimination doctrine, feminist theory and antiracist politics. *University of Chicago Legal Forum, 1*, 139–167.

Crenshaw, K. (1990). Mapping the margins: Intersectionality, identity politics, and violence against women of color. *Stanford Law Review, 43*(6), 1241–1299. doi:10.2307/12219039

Davis, A. Y. (1983). *Women, race, & class*. New York, NY: Random House.

Domonoske, C. (2017, June 5). 'Wonder Woman' smashes domestic box office record for female directors. *NPR*. Retrieved from https://www.npr.org/sections/thetwo-way/2017/06/05/531588482/wonder-woman-smashes-domestic-box-office-record-for-female-directors

Dow, B. (2006). The traffic in men and the *Fatal Attraction* of postfeminist masculinity. *Women's Studies in Communication, 29*(1), 113–131.

Felsenthal, E. (2017, December 18). The silence breakers: The voices that launched a movement. *Time*, 30–56, 58–62, 64, 66–68, 70–71.

Follman, M., Aronsen, G., & Pan, D. (2018, June 28). A guide to mass shootings in America. *Mother Jones*. Retrieved from https://www.motherjones.com/politics/2012/07/mass-shootings-map/

Genz, S., & Brabon, B. A. (2009). *Postfeminism: Cultural texts and theories*. Edinburgh, United Kingdom: Edinburgh University Press.

Gill, R. (2007). Postfeminist media culture: Elements of a sensibility. *European Journal of Cultural Studies, 10*(2), 147–166.

Gill, R. (2016). Post-postfeminism?: New feminist visibilities in postfeminist times. *Feminist Media Studies, 16*(4), 610–630.

Gill, R. (2017). The affective, cultural and psychic life of postfeminism: A postfeminist sensibility 10 years on. *European Journal of Cultural Studies, 20*(6), 606–626. doi:10.1177/1367549417733003

Haas, A. P., Rodgers, P. L., & Herman, J. L. (2014). *Suicide attempts among transgender and gender nonconforming adults: Findings of the national transgender discrimination survey*. American Foundation for Suicide Prevention, and the Williams Institute, UCLA School of Law. Retrieved from https://williamsinstitute.law.ucla.edu/wp-content/uploads/AFSP-Williams-Suicide-Report-Final.pdf

Hall, S. (1997). *Representation: Cultural representations and signifying practices*. Thousand Oaks, CA: Sage.

Haynsworth, L., Toomey, D. M., & McInerney, S. (1998). *Amelia Earhart's daughters: The wild and glorious story of American women aviators from World War II to the dawn of the space age*. New York, NY: William Morrow.

Hill Collins, P. (2000). *Black feminist thought: Knowledge, consciousness, and the politics of empowerment*. New York, NY: Routledge.

Hill Collins, P., & Bilge, S. (2016). *Intersectionality*. Malden, MA: Polity Press.

Jameson, F. (2005). *Archaeologies of the future: The desire called utopia and other science fictions*. New York, NY: Verso.

Jarrett, K. (2016). *Feminism, labour and digital media: The digital housewife*. New York, NY: Routledge.

Jasinski, J. (2001). The status of theory and method in rhetorical criticism. *Western Journal of Communication, 65*(3), 249–270. doi:10.1080/10570310109374705

Jhally, S. (Producer & Director). (1997). *bell hooks: Cultural criticism & transformation* [DVD]. Northampton, MA: Media Education Foundation.

Jones, H. (2016). New media producing new labor: Pinterest, yearning, and self-surveillance. *Critical Studies in Media Communication 33*(4), 352–365. doi:10.1080/15295036.2016.122 0017

Kelsey, E. (2018, April 2). Actor Dwayne 'The Rock' Johnson says he has struggled with depression. *Reuters Entertainment News*. Retrieved from https://www.reuters.com/article/us-people-dwaynejohnson/actor-dwayne-the-rock-johnson-says-he-has-struggled-with-depression-idUSKCN1H91PC

Lotz, A. D. (2001). Postfeminist television criticism: Rehabilitating critical terms and identifying postfeminist attributes. *Feminist Media Studies, 1*(1), 105–121.

Lynskey, D. (2018, February 7). How dangerous is Jordan B. Peterson, the rightwing professor who 'hit a hornets' nest'? *The Guardian*. Retrieved from https://www.theguardian.com/science/2018/feb/07/how-dangerous-is-jordan-b-peterson-the-rightwing-professor-who-hit-a-hornets-nest

Mason, M. A. (2011, March 9). The pyramid problem. *The Chronicle of Higher Education*. Retrieved from https://www.chronicle.com/article/The-Pyramid-Problem/126614

McGee, M. C. (1990/2009). Text, context, and the fragmentation of culture. *Western Journal of Speech Communication, 54*(3), 274–289. doi:10.1080/10570319009374343

McRobbie, A. (2004). Postfeminism and popular culture. *Feminist Media Studies 4*(3), 255–264.

Modleski, T. (1991). *Feminism without women: Culture and criticism in a 'postfeminist' age.* New York, NY: Routledge.

Moraga, C., & Anzaldúa, G. (Eds.). (2015). *This bridge called my back: Writings by radical women of color* (4th ed.). Albany: State University of New York Press.

Nearmy, T. (2016, June 13). Forbes' most powerful women in the world in 2016. *The Telegraph*, Business section. Retrieved from: https://www.telegraph.co.uk/business/2016/06/06/the-most-powerful-women-in-the-world/oprah-winfrey/

Nicholson, L. (2010). Feminism in "waves": Useful metaphor or not? *New Politics*, XII-4(48). Retrieved from: http://newpol.org/content/feminism-waves-useful-metaphor-or-not

Ott, B. L. (2004). (Re)locating pleasure in media studies: Toward an erotics of reading. *Communication and Critical/Cultural Studies, 1*(2), 194–212.

Ott, B. L. (2007). Television as lover, part II: Doing auto [erotic] ethnography. *Cultural Studies ↔ Critical Methodologies, 7*(3), 294–307.

Ott, B. L., & Burgchardt, C. R. (2013). On critical-rhetorical pedagogy: Dialoging with *Schindler's List*. *Western Journal of Communication, 77*(1), 14–33.

Owen, A. S., Stein, S. R., & Vande Berg, L. R. (2007). *Bad girls: Cultural politics and media representations of transgressive women*. New York, NY: Peter Lang.

Petrosky, E., Blair, J. M., Betz, C. J., Fowler, K. A., Jack, S. D., & Lyons, B. H. (2017, July 21). Racial and ethnic differences in homicides of adult women and the role of intimate partner violence: United States, 2003-2014. *Centers for Disease Control and Prevention, 66*(28), 741–746. Retrieved from https://www.cdc.gov/mmwr/volumes/66/wr/mm6628a1.htm?s_cid=mm6628a1_w

Pollan, M. (1998, October 25). Playing god in the garden. *New York Times Magazine*. Retrieved from https://www.nytimes.com/1998/10/25/magazine/playing-god-in-the-garden.html

Projansky, S. (2001). *Watching rape: Film and television in postfeminist culture*. New York: New York University Press.

Reign, A. (2018). Oscars so white is still relevant this year. *Vanity Fair*. Retrieved from https://www.vanityfair.com/hollywood/2018/03/oscarssowhite-is-still-relevant-this-year

Roth, B. (2004). *Separate roads to feminism: Black, Chicana, and White feminist movements in America's second wave*. Cambridge, United Kingdom: Cambridge University Press.

Rushing, J. H., & Frentz, T. S. (1991). Integrating ideology and archetype in rhetorical criticism. *Quarterly Journal of Speech*, 77(4), 385–406.

Sacks, E. (2018, September 28). During Kavanaugh-Ford hearing calls to sexual assault hotline spiked by 201 percent. *NBC News*. Retrieved from https://www.nbcnews.com/politics/politics-news/during-kavanaugh-ford-hearing-calls-sexual-assault-hotline-spiked-201-n914811

Wilhelm, H. (2018, January 26). The last gasps of outrage culture? Jordan Peterson's popularity as an author and commentator may indicate a coming backlash. *National Review*. Retrieved from https://www.nationalreview.com/2018/01/outrage-culture-backlash-jordan-peterson-12-rules-life-antidote-chaos/

· 1 ·

SUPERFICIAL POSTFEMINIST AND POSTMODERN PORTRAYALS: HEGEMONIC AND HYPERMASCULINE IDEOLOGIES IN *KILL BILL, VOLUMES 1 & 2*

We begin this book where *Bad Girls* (Owen, Stein, & Vande Berg, 2007) left off at the turn of the 21st century. In their analyses of media representations of transgressive women, Owen, Stein and Vande Berg argue that women and people of color are transgressive by their very nature because they are not at the top of the "rhetorically crafted…irrefutable social hierarchy" (p. 3). We agree, and we take this a step further. We claim that media representations of women and people of color not only are transgressive—they are also dangerous. The characters studied here are action heroes and villains, hence we embrace the polysemic nature of the term "danger." Literally, the characters we examine are dangerous to other characters by virtue of their superior abilities to fight, use weaponry, and outwit their enemy. Simultaneously, the characters are dangerous to society as they transgress the boundaries of gendered expectations and offer alternatives to traditional roles. Yet, we offer another conception for the term dangerous. At a cursory glance, the strong characters we examine in this book suggest we are in a postfeminist era, in which feminist aims of equality between men and women have been achieved.[1] Upon further investigation and deeper analysis, however, we find this superficial view dangerous to the millions of audience members and fans who approach these texts with an uncritical eye. The fierce females featured in our analyses transgress norms of femininity, and by disrupting societal expectations of the alignment of gender, sex, and sexuality, they trouble these relationships and reveal their social construction. At the same time, they also reproduce certain norms and codes of gender performance. Thus, the transgressive characters we feature are dangerous because they simultaneously threaten and reaffirm the established patriarchal status quo.

Considering that media maintain the ability to discipline feminist politics (Owen, Stein, & Vande Berg, 2007), that producing meaning is not a politically neutral activity (Hall, 1980), and that "the battles over gender in this country are never over, but only episodic" (Gronbeck, 2007, p. xviii; also see Phillips, 2004), we hear the concern voiced in *Bad Girls* about younger feminists forgetting the past when assaulted with numerous postfeminist depictions of "ass-kicking" female-bodied characters in television, film, gaming, digital spaces, and other mediated contexts.[2] As such, we continue this line of inquiry to explore dangerous mediated women in the first quarter of the 21st century, beginning with Quentin Tarantino's box office successes, *Kill Bill: Volume 1* and *Kill Bill: Volume 2* (Fusion, 2003; "Kill Bill" director, 2004).[3]

Released in October 2003 and April 2004 respectively, *Kill Bill: Volume 1* and *Kill Bill: Volume 2* were originally conceived of as one film. However, after realizing its lengthy run time, director Tarantino decided to split it into two films, releasing them six months apart (Fusion, 2003). The films, a box office success with a combined income of over $332 million worldwide ("Quentin Tarantino plans," 2009), tell the tale of an ex-member of the Deadly Viper Assassination Squad (DVAS),[4] Beatrix Kiddo, codename Black Mamba, known primarily throughout the first film as The Bride. Played by Uma Thurman, The Bride is a highly trained martial arts assassin adept with a katana.[5] After a romantic involvement with the organization's leader, Bill, she learns she is pregnant while on a mission. Within minutes of gaining this knowledge, she is confronted by another assassin. She pleads for her life and the life of her unborn child, promising to end her mission and walk away from her profession. Upon seeing the positive pregnancy test, the assassin spares their lives. Soon thereafter, Beatrix retreats into hiding and begins life anew, planning to marry a man unaware of her past. At the wedding rehearsal, however, Bill and the DVAS enter the chapel and kill everyone present. One final blow comes to The Bride; as she informs Bill it is his child, he shoots her in the head. Four and a half years later, she awakens from a coma and enacts her wrath as revenge, systematically killing all the DVAS members and anyone else who gets in her way, ending with Bill. The films detail her vengeance.

We examine these films because the number of powerful female-bodied characters they feature far exceeds most earlier cinema. Four of the six DVAS members are women. As they split up, one of them employs a female-bodied bodyguard, and a female-bodied assassin was tasked with killing Black Mamba before learning she was pregnant. Notably, upon the films' releases, the popular press highlighted the *femaleness* of the films' violence (Brown, 2006; Corliss, 2003; Medved, 2003; O'Brian, 2003). Although powerful and violent female-bodied characters existed prior to *Kill Bill* (Ripley in the *Alien* series [1979, 1986, 1992, 1997] played by Sigourney Weaver, Sarah Connor in *The Terminator* [1984] played by Linda Hamilton, Le Femme Nikita [1990] played by Anne Parillaud, Tank Girl [1995] played by Lori Petty, M played by Judi Dench in the James Bond series [1995–2012], G.I. Jane [1997] played by Demi Moore, and Lara Croft [2001] played by Angelina Jolie), they acted as solitary female-bodied characters. Given the large number of dangerous dames they include, the *Kill Bill* films pique our interest.

On the surface, *Kill Bill* presents postfeminist and postmodern messages and aesthetics. The films' visual elements establish a nostalgic, fragmented, intertextual, and non-linear spectacle of female-bodied power that seemingly celebrates multiculturalism. In doing so, the films stray from typical expectations of hegemonic femininity. The lead female-bodied characters are unflinchingly brutal as they engage in human death and destruction. By enabling the performance of transgression and gender deviance, these visuals serve to distract viewers from more restrictive patriarchal ideologies embedded within the texts. Postfeminism is markedly different than postmodernism, but the postmodern aesthetics in the *Kill Bill* films undermine the potential feminist and postfeminist messages. Specifically, women's power and strength proclaimed in feminism and postfeminism are essentially mocked with excess and spectacle vis-à-vis the excessive carnage, use of Japanese anime and characters' impossible feats defying gravity and the laws of physics. Ultimately, the films convey modern, patriarchal ideologies enshrouded in postfeminist and postmodern glitter.

Superficial Postfeminist Ideals

As a result of second wave feminists' quest for women's equality, "women are assuming lead roles in action narratives on a fairly regular basis" (Brown, 2015, p. 4; also see Jones, Bajec-Carter & Batchelor, 2014). We witness this increase beginning in 1979 with Ripley in the *Alien* series and continuing through contemporary texts; however, while many action movies incorporate one or two women who remain surrounded by male characters, the *Kill Bill* films are particularly rife with powerfully dangerous female-bodied characters. The members of DVAS include Beatrix Kiddo codename Black Mamba (Uma Thurman), Vernita Green codename Copperhead (Vivica A. Fox), Elle Driver codename California Mountain Snake (Daryl Hannah), and O-Ren Ishii codename Cottonmouth (Lucy Liu). Such prominence of leading female-bodied characters who are strong, capable, in control, and mirror typical male hero and villain behaviors clearly supports the idea that we live in a postfeminist era.

Not only are the films' antagonists and protagonists predominantly female-bodied, but the characters comprising the majority of the DVAS are competent, capable, decisive, determined, skilled, and strong. These positive portrayals align with the postfeminist suggestion that gender is no longer a limiting factor for women's career advancement, achievement, or strength.[6] Indeed, in creating these characters Tarantino aimed to provide role models: "I actually want 13-year-old girls to see this movie. I think this will be very empowering for them" (quoted in Medved, 2003, para. 12). These women were certainly at the top of their elite profession, with only two men—the leader and his brother—among the DVAS. In fact, female-bodied characters are just as likely as male characters to work in white collar and professional occupations (Children Now, 2004; Signorielli & Bacue, 1999; Signorielli & Kahlenberg, 2001; Steinke, 2005). The character Vernita Green (alias Mrs. Bell) was successful enough to retire at a relatively young age (in her 30s), and to marry and have a child as her second career. Elle Driver continued working as an advanced assassin, killing her and Beatrix's mentor, Pai Mei, a revered and feared martial artist, as well as her former colleague, Budd, their leader's brother and former DVAS member.

The second most successful member of DVAS, only behind Beatrix, was O-Ren Ishii. She built her professional reputation by avenging her father's death, killing a Japanese mafia-style boss, Matsumoto, and his two henchmen. According to Beatrix's voiceover, "By 20 she was one of the top female assassins in the world." Upon leaving DVAS, Ishii became her own boss and the leader of the mafia bosses in Tokyo. When Tanaka, a mafia boss, questioned why they should take orders from the half-Japanese, half-Chinese American, she decisively responded by cutting off his head with one swipe of her katana and said:

As your leader, I encourage you from time to time, and always in a respectful manner, to question my logic. If you're unconvinced that a particular plan of action I've
decided is the wisest, tell me so, but allow me to convince you and I promise you
right here and now, no subject will ever be taboo. Except, of course, the subject
that was just under discussion. The price you pay for bringing up either my Chinese
or American heritage as a negative is... I collect your fucking head. Just like this
fucker here. Now, if any of you sons of bitches got anything else to say, now's the
fucking time!

Notably, her ethnicity and nationality, not her sex or gender, generated concerns in her leadership. This particular intersection of interlocking power and
oppression unlocks gender as a possible contributing factor to read her as a
leader. The undertone supports postfeminism in its suggestion that race, not
sex or gender, is the only constraint O-Ren faces on her path to success.

The strong and decisive character Gogo Yubari, O-Ren's 17-year-old
bodyguard also draws on postfeminism, and especially its embrace of femininity and sexual power (Arthurs, 2003; Atwood, Brunt, & Cere, 2007; Lazar,
2006). Gogo's girlish youthfulness was emphasized and eroticized as she wore
a Catholic school girl outfit complete with a white button-up blouse, short
plaid skirt, long white socks, and Buster Brown shoes. She was further infan-
tilized (and sexualized) with her hair in pig-tail style braids and often seen
sucking on a lollypop. Rather than associating her age with innocence, it was
connected to her ruthless power, sexual desirability, and deficient self-control.
As Beatrix described: "what she lacks in age she makes up for in madness." In
one exemplary scene, Gogo propositioned a man at a bar, asking if he wanted
to "screw her." Surprised and excited, he answered "yes." She responded by
stabbing him in the gut, and as she pressed up against him with a firm grasp
on the impaled knife, thereby not allowing him to double over as he bled to
death, she challenged, "Do you still want to penetrate me or is it I who penetrate you?" This postfeminist scene reconfigures patriarchal notions regarding
who wields phallic (and deadly) power. Yet, her "madness" aligns with how
female-bodied power is subsumed within a patriarchal structure, positioning
her outside of masculine norms of rationality. Portraying her as out-of-con-
trol limits her power as she is unpredictable and, therefore, untrustworthy.
As with Lorraine in *Atomic Blonde* and Mary in *Proud Mary* (Chapter 4), she
aligns with the femme fatale/Eve figure who lures in men through (sexual)
deception causing him to face his mortality (Hallissy, 1987). Nevertheless,
audiences may hastily view her as a dangerously powerful teenage girl who can
easily measure up to or surpass adult male characters' abilities, thus suggesting
postfeminism has arrived.

The strongest and most successful dangerous dame is clearly the protagonist, Beatrix, who undoubtedly serves as a sign that postfeminism is part of our contemporary culture. Surrounded by formidable opponents, Beatrix's ability to defeat them positions her at the pinnacle of career success as a powerful, and unconquerable, assassin. Indeed, Elle noted her respect for her ex-colleague, describing her as "the greatest warrior that I have ever met." Viewers witness her survive being shot in the head, buried alive, and numerous other assassination attempts. Not only did she slay her former colleagues Vernita, Elle, O-Ren, and Bill, but she killed Gogo, a rapist, a potential rapist, and approximately 38 members of the Crazy 88 (O-Ren's assassin squad). Although she experienced hardships, she ended triumphant. This hearkens postfeminist heroism; these "heroines are sometimes simultaneously worshipped as goddesses, reviled as villainesses, raped and beaten as victims, lusted after as sex objects, [and] placed on pedestals as positive role models" (Jones, Bajec-Carter & Batchelor, 2014, p. ix).

Clearly, the *Kill Bill* films present strong, powerful women who are extremely competent in their dangerous profession. After the release of the first film, the *New York Times* reported women's favorable opinions; they deemed it empowering to women and claimed they would take their daughters to see it (Leland, 2003). Despite being trained by or lead by men, these assassins ended up killing the men, demonstrating not only their equality to men, but appearing to dominate and surpass the men's abilities. *Kill Bill Volumes 1* and 2 illustrate "the perception that we now live in a postfeminist era—where women can be heroic and independent, where they can do whatever they want, and where they can overcome oppressive patriarchal systems" (Brown, 2015, p. 11). These films make arguments about women's empowerment via a strong female-bodied lead who fights against strong female-bodied adversaries. By demonstrating that women can be just as heroic, successful, and powerful as men, if not more so, the films convey the postfeminist myth that equality has been achieved and that feminism is outdated and no longer necessary.

The Façade of Postmodern Imagery, Excess and Spectacle

In addition to postfeminism, the *Kill Bill* films embrace postmodernism in Tarantino's auteur style rife with intertextual references. Marked by excess and spectacle, postmodern films may include nostalgia, fragmentation, intertextuality, non-linearity, and the apolitical embrace of difference (Borchers & Hundley, 2018; Denzin, 1991; Hodkinson, 2011; Turner, 1990). From the opening credits which pay homage to kung-fu films and appropriate the Shaw Scope logo, to its intertextual winks to a soundtrack spanning multiple decades, the Kill Bill films exemplify postmodern aesthetics.

Excess and spectacle are apparent in the films' bloodshed, death, and carnage. The lead character killed approximately 45 characters on camera, and the other characters combined killed an additional 16 on camera and 1 off camera. This totals 62 deaths in the 4 hours and 10 minutes of the films' total run time; this is roughly a death every 4 minutes. Beyond the number of deaths, the blood and gore are equally extreme; in many scenes, blood is shown spewing and gushing from limbs severed with a single swipe of a sword. In fact, according to special effects artist Christopher Nelson, over 540 gallons of fake blood were used in the two films (Kill Bill trivia, 2003, para. 9).

Beyond excess and spectacle, viewers possessing popular cultural capital can easily identify additional signifiers of postmodern aesthetics, pointedly, the films' nostalgic intertextuality and pastiche. The Kill Bill films are a "postmodern barrage of references to other filmic sources" (Grady, 2014, p. 70). These include nostalgic intertextual throwbacks to grindhouse films like Clint Eastwood's spaghetti westerns,[7] Bruce Lee's kung-fu films, and blaxploitation films of the late 1960s and early 1970s. Additionally, the soundtrack comprises a pastiche of hip hop (The RZA's "Banister Fight"), rockabilly (Charlie Feathers' "That Certain Female"), Latin funk/soul (Santa Esmeralda's "Please Don't Let Me Be Misunderstood"), soul/funk/disco (Isaac Hayes' "Run Fay Run"), instrumental (Vincent Tempera "Ode to O-Ren Ishii"), and 1950s pop (Nancy Sinatra's "Bang Bang") music.

The films' production values and narrative cement their postmodern aesthetic. Specifically, Tarantino's signature nonlinear narrative style unfolds in a series of flashbacks, with each scene titled as if it were a chapter in a book of one's life. The subtitles provide markers and insights for audiences, establishing expectations and navigation for the complex storyline. For example, the first segment after the opening scene is simply called Chapter One, and it shows The Bride confronting Vernita in her Pasadena home. Chapter Two occurs four years earlier, when the sheriff enters the bloody chapel. Then the film jumps to The Bride laying comatose in the hospital. As Elle prepares to kill her, Bill calls and cancels the mission. Next, The Bride awakens from her coma, four years later. Chapter Three, subtitled Origin of O-Ren goes back in time to trace how she came to power. This story fragment juxtaposes anime-style visuals with spaghetti western music. At the end of this segment, audiences are thrust thirteen hours forward to the hospital's parking garage.

The remainder of the film and its sequel continue to employ this postmodern aesthetic and narrative structure, jumping back and forth in time, changing from color to black and white, and fragmenting the story into chapters with sectional subtitles.

Finally, *Kill Bill* signifies postmodernity by seemingly embracing and celebrating difference. Of the four female-bodied DVAS members, Elle and Beatrix were white, Vernita was African American, and O-Ren was Chinese-Japanese American, but all the characters had equal status. Gilpatric's (2010) content analysis of violent female-bodied action characters from 1991 to 2005 found Asian and Latinx people were missing from U.S. American cinema; however, in the films under investigation Asian characters and cultures are especially prominent. Myriad Asian characters were included as audiences learned O-Ren's backstory and Beatrix travelled to China for training and to Japan to obtain her katana and then to take on O-Ren's posse, bodyguard, and ultimately defeat O-Ren herself. Beatrix and others also oscillate between speaking Japanese and English in Chapters Three, Four, and Five of the first five-part movie. In the second film, Beatrix and her sensei Pai Mei speak Cantonese and English in Chapter Eight.

Moving beyond the fact of inclusion to consider how the characters were illustrated, non-white characters were not only featured but often respected as powerful, dangerous, and dignified. For instance, white characters Bill, Elle, and Beatrix all sought instruction from a Chinese mentor, Pai Mei, and DVAS members prized the work of a Japanese swordsmith, Hanzo Hattori. Hence, the films portrayed the value, skill, and respect of people of differing ethnicities and cultures without trying to impose Eurocentric norms or standards on Others. This suggests that *Kill Bill's* postmodern aesthetic celebrates multiculturalism by engaging in representation without assimilation.[8] Thus demonstrating that white people accept, appreciate, and accommodate Others. Simultaneously, the films also at times reproduce stereotypes, such as the gendered, racialized stereotype of the Dragon Lady fulfilled by O-Ren's portrayal (Shah, 1997), and the focus on martial arts as the enabling vehicle for Asian representation.

Similar to the postfeminist portrayals of gendered and sexual equity, the films' postmodern construction of multicultural characters as equally or more powerful than white characters simultaneously suggest that we live in a postracial society as well. In a corresponding logic to postfeminism, postracialism dangerously implies that racism is an obsolete concern not applicable to today's culture. Yet, upon deeper reflection and analysis, both the postfeminist and postmodern elements of the films merely serve to conceal more problematic representations.

Specifically, the postmodern aesthetic curtails women's empowerment when considering Baudrillard's (1995) fourth phase of media transformation. Baudrillard posited that mediated images make us think they represent reality, but, because the real and the image have imploded, they are hyperreal. *Kill Bill's* hyperreality is evident in the films' shift from live action to anime, where the use of real people and animated characters flow seamlessly. Hyperreality is also evident in the characters' accomplishing of impossible feats that exceed reality.

Beatrix engages in several impossible feats. In Chapter One, she dodges a bullet at close range, responding by throwing a knife killing Vernita. In Chapter Five: The House of Blue Leaves, the fight scene changes from color to black and white, from real time to bullet time, and includes gravity-defying action. In this scene, Beatrix effortlessly spins and flips through the air and easily jumps to a second floor bannister while combatting the Crazy 88s. During the battle, she catches a hatchet thrown at her head, splits a man in half length-wise with her sword, stands on one man's shoulders while stabbing another man, and holds up a dead body with her sword, using him as a shield. Most of this fighting takes place on a dance floor reminiscent to the iconic scene in the 1978 hit film *Saturday Night Fever* while the 1960s Isley Brothers' pop song "Nobody but Me" plays in the background, reinforcing the postmodern pastiche. The action continues as the battle appears to take place on stage, with opponents in silhouette with a blue light outlining their figures and a blue grid background providing the backdrop. Such imagery suggests a theatrical performance and hails Elvis Presley's "Jail House Rock" performance on the *Ed Sullivan Show*. After defeating over 30 attackers, Beatrix faces one final member of the Crazy 88, who stands shaking in fear. Demasculinizing him to validate her conquest, Beatrix spanks him and tells him to "go home to your mother!" She then demonstrates amazing balance by standing on the second-floor railing and telling everyone still alive to go but to leave their dismembered limbs behind because "they belong to me."

Beatrix repeats her ability to defy reality in Chapter Seven: The Lonely Grave of Paula Schultz and Chapter Eight: The Cruel Tutelage of Pai Mei. After being shot in the chest at close range with a shotgun loaded with rock salt, Beatrix is tied up and buried alive. Fortunately, because of her training, she was able to punch her way out of the pine coffin and break through the soil, freeing herself. In the following chapter, viewers learn that Beatrix acquired her gravity-defying acrobatic skills from her elderly trainer, Pai Mei. When she meets him to begin training, he demonstrates his gymnastic moves while testing her fighting abilities. In addition to successfully dodging her attacks, he effortlessly jumps in the air and lands on her extended sword, five feet above the ground, parallel to the earth. Later in this test of her skills, he throws his sword up in the air and catches it with the scabbard strapped to his body. This ancient artist, with long white hair and an equally long white beard, apparently defies time, space, and gravity.

Beatrix similarly defies physics and demonstrates impressive martial artistry adding more examples to the excess and spectacle apparent in the films. In Chapter Nine: Elle and I, the fight concludes when Beatrix pulls out Elle's only eyeball.[9] She uses lightning fast reflexes and squishes it between her bare toes as she leaves the blinded Elle in Budd's trailer home with a deadly Black Mamba snake.[10] In the Last Chapter: Face to Face, Bill met his demise when Beatrix performed the deadly five-point-palm exploding-heart technique that Pai Mei taught her. A lightning-quick, precise punch to the heart kills the recipient. Bill had heard about this method but was surprised that Pai Mei taught it to Beatrix; he was never afforded the opportunity to learn it himself. By presenting the feminine characters' strength in an over-the-top manner that places them outside the realm of the real, these repeated violations of reality actually serve to mock and undermine women's power and strength proclaimed by postfeminism. Despite Tarantino's claim of providing positive portrayals for girls, his work counters his goal as the excess and spectacle of the hyperreal distract audiences from the traditional patriarchal ideologies embedded within the films.

Modern Patriarchal Ideologies

In concert with the films' postfeminist and postmodern limitations, the *Kill Bill* films co-opt and repackage modern patriarchal ideologies. To begin with, hegemonic masculinity (Connell, 2001; Hundley, 2013; Trujillo, 1991) manifests in the *Kill Bill* films in numerous forms. Although the story is about a woman's quest for revenge, a man's forceful actions (Bill shooting Beatrix) catalyzes the narrative. If not for Bill's decision, the story would never have taken place. Moreover, he shot her because he was jealous she was marrying another man. Hence, due to two men's actions, myriad lives, including their own, were lost.

Another signifier of hegemonic masculinity is that women submit to men, maintaining a patriarchal power structure in the *Kill Bill* films. The majority of DVAS were women, but a man remained at the top of the organizational hierarchy. Bill was the boss, and he directed the DVAS missions. His code-name, Snake Charmer, reinforced his position of power as all of the assassins' codenames are snake breeds (Black Mamba, Copperhead, Cottonmouth, California Mountain Snake), suggesting that he controlled them with his ability to "charm" them.[11]

In addition to a man being the center of action and the heterosexual over-tones in their codenames, biological determinism cements women's domestic role and the patriarchal culture embedded within the films. Beatrix's quest for revenge takes place after she learns she lost her unborn child. The loss of the child fuels her rage and drives her revenge quest. Tasker (1998) argues that the heroic mother/wife motif is a common frame for female-bodied characters who risk themselves for their children's safety and survival (Gilpatric, 2010). Like Katniss in *The Hunger Games* (Chapter 2) and Mary in *Proud Mary* (Chapter 4), Beatrix is no exception. Brunsdon (2013) concurs that maternal instincts are accepted as justifiable reasons for women to kick ass, drawing attention to female-bodied heroes in *Aliens* (1986), *Terminator 2: Judgment Day* (1991), *Kill Bill* (2003 & 2004), *Xena: Warrior Princess* (1995–2001), *Alias* (2001–2006), and *Underworld: Awakening* (2012), among others.

Apparently, other female-bodied assassins also acquiesce to women's inherent biological nature. For example, the female-bodied assassin sent to kill Beatrix disengages when she learns Beatrix is pregnant. In an earlier scene Beatrix allows a temporary truce when Vernita's child exits the school bus and enters her ransacked home. These scenes suggest that when it comes to children, women's "maternal instincts" supersede their violence and, even as assassins, their implied decorum protects children (also see Chapters 2 and 4).

Unlike most action-oriented characters, Beatrix was not rewarded with a love interest at the films' conclusion (also see Chapter 3 regarding Wonder Woman). Instead, she was "rewarded" with the return of her child to assume her "true" place in society—that of a mother. Unlike the reward of an adult sex partner, motherhood does not provide her with sexual pleasure or assistance raising the child; it annihilates her independence, ends her career, returns her to the domestic sphere, and forces her into a position of responsibility as a caretaker for another person. Indeed, her fate is sealed when the film concludes, and viewers see the following statement on screen: "The lioness has rejoined her cub and all is right in the jungle."[12] This reifies the idea that women's violence is permitted and forgiven if it is aimed at protecting children.

Women's traditionally subordinate and stereotypical roles are further naturalized by reaffirming gendered stereotypes of domesticity that maintain patriarchal dominance. Specifically, two of the powerfully deadly women leave their profession to settle down in domestic roles. Beatrix leaves DVAS to marry Tommy, give birth to her child, and work at a video store in El Paso, Texas. Similarly, Vernita departs DVAS, marries Dr. Bell, and becomes a housewife and stay-at-home mother in Pasadena, California. How these women, who were globally feared and at the top of their profession, were content (or would be content) as domestic dependents is never addressed.

Even the fighting skills of female-bodied characters are partially demonstrated within the domestic sphere. For instance, two fights among women warriors occurred within homes—Vernita's and Budd's. In both instances, Beatrix prevailed. She defeated Vernita (an ex-DVAS colleague turned housewife and stay-at-home mother) in a fight beginning in the living room and ending in the kitchen, where pots, pans, and kitchen knives were employed as weapons. The fight culminated when Vernita secured a gun she had hidden and shot at Beatrix through a cereal box. After dodging the bullet, Beatrix retaliated by throwing a kitchen knife and ending Vernita's life. In a later scene, Beatrix defeated Elle in Budd's trailer home. While most of the fighting was hand-to-hand combat, Beatrix used a television antenna as a weapon, attempted to drown her in the toilet, and after resorting to katanas without the desired result, Beatrix ended up ripping out Elle's remaining eye leaving her blinded in the company of a lethally venomous Black Mamba snake. In both scenes, Beatrix and her female-bodied adversaries channeled the weapons readily available to women in their stereotypical everyday life thereby demonstrating their comfort and superiority in domesticated space.

Hegemonic masculine messages are further reinforced as (white) female-bodied colleagues compete for their boss's admiration, attention, love, and release. The film's narrative centers heteronormativity. To begin with, Beatrix's attempt to move on from Bill and the DVAS by marrying another man is thwarted by Bill's attempt to possess her, which is exacerbated when he finds out she was carrying his baby and shoots her out of jealousy. Moreover, while Bill and Beatrix's prior romantic involvement is the story's catalyst, Elle also displays signs of being in love with Bill and envying Beatrix's past relationship with him. When Elle poses as a nurse and prepares to kill the comatose Beatrix, her action is motivated by her interest in Bill.

Elle's attempt to take out "the other woman" goes awry, however, when Bill calls Elle to direct her to abort the mission. Bill claims, "one thing we won't do is sneak into her room in the night like a filthy rat and kill her in her sleep. And the reason we won't do that thing is because…that thing would lower us." Although disappointed, Elle acquiesces to his orders, but before ending the phone conversation confesses to Bill that she loved him. Thus, despite its postfeminist façade, the dangerous dames of *Kill Bill* still vie for the love and approval of a man (Dow, 2006). Portraying the love of a man as the ultimate prize—or in Kiddo's case, love's reversal in the form of revenge—naturalizes heteronormativity and constructs women's motivations as determined by men's affections.

The *Kill Bill* films further demonstrate hegemonic masculinity by portraying a "man's world" in which the dangerous dames of the DVAS are an exception rather than a rule. For example, the El Paso law enforcement officers sent to investigate the chapel massacre are father and son. During the wedding rehearsal, the obedient wife sits by her minister husband's side. The strip club owner is a man, and his bouncer, Budd, and the strippers are submissive to him. Hattori Hanzo, who is the best swordsmith in the world, Beatrix's and Elle's kung fu master Pai Mei, and all of the Japanese mob bosses are men. Beatrix had to rely on another man, Estában, to help her locate Bill. Even though women engage in the majority of the action in these films, men thus retain their dominant place, serving as privileged leaders and expert artists who dictate and regulate women's actions.

The films also reject feminist and postfeminist messages by duplicating rape culture reminding viewers that regardless of how powerful or dangerous women may be, they can still be overcome with the male phallus. For example, even while averting the female-bodied nurse stereotype, *Volume 1* includes Beatrix's nurse, Buck, who collected money from other men by allowing them to rape her while she was hospitalized in a coma. Between being buried alive and repeatedly raped while in a coma, the link between torture and sex reaffirm a masculinist heterosexual desire for maintaining patriarchal control. Brown (2014) notes how dangerous this can be: "When heroines are victimized in torture scenes, often to the point of actual rape, the films risk eroticizing images of violence against women, even if the women do eventually triumph over their torturers" (p. 47). Clearly, the fact that the "greatest warrior" in the world can be victimized and penetrated against her will demonstrates the phallic power perpetuated by patriarchy is greater than any sword or skill a woman may possess.

Within the "man's world" of the films, the dangerous dames' access to power is, in fact, reliant on their ability to temporarily possess the phallus. Other scholars have interrogated filmmakers' creation of female-bodied action heroes in men's image as incorporating and reproducing masculine (fighting) behaviors (Brunsdon, 2013; Eschholz & Bufkin, 2001; Gilpatric, 2010; Grady, 2014; Halberstam 1998; Tasker, 1998). *Kill Bill's* hyperreality, likewise, co-opts and caters to the norms of hypermasculine violence. The *Kill Bill* films celebrate and perpetuate violence that, even when perpetrated by women, is coded as masculine. Specifically, the female-bodied assassins engage in masculine fighting, serving as an example of female-bodied masculinity (Grady, 2014; Halberstam 1998) that reifies the preference for male norms and dominance that typifies patriarchal culture.

Not only do women fight like men in the films, their possession of the phallus is further evidenced by their targeting of male-centered weaknesses by kicking each other in the crotch. Early in *Volume 1*, for instance, Beatrix kicks Vernita in the crotch before dropping her through the glass coffee table. Later in *Volume 2*, Beatrix and Elle exchange kicks to the crotch as they fight each other in Budd's trailer home. Continuing with their hand-to-hand combat, Beatrix plunges Elle's head into the toilet yet Elle escapes by elbowing Beatrix in the crotch. Melding stereotypical hypermasculine violence with stereotypical feminine artistic expression, one journalist praised, "the bloodletting is so over the top it turns the carnage into a blood-soaked ballet" (Brown, 2006, p. 104), a comment that suggests that women's violence is performative, stylized, and unnatural.

Finally, despite a superficial conclusion that the films affirm diversity through inclusion, this postmodern aesthetic disguises latent racism. That is, while the *Kill Bill* films suggest a postracial society by assembling a bricolage of film and music genres, geopolitical and ethnic identities, and different languages, the construction of apolitical difference (representation as a stand in for structural change) enables the reinscription of whiteness.[13] Specifically, the inclusion of black, Chinese, and Japanese female-bodied characters support Tarantino's postmodern imagery; however, they remain antagonists defeated by the white female-bodied warrior as Beatrix kills them all. Tierney (2006) notes that "the ability of the White practitioner to defeat Asians, using an Asian skill, in Asia, propagates the theme of ubiquitous, even inevitable White supremacy of global proportions" (p. 614). Beatrix's emergence as a female-bodied hero thus reinscribes white women's advancement at the expense of women and men of color, reinscribing white superiority (Tierney, 2006).

Repackaging Patriarchal Ideologies

The *Kill Bill* films palpably communicate postfeminist and postmodern aesthetic and structural messages. We find these messages to be dangerous because they superficially allow audiences to be pleased with women's and people of color's "positive" presence in 21st century film. In essence, this simplistic conclusion serves as a façade for modern patriarchal ideologies embedded within the texts including the reproduction of hegemonic masculinity, rearticulation of gendered stereotypes, co-option of hypermasculine violence, and representation of a superficial politics of difference.

Although viewers may be lured by the promise of empowerment proffered by postfeminist portrayals and postmodern aesthetics, they ought to be wary of such dangerous offerings, which merely repackage traditional ideologically patriarchal fare. Clearly, postfeminist representations of powerful women serve as a marketing ploy (Sklar, 1994). Despite the increased number of female-bodied assassins in *Kill Bill*, the quality of portrayal matters more than the quantity. They definitely have power, but they are certainly not empowering. Gilpatric (2010) concurs that female-bodied action heroes do not provide ideal feminist role models. "The majority of female action characters shown in [U.S.] American cinema are not empowering images, they do not draw upon their femininity as a source of power, and they are not a kind of 'post woman' operating outside the boundaries of gender restrictions" (Gilpatric, 2010, p. 744; also see Chapters 5 and 6).

Focusing specifically on Beatrix, we note that she is a lone warrior lacking care or concern from others. The saga that unfolds in the *Kill Bill* films detail how Beatrix responded after her professional organization, much like a sisterhood, was dissolved. Rather than relying on other women to complete her mission, Beatrix and the other DVAS members turned on each other in reaction or support of male jealousy. What was once a band of women became a fragmented display of petty jealousies and catty behavior. Unlike most heroic protagonists, Beatrix is denied a sidekick and turns on other powerful women who were once her compatriots, thus supporting the patriarchal notion of competition rather than support and camaraderie.

Comparing Beatrix further with traditional male heroes, she even lacks someone to save. Instead, she engages in a "roaring rampage of revenge." As she informs viewers at the beginning of *Volume 2*, "I roared, and I rampaged, and I got satisfaction." Thus, her quest is presented as selfish revenge rather than serving the greater good—narratives more typical in superhero epics.

Clearly, this postfeminist message suggests that women are defending themselves and making a statement based on their biological status as mothers and gendered status as wives and lovers rather than their concern for the greater good.

Tarantino's postmodern exhibition undercuts the films' potentially progressive representations and counteracts any ostensibly positive messages offered to girls and women by these films. Despite the protagonist's victorious conclusion in the saga, the films house modern hegemonic ideologies and hypermasculine behaviors in female bodies that are stripped of their power, one by one, and then tamed by a return to the domestic sphere. In light of these lessons, we agree with Brown (2015), who observes that "feminism is still very much needed and the world has a long, long way to go before real gender equality is achieved" (p. 11).

Notes

1. Douglas (2010) interrogates two contradictory trends that together characterize postfeminist media and the "fantasies of power" it offers (p. 1). The first of the trends she identifies is the televisual overrepresentation of high-power women in roles like lawyers, surgeons, politicians, and police chiefs. This trend is the result of what she calls "embedded feminism," or the integration of the goals of feminism into our cultural fabric to the extent that media (falsely) suggest women have made it, and full equality has been achieved (p. 9). The second of the trends she identifies is the resurrection of sexist images of women in media under the guise of irony and/or empowerment. Together, these produce what she refers to as "enlightened sexism": media fare a media that is "feminist in its outward appearance...but sexist in its intent" (p. 10).

2. Owen, Stein and Vande Berg (2007) discuss the historical disconnect perpetuated by postfeminism (pp. 8–14, 231–244). They are concerned that mediated postfeminist representations may erase decades of feminist work.

3. Considering political economy, we recognize established power structures on multiple levels. After the successes of Reservoir Dogs and Pulp Fiction, Tarantino gained tremendous power in Hollywood. Thus, the dangerous dames constructed in the Kill Bill films were crafted and shaped by a man, e.g., his vision, his decisions, his execution. His power created tension on the set (Respers France, 2018) but nevertheless, Tarantino prevailed. Additionally, in the aftermath of the #MeToo movement we recognize the power imbalance and potential assaults between producer Harvey Weinstein and Uma Thurman. Tarantino later admitted he was aware of these issues and failed to act on them (Kantor, 2017). Finally, we also acknowledge criticisms of Tarantino's co-optation of kung fu and blaxploitation films (Walker, 2012).

4. We recognize the double entendre with the acronym DVAS read divas. We also note the snake metaphor employed in the portrayal of the female-bodied assassins as "deadly vipers"

and their snake breed codenames whereas the leader is known as "the snake charmer." The repurposing of snakes as symbols of feminine fertility to agents of women's betrayal occurred when Christianity absorbed goddess religions.

5. A katana is a long, single-edged sword used by Japanese samurai.

6. Douglas (2010) discusses the danger of positive portrayals of powerful women for whom gender is not a limiting factor, noting that, "in the end, embedded feminism and enlightened sexism serve to reinforce each other: they both overstate women's gains and accomplishments, and they both render feminism obsolete" (p. 15).

7. Spaghetti westerns are a subgenre of Western films that were inexpensively produced in Europe, usually by an Italian producer and director. Clint Eastwood helped popularize them in the 1960s with films such as A Fistful of Dollars (1964), For a Few Dollars More (1965), and The Good, the Bad and the Ugly (1966).

8. Although Tanaka shared his racist perspective, Ishii immediately punished him by cutting off his head showing that there is no place for such discrimination.

9. Elle tells Beatrix that Pai Mei pulled out her first eyeball. In response, Elle killed Pai Mei by poisoning his rice. Thus, Beatrix avenged her tutor.

10. Elle surprised Budd with the Black Mamba, which killed him. However, after Beatrix blinded Elle, the snake sealed her fate as well. We note that Black Mamba is also Beatrix's codename.

11. Although Budd was a member of DVAS, he did not have a codename. Thus, he could not be charmed by his leader-brother Bill. Additionally, it does not elude us that Beatrix's last name is Kiddo, sounding childlike, adolescent, and a buddy/friend to Bill even though they were romantically involved. This appears to be yet another attempt of men infantilizing women to maintain their position of authority.

12. This conclusion is exacerbated as we note that lions do not live in the jungle, they live in the savanna. Yet, it suggests a "mother bear" protecting her "cub." See Gibson and Heyse (2013) regarding how Sarah Palin's postfeminist and frontier feminism defines the mama grizzly as an exclusionary construct.

13. From a political economy perspective, we also recognize how Tarantino profits from the co-optation and colonization of a wide range of cinematic styles developed by people of color, music from an array of eras and cultures, and nods to Chinese kung fu films including Jackie Chan as Beatrix dons the iconic yellow track suit. This is yet another example of white appropriation.

References

Arthurs, J. (2003). Sex and the City and consumer culture: Remediating postfeminist drama. Feminist Media Studies, 3(1), 83–98. doi:10.1080/1468077032000080149

Attwood, F., Brunt, R., & Cere, R. (Eds.). (2007). Mainstreaming sex: The sexualization of culture. London, United Kingdom: I. B. Tauris.

Baudrillard, J. (1995). Simulacra and simulation. Ann Arbor: University of Michigan Press.

Bender, L. (Producer), & Tarantino, Q. (Director). (2003). Kill Bill: Volume 1 [Motion picture]. USA: A Band Apart.

Bender, L. (Producer), & Tarantino, Q. (Director). (2004). *Kill Bill: Volume 2* [Motion picture]. USA: A Band Apart.

Borchers, T., & Hundley, H. (2018). *Rhetorical theory: An introduction*. Long Grove, IL: Waveland.

Brown, D. M. (2006). Tarantino and the re-invention of the martial arts film. *Metro Magazine: Media & Education Magazine, 148,* 100–105.

Brown, J. A. (2014). Torture, rape, action heroines, and *The Girl with the Dragon Tattoo*. In N. Jones, M. Bajac-Carter, & B. Batchelor (Eds.), *Heroines of film and television: Portrayals in popular culture* (pp. 47–64). Lanham, MD: Rowan & Littlefield.

Brown, J. A. (2015). *Beyond bombshells: The new action heroine in popular culture*. Jackson: University Press of Mississippi.

Brunsdon, C. (2013). Television crime series, women police, and fuddy-duddy feminism. *Feminist Media Studies, 13*(3), 375–394. doi:10.1080/14680777.2011.652143

Children Now. (2004). *Prime time diversity report*. Retrieved from http://www.childrennow.com

Connell, R. W. (2001). The social organization of masculinity. In S. M. Whitehead, & F. J. Barrett (Eds.), *The masculinities reader* (pp. 30–49). Cambridge, United Kingdom: Polity.

Corliss, R. (2003, October 20). And now…pulp friction. *Time, 162*(16), 70.

Denzin, N. K. (1991). *Images of postmodern society: Social theory and contemporary cinema*. London, United Kingdom: Sage.

Douglas, S. J. (2010). *Enlightened sexism: The seductive message that feminism's work is done*. New York, NY: Times Books/Henry Holt and Company.

Dow, B. (2006). The traffic in men: Fatal attraction, postfeminist masculinity, and the 1980s media. *Women's Studies in Communication, 29,* 113–131.

Eschholz, S., & Bufkin, J. (2001). Crime in the movies: Investigating the efficacy of measures of both sex and gender for predicting victimization and offending in film. *Sociological Forum, 16*(4), 655–676.

Fusion, B. (2003, October 13). 'Kill' fills box office bill: With $22.7 mil booty, 'Vol I' rubs out competitive. *The Hollywood Reporter,* 1, 55.

Gibson, K. L., & Heyse, A. L. (2013). Depoliticizing feminism: Frontier mythology and Sarah Palin's "the rise of the mama grizzlies." *Western Journal of Communication, 74,* 97-117.

Gilpatric, K. (2010). Violent female action characters in contemporary American cinema. *Sex Roles, 62,* 734–746. doi:10.1007/s11199-010-9757-7

Grady, M. (2014). The maternal hero in Tarantino's *Kill Bill*. In N. Jones, M. Bajac-Carter, & B. Batchelor (Eds.), *Heroines of film and television: Portrayals in popular culture* (pp. 65–75). Lanham: MD: Rowan & Littlefield.

Gronbeck, B. (2007). Foreword: The politics of representation. In S. A. Owen, S. R. Stein, & L. R. Vande Berg (Eds.), *Bad girls: Cultural politics and media representations of transgressive women* (pp. xiii –xix). New York, NY: Peter Lang.

Halberstam, J. (1998). *Female masculinity*. Durham, NC: Duke University Press.

Hall, S. (Ed.). (1980). *Culture, media, language: Working papers in cultural studies 1972–1979*. London: Centre for Contemporary Cultural Studies, University of Birmingham.

Hallissy, M. (1987). *Venomous women: Fear of the female in literature*. Westport, CT: Greenwood Press.

Hodkinson, P. (2011). *Media, culture and society: An introduction*. Los Angeles, CA: Sage.

Hundley, H. L. (2013). Mediated portrayals of masculinities. In A. N. Valdivia (Ed.), *The international encyclopedia of media studies: Content and representation* (pp. 240–262). Oxford, United Kingdom: Blackwell.

Jones, N., Bajec-Carter, M., & Batchelor, B. (Eds.). (2014). *Heroines of film and television: Portrayals in popular culture*. Lanham, MD: Rowan and Littlefield.

'Kill Bill' director hits no. 1 with 'Vol. 2'. (2004, April 19). *The Boston Herald*, p. 36.

Kill Bill: Vol 1. (2003). *Trivia*. IMDB. Retrieved from https://www.imdb.com/title/tt0266697/trivia

Kantor, J. (2017, October 17). Tarantino on Weinstein: 'I knew enough to do more than I did.' *The New York Times*. Retrieved from https://www.nytimes.com/2017/10/19/movies/tarantino-weinstein.html

Lazar, M. M. (2006). "Discover the power of femininity!": Analyzing global "power femininity" in local advertising. *Feminist Media Studies*, 6(4), 505–517. doi10.1080/14680770600990002

Leland, J. (2003, October 19). I am woman. Now prepare to die. *New York Times*. Retrieved from https://www.nytimes.com/2003/10/19/style/cultural-studies-i-am-woman-now-prepare-to-die.html

Medved, M. (2003, October 22). *Kill Bill* mocks innate revulsion toward cruelty. *Catholic Exchange*. Retrieved from https://catholicexchange.com/kill-bill-mocks-innate-revulsion-toward-cruelty

O'Brien, G. (2003, November/December). Battle royale. *Film Comment*, 39(6), 22–25.

Owen, S. A., Stein, S. R., & Vande Berg, L. R. (2007). *Bad girls: Cultural politics and media representations of transgressive women*. New York, NY: Peter Lang.

Phillips, K. R. (Ed.). (2004). *Framing public memory*. Tuscaloosa: University of Alabama Press.

Quentin Tarantino plans 'Kill Bill 3' for 2014 release: Movie news recap. (2009, October 2). *The Independent: Arts & Entertainment*. Retrieved from https://www.independent.co.uk/arts-entertainment/films/quentin-tarantino-plans-kill-bill-3-for-2014-release-movie-news-recap-5504181.html

Respers France, L. (2018, February 6). Quentin Tarantino responds to Uma Thurman allegations. *CNN Entertainment*. Retrieved from https://www.cnn.com/2018/02/06/entertainment/quentin-tarantino-uma-thurman/index.html

Shah, S. (1997). *Dragon ladies: Asian American feminists breathe fire*. Boston, MA: South End Press.

Signorielli, N., & Bacue, A. (1999). Recognition and respect: A content analysis of prime-time television characters across three decades. *Sex Roles*, 41, 527–544.

Signorielli, N., & Kahlenberg, S. (2001). Television's world of work in the nineties. *Journal of Broadcasting and Electronic Media*, 45, 4–22.

Sklar, R. (1994). *Movie-made America*. New York, NY: Vintage Books.

Steinke, J. (2005). Cultural representation of gender and science. *Science Communication*, 27, 27–63.

Tasker, Y. (1998). *Working girls: Gender and sexuality in popular cinema*. New York, NY: Routledge.

Tierney, S. M. (2006). Themes of whiteness in *Bulletproof Monk*, *Kill Bill*, and *The Last Samurai*. *Journal of Communication, 56*(3), 607–624. doi:10.1111/j.1460-2466.2006.00303.x

Trujillo, N. (1991). Hegemonic masculinity on the mound: Media representations of Nolan Ryan and American sports culture. *Critical studies in mass communication, 8*, 280–308.

Turner, B. S. (Ed.). (1990). *Theories of modernity and postmodernity.* London, United Kingdom: Sage.

Walker, T. (2012, December 26). Quentin Tarantino accused of 'blaxploitation' by Spike Lee... again. *Independent.* Retrieved from https://www.independent.co.uk/news/world/americas/quentin-tarantino-accused-of-blaxploitation-by-spike-lee-again-8431183.html

· 2 ·

APPROPRIATING FEMINISMS: THE NATURALIZATION OF PATRIARCHAL POWER STRUCTURES IN *THE HUNGER GAMES*

Soon after the release of the *Kill Bill* films, women in action roles appeared primarily as sole characters. Films such as *Underworld* (2003), *Catwoman* (2004), *Elektra* (2005), *Underworld: Evolution* (2006), *Underworld: Rise of the Lycans* (2009), and *Avatar* (2009) included dangerous dames surrounded by a mass of masculinity. At the dawn of the next decade, *Salt* (2010), *Underworld Awakening* (2012), *Her* (2013), *Fast and Furious 6* (2013), *Guardians of the Galaxy* (2014), *Maleficent* (2014), and *Divergent* (2014) offered audiences strong female-bodied protagonists; however, unlike *Kill Bill, Volumes 1 and 2*, these films failed to feature a collective of strong and powerful women. In fact, the only ensemble cast of women to appear early in the decade starred in the postfeminist romantic comedy *Bridesmaids* (2011), in which the characters turn on each other based on petty jealousies and competition. Although the increase of female-bodied action heroes compared to the prior century may suggest feminist progress in representing women, the narrow range of portrayals proves otherwise.

The *Hunger Games* films (2012, 2013, 2014, and 2015) feature a strong female-bodied lead supported by additional women in active roles. As an extended series whose books and films were globally popular, *The Hunger Games* warrants attention. Over 100 million copies of the young adult books were printed worldwide and spent five years on the *New York Times'* best-seller list (Levithan, 2018). The films, based on the best-selling books, earned a combined box office income grossing $2.9 billion worldwide ("Box office revenue," 2019). Critics hailed the films, particularly the leading character, comparing her to Lara Croft and Ellen Ripley, writing, "Katniss is gritty, she's flinty, she's intimidating—and she doesn't have to compromise one iota of her femininity for it" (Scott, 2012, para. 3).

The Hunger Games narrative occurs in a dystopian world in the aftermath of an attempted revolution. The fictional nation of Panem, comprised of 12 districts, is ruled by the Capitol and its centralized, totalitarian government. Class politics are obvious, as the proletariat live in squalor and are forced to labor in occupations determined by their individually distinct, and often natural, resources, such as fishing (District 4), forestry (District 7), agriculture (Districts 9–11), and mining (District 12). In contrast, the bourgeoisie live in exuberant luxury in District 1 and the Capitol, and they are allowed a wider range of white-collar occupations (e.g., television host, costume designer, gamemaker). In this exploitative system, all manufacturing from the districts serves and supports the government.

Detailed in the Treaty of Treason and enforced by President Snow (Donald Sutherland), The Hunger Games is an annual competition that serves as the public memory of a previous rebellion. It begins with the Reaping, which is a lottery selection of one boy and one girl between 12 and 17 years in age from each district. Once 24 Tributes are selected, they travel to the Capitol's training center, and are styled thematically to be paraded around for audiences. The Tributes enter an elaborate arena controlled by gamemakers, and they fight to the death until one victor remains. Mimicking modern reality television, The Games are televised throughout the country, betting odds are assigned to Tributes, political alliances are formed, and outside assistance may be bartered.

In the first film, *The Hunger Games* (2012), the main protagonist Katniss Everdeen (Jennifer Lawrence) volunteers as a Tribute, replacing her younger sister, Primrose "Primm" (Willow Shields), who was selected during the Reaping. Katniss survives The Games with her skill, cunning, and persistence, saving her male counterpart, Peeta Mellark (Josh Hutcherson). In an unprecedented turn of events, they both hail as Victors.

In the second installation, *The Hunger Games: Catching Fire* (2013), President Snow targets the two, fearing their victory called The Games into question. He believes their success offers disenchanted district citizens a model for resistance. Concerned about a rebellion, Snow attempts to elim-inate Katniss and Peeta by announcing that the contestants for the next Hunger Games will be drawn from previous District Victors.[1] Angered by this betrayal, many of the Victors team up during The Games, foiling Snow's plans, saving Katniss and Peeta, and launching a revolution.

The third and fourth films were produced as one, adapted from the third installment in the book trilogy, but, similar to *Kill Bill*, after filming it the director and producers noted its excessively long run time and broke it into two: *The Hunger Games: Mockingjay – Part 1* (2014) and *The Hunger Games: Mockingjay – Part 2* (2015).[2] The third film begins as viewers learn that Katniss and some colleagues were rescued by rebels and the underground District 13 led by President Alma Coin (Julianne Moore), whereas Peeta and other colleagues were captured and tortured in the Capitol. With some con-sternation, Katniss joins the rebellion and agrees to serve as their Mockingjay (an inspirational propaganda figurehead), in part to save Peeta and the others. Finally, in *Part 2*, the rebellion overthrows Snow's totalitarian government, Katniss prevents the installation of a similar governmental system by assassi-nating President Coin, and the nation adopts democracy. Katniss and Peeta are reunited, and, in the last scene, appear content living as a nuclear family.

The Hunger Games and Its (Post)Feminist Presence

The Hunger Games series supports feminist and postfeminist ideals in numerous ways, including representing "empowered female characters who resist tradi-tional gender scripts" (Lashley, 2018, p. 1). These women engage in an array of occupations traditionally reserved in action-adventure films for men. Indeed, postfeminist media give the impression that gendered representations have evolved over the past decade with a "shift from the traditional subordinate supporter female role to a more equal view of a co-hero/ine" (Boncori, 2017, p. 95). In *The Hunger Games*, for example, given that half of the Tributes in The Games were girls, viewers witness gender parity, which supports a superfi-cial reading of equitable representation. However, the female-bodied Tributes were not necessarily strong or powerful. In fact, in The Games in the first film, five of the female-bodied Tributes' weaponry skills were not disclosed, and the youngest (age 12) female-bodied Tribute's weaponry skill was stealth and slingshot ("The Hunger Games," n.d.). Clearly, these skills were no match against their male-bodied counterparts' knife, axe, and javelin specialties. In the second film's 75th Hunger Games, contestants were selected from existing Victors. Again, half of them were girls, but as former Victors, they excelled in areas such as applying intelligence (Wiress), throwing axes (Johanna Mason) and knives (Cashmere), and slashing with swords and teeth (Enobaria). Thus, as a postfeminist text, viewers may be encouraged to see that girls and women were not just recruited and killed in The Games, but some obtained formidable skills and training helping them to survive.

Other than the Tributes, strong and powerful women appear in a range of roles in the series. For example, Alma Coin leads District 13, the rebels, and, for a fleeting moment, becomes the nation's president. Several women serve as rebel military personnel, including Commander Paylor (Patina Miller), Lieutenant Jackson (Michelle Forbes), Leeg 1 (Misty Ormiston), and Leeg 2 (Kim Ormiston). Cressida (Natalie Dormer) directs the rebels' propaganda films.[3] Most prominently, however, the films, and we, focus on the main protagonist, Katniss Everdeen.

Katniss as a (Post)feminist Hero

Like the powerful female-bodied protagonists in postfeminist media in Chapter 6, Katniss is quite young. As a 16-year-old fighting in her first Hunger Games, the "teenage action heroine taps into a *belief* that exists in younger viewers that women are capable of being their own heroes" (Brown, 2015, p. 11). A teenage girl participating in a revolution stands in stark contrast with a media landscape in which war is most frequently portrayed as a masculine, adult activity (Bignell, 2016). War stories are incompatible with traditional views of children, who are conceived of as "incomplete, irrational and disposed to disordered behavior" as well as "uncorrupted, innocent and authentic, so that they need to be protected from the adult world" (Bignell, 2016, p. 200).

These qualities propel Katniss as the story's hero. She functions as a revolutionary catalyst who "inspire[s] masses of downtrodden citizens to rise up against oppression" (Brown, 2015, p. 22). Juxtaposing her youth with her power to spark a revolution, scholars compare her to Joan of Arc (Brown, 2015; Mumford, 2012) and argue that she is simultaneously docile and dangerous (Green-Barteet & Gilbert-Hickey, 2017). As a renegade, Katniss does not follow a systematic plan; she shoots from the hip. Unresponsive to the rules, the rebels trust her authentic, genuine nature. Despite her youth, she is forced to mature at an early age after her father dies in a coal mining explosion, leaving her mother emotionally unavailable. She is neither "too militant" nor "too girly" (Frankel, 2017, p. 263). Instead, she mirrors characteristics of the Final Girl (Clover, 1992; Laird, 2017; Owen, Stein & Vande Berg, 2007). Katniss teeters between emotional outbursts as a surrogate mother protecting those more vulnerable than herself and rational, parental responsibilities like providing food, earning a paltry income, and caring for her younger sister.

As a (post)feminist hero, Katniss resists gendered norms (Connors, 2014; Miller, 2012; Rauwerda, 2016) and stereotypical conceptions of femininity. Early in the first film, as Katniss and Primm prepare for the Reaping, simple cotton prairie dresses are laid out on the bed for them to wear. Their mother demonstrates her knowledge of styling as she braids Katniss's hair, but Katniss is not overly feminine, wearing no jewelry or makeup, and seeming much more comfortable in pants than in her dress. Rather than placing emphasis on her appearance, she spends her time foraging for food, trying to survive, and providing for her family.

Once selected to fight in The Games, viewers are privy to the extreme body maintenance required to make Katniss appear acceptable and conform to feminized beauty. Her Games escort Effie Trinket (Elizabeth Banks) raves on about the need for her to wash up and bathe. A team of beauticians make over Katniss by plucking her eyebrows, waxing her legs, applying makeup, and styling her hair. This beauty regimen aligns with the constructed notions of attractiveness found in femme fatales (see Chapter 4): creating a beautiful killer who can use her sexual wiles to lure men. Juxtaposed with Katniss's aversion to gendered norms, this beauty work markedly reinforces her desired natural state and signals her disdain for superficially constructed exhibitions of beauty.

Katniss's disinterest in conforming to traditional conceptions of feminized beauty is exemplified when she meets her Games stylist and costume designer, Cinna (Lenny Kravitz). She asks him, "So you're here to make me look pretty?" He answers, "I'm here to help you make an impression." After dressing her in a red evening gown, applying cosmetics, and styling her hair, Cinna comments, "Amazing." Katniss responds, "I don't feel amazing." He asks, "Don't you know how beautiful you look?" "No," Katniss flatly replies. Rather than admiring her own beauty, she concerns herself with surviving The Games.

In the second film installation, fearing her potential to encourage a rebellion, President Snow attempts to discipline Katniss back into traditional gendered norms by requiring her to wear a wedding gown. In response, Cinna takes advantage of her willingness to challenge gender stereotypes and he and Katniss defy Snow's castigation. During a televised interview, she spins in her full petticoat accentuating her layered ballgown, which appears to catch fire and transmutes into a black mockingjay dress. Once fully transformed, she slowly unfurls the wings attached to her arms and, though still in a dress, she stands in defiance to the pure, wholesome, innocent image conjured by the wedding gown that was imposed upon her. This demonstration not only mocks authority and somewhat challenges standardized notions of beauty, but it reveals something beyond mere beauty: her power and agency to express herself.

Not only does Katniss resist contemporary standards of beauty, she also resists traditional gendered scripts, thereby presenting a more masculinized femininity. Likewise, her male counterpart and eventual love interest, performs a more feminized masculinity. Early on, viewers see that she fulfills a familiar role in her father's absence by hunting and providing food for her family. Peeta, on the other hand, is a baker's son skilled in cake decorating. While her responsibility takes her outdoors in the public domain, his keeps him inside the private realm. More specifically, Peeta is contained within a kitchen, a space traditionally reserved for feminine labor. At the end of the last film, he plants flowers and plays with a child, again demonstrating traditionally feminine activities. These challenges to gender norms and scripts reinforce the understanding that gender is fluid and flexible (Guanio-Uluru, 2016; Lashley, 2018; Lupold, 2014; Miller, 2012; Mitchell, 2012; Romøren & Stephens, 2009).

As a (post)feminist hero, Katniss embodies contradictions. She is young but assumes mature responsibilities. She is naturally beautiful but dismisses the extreme maintenance required to conform to civilized standards of beauty. She is a powerful symbol of rebellion but discards feminized beauty as a source of power. Ultimately, Katniss challenges traditional ideas about beauty as a superficial power, reinforces the postfeminist belief that a woman can be anything without sacrificing desirability, and provides messages of empowerment (Brown, 2015).

Due to this representation, millions of viewers are encouraged to believe that women and girls have the same opportunities, liberties, and constraints as men and boys, and either can challenge gender norms and scripts without consequence. This presents an inspiring message, but in doing so, the films also reinscribe and naturalize patriarchal power structures. By associating nature with femininity and civilization with masculinity (Connors, 2014; Guanio-Uluru, 2016; Murphy, 1995), viewers learn that nature (good) conquers civilization (evil). The veneration of the natural world juxtaposed with the demonization of hypercivilization reaffirms stereotypical gender roles, naturalizes heteronormativity, and reifies biological determinism. Katniss, as a powerfully strong feminist, is thereby appropriated, supporting traditional patriarchal ideologies espoused in the story.

Katniss and the Natural World

In many ways, The Hunger Games links Katniss and her (often feminized) colleagues with nature (Connors, 2014) and the primitive. We begin with nomenclatures. Four of the 12 female-bodied Tributes in the 74th Hunger Games are associated with nature: Clove, Fox Face, Rue, and Katniss[4]; and the lone male Tribute's name associated with nature, Peeta Mellark (lark), points to a feminized male. The 75th Games connect two more female-bodied Tributes with nature: Cashmere and Seeder. The three male Tributes' names are also related to nature: Chaff, Woof, and Blight.[5]

Beyond naming, Katniss often appears in natural environments, connecting with flora and fauna. For example, in the opening scene of the first film, she cuts through a fence into a wilderness area. She seems attuned to the environment as she balances on a log and crushes dried leaves, releasing them to check the wind direction. She hunts with a bow and arrow, which requires her to be much closer to her prey, quieter in the environment, and aware of which way the wind casts her scent. In the same scene, she takes aim at a deer, but is stopped from letting go of the arrow by her friend Gale Hawthorne (Liam Hemsworth).[6] Later, he attempts to encourage her as she prepares to participate in The Hunger Games, reminding her, "You know how to hunt." To which she responds, "Animals."

The opening scene of the second film shows Katniss in the wilderness, gazing out over a serene lake. She takes aim at a wild turkey but decides not to proceed. Even in the third film, when they engage in revolutionary war, she and her colleagues take time enjoying nature, sitting by a stream or lake and listening to the babbling brook and nearby mockingjays. Again, she takes aim at an elk, but she refuses to let go of the arrow, observing, "He's not even afraid of us." Gale responds, "Because he's never been hunted before. It's almost not fair." Katniss's hunting skills precede her; former District 12 Victor and current mentor Haymitch Abernathy (Woody Harrelson) discloses, "I hear you can shoot." Katniss downplays her abilities, acknowledging, "I'm alright." Peeta clarifies, "She's better than alright. My father buys her squirrels. He says she hits them right in the eye, every time." Although audiences do not see Katniss kill any big game, it is clear that she only hunts for food or for meat to trade (Atkins, 2016).

Thrust into The Games arena, Katniss takes refuge in the woods, and a butterfly lands on her hand. Although being hunted, she stops to admire the butterfly; she brings it up to her face and smiles before it flutters away. She continues fusing with nature in the arena by touching moss and dirt while locating water, traipsing through the woods, and sharpening sticks. Katniss's keen aptitude to operate within nature literally saves her life. For example, her climbing skills prove convenient, allowing her to seek safety, rest, and hide in trees. In the first film, this ability enables her to escape a band of Tributes hunting her. Attempting to wait her out, the hostile Tributes fall asleep at the tree's base. Hiding in a nearby tree, Rue (Amandla Stenberg) assists Katniss by pointing out a hive of tracker jackers, genetically engineered wasps whose stings cause severe pain, hallucinations, and potentially death. Enduring a few stings, Katniss saws through the limb holding the hive, dropping it on the group below her. The band of Tributes scramble to evade the swarm, yet one is fatally overcome. Hence, Katniss works in concert with the natural resources around her, employing them for her benefit.

Katniss's connection to nature extends to another female-bodied Tribute: Rue. Specifically, when Katniss wakes from the effects of the wasp stings, she sees that Rue had covered her arms in leaves to draw out the venom. Later, the two companionably share food they foraged in the forest, further demonstrating their harmony with nature. Continuing this theme, after another Tribute impales Rue, Katniss encases her dead body with flowers, leaving only her young, peaceful face visible. Much later, Katniss tells Rue's district, "I did know Rue. She was not only my ally; she was my friend. I see her in the flowers that grow in the meadow by my house. I hear her in the mockingjay song." These examples illustrate that Katniss and nature have a deeply rooted, symbiotic relationship.

Metamorphosis into a Mockingjay Rising

Beyond her association with nature, Katniss is featured *as* nature. As the films progress, her previous form is subsumed by her Mockingjay persona. This connection begins early in the first film. When Katniss and Primm prepare for the Reaping (to select Tributes for The Games), Katniss gives Primm a mockingjay pin as a protective charm. Once Katniss volunteers to take Primm's place, the pin returns to her. Her fashion designer Cinna, secretly a rebel, hides the pin inside her jacket as a good luck charm, revealing it to Katniss just prior to her deployment to the arena for the 74th Games. In the second film, audiences see her Mockingjay form embodied when she transforms the wedding dress into a black mockingjay costume. Akin to a phoenix rising in Greek mythology, the mockingjay imagery connects with fire and represents new life possible from rebelling.

By the third and fourth films, Katniss is known simply as The Mockingjay. The Head Gamemaker and rebel Plutarch Heavensbee (Phillip Seymour Hoffman) introduces her to President Coin: "Madam President, may I present you with The Mockingjay." Later, wearing an armored version of the mockingjay costume, Katniss informs Coin, "I'll be your Mockingjay." Coin confirms the conflation of Katniss with her role when addressing the District 13 citizens, stating, "I stand here with The Mockingjay to announce that our moment has arrived." Clearly, human-animal lines blur as Katniss is subsumed into The Mockingjay (Guanio-Uluru, 2017).

Connections with Fire

The films demonstrate several symbolic and literal connections to the natural element of fire. Explicitly, because her costumes for the 74th and 75th Hunger Games promotional events were designed to appear on fire, Katniss becomes known as "the girl on fire." Cinna first toasts, "To Katniss Everdeen. A girl on fire!" and later, the television host, Caesar Flickerman (Stanley Tucci), introduces her to the audience as "The girl on fire." In the third film, Plutarch joins in addressing her in this manner: "There she is. Our girl on fire." This catchphrase bolsters Katniss's connection with nature, including its elements.

Metaphoric fire is associated with Katniss as well. For example, Katniss asks Coin, "do you want me to fire up the troops?" Coin tells the rebels, "Spread the word that we're going to stoke the fire of this rebellion" with The Mockingjay. Harnessing fire to transform into the mockingjay, rising phoenix-like from the ashes, extends Katniss's symbolic connection to this natural element.

In a shot framing her with actual flames, Katniss threatens Snow, "Fire is catching, and if we burn, you burn with us!" Like her use of natural resources such as wind, water, trees, and plants, Katniss employs fire, as well. For example, during The Games, she dodges fireballs shot at her, starts fires to keep warm, and, while in training, teaches two Tributes how to start a fire with a stone and a stick. Combined, her ability to manipulate fire validates her survival skills and comfort working with nature, as if they are one and the same.

Uncivilized and Untrainable

Like nature itself, Katniss is difficult to control.[7] For example, although he tried, Snow was unable to contain her. She starts the rebellion, and later the revolution, by thwarting The Games. As Coin explains, "When you fired your arrow at the forcefield you electrified the nation." Katniss's wild nature appears when she asks her mentor how to acquire shelter during The Games. When he fails to answer, she plunges a knife into the dining table, dangerously close to his fingers. Haymitch responds by explaining that survival depends on getting people to like her, declaring, "right now, sweetheart, you're not off to a very good start." In the second film, Katniss's uncivilized nature leads her to wake him by pouring a pitcher of water over his head. Startled, he rebukes, "I asked you to wake me without giving me pneumonia! You are a strangely dislikable person." Once more, Katniss reveals her unbridled nature when touring Panem with Peeta after their victory in The Games, refusing to read a prepared speech. Instead, she speaks from her heart, demonstrating her wildly independent nature and launching a national firestorm.

This characterization continues when Haymitch tasks a group with brainstorming how to harness The Mockingjay's passion. In response, they offer examples of times she inspired them. Identifying the underlying theme, Gale observes they are all moments "when no one told her what to do." Former Tribute, Beetee (Jeffrey Wright) concurs, "Unscripted, yes," and suggests, "Then maybe we should all just leave her alone." Noting her aversion to follow directions, Plutarch determines that Katniss should be filmed, unscripted, during combat for the propaganda films. Coin objects, but Haymitch asserts, "It has to come from her. That's what the people need. You want a symbol for the revolution. She cannot be coached into it. Trust me, I know." Haymitch and the room of rebels agree that Katniss is wildly independent, even undomesticated. Her natural emotions must be sparked organically, naturally, rather than staged and manipulated in a studio.

The last time audiences see Katniss as uncivilized and undisciplined occurs at the end of the fourth film, after the rebellion succeeds and the new government assumes power. Dressed in her Mockingjay costume, bow and arrow in hand, Katniss enters the Capitol's public arena, where Snow is tied to a pole. At this event, staged for Katniss to avenge her sister's death by killing Snow, she defies Coin and kills her instead. Immediately, the mob rushes Snow and ends his life while Katniss is whisked away and placed under guard. Again, Katniss does not follow orders and resists efforts to tame her. Haymitch affirms, "I'll say this for you Katniss. You don't disappoint." Haymitch continues, "You never make it easy, do you?" Ever wild and uncivilized, these traits are attributed to her nature. That is, rather than carry out the agreed upon plan, she independently makes her own decisions without anyone's approval. Thus, her wild nature is evident when she trusts her thoughts and instincts despite impending ostracization.

The Demonization of Hypercivilization

Juxtaposed with Katniss and her association with nature, the series demonizes civilization, presenting it as the antagonist.[8] Thus, rather than an evolution of nature, civilization is set in contrast to nature. As a concept, civilization entails taking from others, making it a fundamentally oppressive institution (Diamond, 1974; Jensen, 2006; Quinn, 1999; Zerzan, 2015). The Panem government maintains necropolitical relations between the Capitol and the districts, deciding which people live and which die (Mbembe, 2001). They also employ biopower (Foucault, 1976) to regulate how people live, as displayed through the Capitol's extensive weaponizing of technology, militant practices, and superfluous excess. The Capitol exceeds civilization; they have created a hypercivilization.

Exerting Control through Militant Technology

Technology permeates *The Hunger Games*, particularly as a form of weaponized control deployed by the Capitol and Panem government. In fact, all of the Hunger Games pageantry would not be possible without advanced technology. Each Game takes place in an arena constructed and manipulated in every way. The borders and dome are invisible and appear limitless, and the Head Gamemaker herds the Tributes with fire, flood, or mutant animals if they come too close to discover or reveal the illusion. Indeed, even the "natural" parts of the arena are manufactured, and surveillance is accomplished using hidden cameras. Technology weaponizes the natural world in the are-nas, as well. For example, jabberjays, bioengineered birds who mimic what they hear, are programmed to parrot the voices of Tributes' loved ones, mak-ing the Tributes worry these people are nearby and in danger. Other beasts the Capitol and the gamemakers create include mutant mandrill baboons, dogs, and lizards the size of humans. Other "natural" threats amended and controlled by the Capitol include lightning, giant waves, fire, blood rain, tar, and acidic fog.

The government implements this technology to maintain order and uphold civilization with militant force. Akin to Star Wars' Stormtroopers, the Peacekeepers are technologically militarized, encased completely with hel-mets and visors, chest plates, gloves, leather boots, and knee pads. Their belts hold a baton and a sidearm, and they carry an assault rifle or submachine gun. Because people cannot look them in the eye or see any skin, the Peacekeepers lack individuality. Instead, they appear as interchangeable law enforcement robots devoid of humanity.

Panem's citizens are subjected to the Peacekeepers' militant extremes throughout the series. For example, in Catching Fire, when Katniss and Peeta tour Panem and speak to Rue's district, one man in the crowd raises a three-finger salute and whistles a tune supporting the impending revolution.[9] The Peacekeepers respond by dragging him onstage and shooting him in the back of the head. Then, as part of a nationwide crackdown, the Peacekeepers raid District 12 and burn their black market, looking for signs of rebellion.

Such militancy continues after Snow announces that the 75th Games will consist of former Victors and the Peacekeepers round up Katniss, Peeta, and Haymitch for the Reaping. After the lottery yields Haymitch's name, Peeta volunteers to take his place. The District 12 citizens salute Katniss and Peeta as Victors with the three-fingered sign of rebellion, and they reciprocate. Quickly and aggressively, the Peacekeepers force them off the stage. The Peacekeepers, extending faceless and uncaring technologies of control, fear, and destitution, maintain Panem's necropolitical relations with the citizenry.

Visual Imagery and Excess

Along with militant technology, the films' imagery and depictions of excess reinforce this demonization of hypercivilization by demarcating class sta-tus between the Capitol and surrounding districts. Dim colors and dramatic lighting cast the districts in dark grey and blue hues, with gritty and dreary settings. In contrast, the Capitol has bright, flat lighting, seamless transitions, and garish, peacock colors. Its citizens don bold, elaborate outfits whereas district citizens wear drab, tattered clothes, poorly protecting them from the elements. These visual differences alert viewers to divergent standards of living and aesthetically present the civilized Capitol as the livelier and superficially more desirable location. However, the narrative quickly dispels this myth, revealing that the Capitol merely placates its citizenry, using excess as a form of biopower to extend the government's control.

Effie Trinket epitomizes this oversaturated, shallow and frivolous imagery; she dresses like a Dr. Seuss caricature reminiscent of Lady Gaga. As an eccentric fashionista, Effie attempts to keep moods light and encourages her Tributes to feel honored to participate in The Games, knowing they most likely will be massacred. Throughout the films, she sports ornate wigs coifed in outlandish styles and often ornamented elaborately, in colors far from those found in natural hair such as pink, metallic gold, platinum blonde, pumpkin, and bright orange. She accessorizes with fascinators, precarious wedges, decorative gloves and cuffs, and elaborate statement makeup. Her outfits include a purple dress with puffed sleeves, an exaggerated peplum, and purple high heels with black socks; a pink and purple mini dress with a puffed skirt and yellow trim; a sleeveless, high-necked mini dress that appears to be constructed out of monarch butterflies; and a ruffled, furry red dress with matching feathered shoes, pink and purple gloves, and silver finger ornaments.[10] Even when incorporating elements found in nature, such as butterflies, fur, and feathers, their outlandish manipulation highlights the capture and control of nature. In essence, fashion is gained at the expense of nature, further demonizing the hypercivilization illustrated in the Capitol. The oversaturated visuals, including the colors, lighting, and fashion styles, particularly highlighted by Effie and contrasted with district citizens, illuminate the distinctions between hypercivilization and nature advanced in The Hunger Games.

Excess and poverty illuminate class divisions in myriad ways, including the availability of food. District citizens appear malnourished, and they are desperate for food. Katniss hunts for her family's food and to trade, exchanging squirrels for bread at Peeta's family bakery. In sharp distinction, the high-speed train and training centers for the Tributes and Victors surround them with elaborate, expensive décor like crystal and mahogany and an overabundance of alcoholic and nonalcoholic beverages, fruit, cheese, meats, cakes, and other delicacies. At a ball celebrating their victory, Peeta and Katniss learn that citizens in the Capitol drink purgatives, so they can vomit and continue partaking from the buffet. The contrast of extreme deprivation in the districts with the waste in the Capitol reinforces hypercivilization's exploitive power.

Civilization clearly is demonized. The Capitol's extensive use of militarized technology, oversaturated hues and loud colors, elaborate and gawdy outfits, expensive décor, and other marks of excess present an over-the-top vision of civilization, a form of hypercivilization. Combined, these elements are powerful biopolitical tools employed to control and manipulate the environment and its constituents, extending beyond the Capitol to the surrounding districts.

The Naturalization of Power Structures

In aligning Katniss with nature and the Capitol with hypercivilization, the story concludes when rebel forces symbolized by The Mockingjay successfully overthrow the necropolitical government. Hence, not only can civilization not contain or control nature, but civilization falls to nature. Indeed, *The Hunger Games* demonstrates potential dangers posed by advanced technology (Guanio-Uluru, 2017). Although Katniss, and nature, emerges victorious in the battle with the Capitol, and civilization, she is tamed as feminism is appropriated, maintaining and even strengthening the status quo. Specifically, *The Hunger Games* naturalizes gender roles, reaffirms heteronormativity, and purports biological determinism, thereby reinforcing patriarchal ideologies extant in contemporary society.

Reaffirming Traditional Gender Roles

Paradoxically, *The Hunger Games* simultaneously disrupts and reifies stereotypical gender roles. As a (post)feminist hero, Katniss initially rejects femininity and exhibits traditionally masculine traits. She thwarts the government's biopolitical attempts to control and regulate her body. Conversely, in other ways stereotypical gendered scripts manifest (Guanio-Uluru, 2016; Palmieri, 2017) as men frequently determine plans of action and overrule women.

In the Capitol, all key decision-makers are male. This includes the Head Gamemakers, who take orders directly from Snow and direct The Games. Although the peacekeepers appear genderless, their body shape suggests they are male, militantly ensuring the Capitol's dictates are obeyed. Other male decision-makers include the Head Peacekeepers, who command in each district. Indeed, the hypercivilized government is led and run by men, and women are symbolically annihilated, not visible in any position of power. Among the rebels, Plutarch and Coin's relationship reaffirms traditional gender roles. In the third film, he often confronts her. To begin, they argue about whether Katniss should serve as the rebellion's symbolic source of inspiration. Plutarch declaratively urges,

> This is the only choice you have. ...that anger-driven defiance. That's what we want, and we need to redirect it. We need a lightning rod. They'll follow her. She is the face of the revolution. Let her see it. Let her go home.

Coin acquiesces, allowing Katniss to see the damage inflicted upon her home district by the Capitol. Upon her return, Katniss agrees to serve as The Mockingjay and presents Coin with conditions. When Coin asserts that she will not meet Katniss's demands, Plutarch argues with her and Coin concedes again. Later, Coin addresses her constituents and informs them that Katniss has agreed to be the face of the cause. Plutarch criticizes, "May I speak freely?" Coin responds, "You don't appear to do anything else." Plutarch remarks, "I'm only talking about salesmanship. The thing with revolutions. They're a tender flame and need to be nurtured, with a little kindling and warmth, a little bit of oxygen." Coin queries, "Oxygen?" Plutarch answers, "One sure way to put it out is to smother it." Coin wryly responds, "Or to use up all the air in the room." More often than not, Plutarch, despite being Coin's subordinate, gets his way and simply uses Coin as a puppet. During the next speech Coin delivers, Plutarch mouths it in the background, blatantly revealing that he wrote it and she merely embodies and delivers his decisions. This further illustrates how *The Hunger Games* oscillates between presenting a strong female-bodied character and upholding traditional, stereotypical gender roles. That is, the films present a bifurcated depiction of Coin. One the one hand, the films include a strong powerful female-bodied president. On the other hand, she appears to be Plutarch's puppet merely serving as a front person to his plans. Despite confronting him, she ultimately gives in to him. Thus, rather than depicting a positive woman role model, the films reveal her subservience to a man.

Similar stereotypical gender roles arise during the abysmal filming of the first propaganda video starring The Mockingjay. Haymitch blames Katniss's inability to act rather than criticizing Plutarch's inability to direct. To remedy the situation, Haymitch addresses the entire group, but the men create the new plan. All the while, Katniss sits idly by, as if she were not in the room. When Coin queries the new plan, the men argue with her and eventually prevail. This questions her role as a leader and demonstrates men's assertiveness, their vocal power, and suggests they have the best ideas and should determine the correct course of action.

In *Mockingjay Part 2*, the men strategize without women's input or consideration once again. Specifically, three male-bodied rebels develop plans to enter the Capitol, even superseding the woman leader's authority. Then, as three female-bodied leaders argue among themselves, a man interrupts them to present his plan. The men ignore the women leaders and begin working out the details. Once one woman shows support for another woman's plan, she flips to support the men's plan. Rather than women working together, as men are depicted doing, this scene pits the women against one another. Pointedly, Coin worries that Katniss will lead or will endorse another leader after the revolution. Such jealousies, insecurities, and infighting prevent women from banding together. This supports the postfeminist narrative and reveals the hypocrisy of featuring strong, powerful women but limiting them to traditional, stereotypical gender roles.

Espousing Heteronormativity

Exacerbating the feminist pretense, the narrative naturalizes heteronormativity with the love triangle between Katniss, Peeta, and Gale. The first film initially favors Gale, but this begins to shift when, during Peeta's interview prior to the 74th Games, he discloses, "There is this one girl that I've had a crush on forever." Upset this information could make her look weak, Katniss responds by violently slamming him against the wall when he exits the stage. Haymitch convinces her that this narrative could save her life, noting, "He made you look desirable. Now, I can sell the star-crossed lovers from District 12." Later, in a parade while riding in a chariot, Peeta reaches for her hand, and she pulls away from him. After he cajoles her, she complies, clasping his hand and raising their hands together triumphantly overhead. Even though she initially resists him, Katniss eventually learns his romantic interest is genuine. A strategy to survive blossoms over time. Thus, not only is heteronormativity encouraged, but men work to discipline and regulate Katniss's feelings and desires.

Over time, Katniss develops feelings for Peeta. During The Games, she finds him injured and vows, "I'm not going to leave you." While nursing him back to health, she lies down with him, rests her head on his chest, and kisses him. They sleep in embrace and, as he recuperates, he kisses her in return.

Having bonded, as the only two Tributes remaining at the end of The Games, they agree to die together by simultaneously ingesting poisonous berries.[11] Just as the fruit touches their lips, an announcer stops them, declaring, "Ladies and gentlemen, may I announce the winners of the 74th annual Hunger Games!"

Although they shared moments of intimacy, Katniss rejects attempts to regulate her love. Aware of her untamable nature, Snow threatens her family and informs Katniss she must convince him and the country that her love for Peeta is authentic. At the beginning of Catching Fire, Katniss perpetuates the ruse and pretends to be in love with Peeta while on camera. In a feeble attempt to be dismissed from The Games, Peeta claims they secretly married and are expecting a child. Snow is unmoved and forces them to compete.

After oscillating between Gale and Peeta, Katniss's feelings once again gain strength in the arena, when she and Peeta compete in the 75th Games. Peeta declares, "If you die and I live, I have nothing to live for. Your family needs you. You have to live for them." Katniss wonders, "What about you?" Peeta notes, "Nobody needs me." Katniss shares, "I do. I need you." They kiss. She realizes that they share common traumatic experiences, and, unlike Gale, Peeta can comfort her after she experiences nightmares. Because she has proven her ability to take care of herself and her family, he provides emotional support that others cannot. Following this actualization, Katniss and Peeta take turns protecting each other, emotionally and physically, in the two Mockingjay films.

In the final film installation, although Gale is not yet forsaken, he and Peeta discuss their personal situation. Gale laments, "I should have volunteered to take your place in the first Games." Peeta responds, "No, she needed you to take care of her family. She can't lose you. She really loves you." Gale points out, "The way she kissed you in the Quarter Quell? She never kissed me like that." Peeta dismisses this, suggesting, "It was just part of the show." Gale disagrees, "No, you won her over. You gave up everything for her. It's not going to be an issue much longer. I doubt all three of us are going to make it out of this, and, if we do, it's her problem, and she'll have to choose. I know Katniss will pick whoever she can't survive without." Setting aside their omission of Katniss from the conversation regarding her romantic life partner, it is clear they become her prize; she is rewarded with selecting which of the two she wants. Ultimately, Katniss selects Peeta, which aligns with Dow's (2006) claim that postfeminist masculinity presents the sensitive man as the woman's reward. Furthermore, the men's conversation points to the inevitability of heterosexual coupledom espoused by the series, suggesting that a heterosexual relationship is necessary for love and survival.[12]

Promoting Biological Determinism

In addition to espousing heteronormativity, the series promotes biological determinism. Despite stating she does not want to have children, Katniss stands in as surrogate mother to her sister and extends that role later to Rue, protecting the weak and vulnerable (Atkins, 2016; Green-Barteet & Gilbert-Hickey, 2017). Early in the first film, she discloses to Gale that she does not want children because of The Games and the Reapings. That is, she cannot conceive how anyone could bring children into a world where they are subjected to a lottery for death and, therefore, she claims that she will not impose that risk on anyone. By the end of the narrative, she gives birth to two children, signaling that the world is now safe. Viewers are left to decide if she legitimately did not desire children (but used The Games as an excuse) or if she sacrificed her desire to not expose them to the risk of The Games.

Stereotypically, "the traditional heroine was self-sacrificing and extremely caring of others" (Newsom, 2004, p. 66; see also Douglass, 1994). Katniss's sacrificial bent appears early in the first film, when she volunteers for The Games in place of Primm. Her care extends beyond Primm to Rue, Peeta, and countless others, including the innocent men, women, and children killed when the Capitol bombs a hospital. As a woman, Katniss is burdened with this nurturing, mothering role. This same expectation appears in *Kill Bill* (see Chapter 1), *Wonder Woman* (see Chapter 3), and *Bionic Woman* (see Chapter 5), with powerful women contained by the "weight of protecting family members" (Brown, 2015, p. 15), which serves as yet another form of biopower regulating gender roles.

Surrogate motherhood turns into actual motherhood by the story's conclusion, thereby returning Katniss to her "natural" feminine role as a nurturing mother. Once the revolution is long over, Katniss and Peeta resume life in District 12. Domestic bliss is evident, as viewers see Katniss lying in bed with Peeta, who affirms, "I love you." Approximately 15 years later, they remain coupled, and have transformed into a nuclear family, with a toddler and an infant. The narrative proffers contradictions. For example, in the first film when audiences are introduced to Katniss and Gale, they are discussing the upcoming Games. Fearing offspring would be subjected to such risk, she declares, "I'm never having children." After victory is claimed and peace reestablished, however, she not only is rewarded with her selection of a mate, but she extends Dow's (2006) claim; she is rewarded with children. Such an outcome implies that women are fulfilled with their own children, rounding out a "traditional" family (Cain, 2001). Thus, the message reifies compulsory heterosexuality and limits a broader array of womanhood. Combined, these scenes demonstrate how *The Hunger Games* films "conform to the established heterosexual patriarchal norms after the rebellion's end" and how the characters are "ultimately contained through a traditional dichotomy" (Lashley, 2018, p. 1). Thus, the once uncivilized and untrainable Katniss concedes to patriarchal regulation and is disciplined into adhering to heteronormativity and biological determinism.

Because the story's hero is associated with nature, her actions and words are upheld, valorized, and naturalized as the "correct" way to behave and think. Although she resists being manipulated and controlled, Katniss eventually acquiesces, thereby reifying stereotypical gender roles, heteronormativity, and biological determinism. Through this, patriarchal power structures become seamlessly naturalized. Framed this way, Katniss makes the "right" decisions and is socially rewarded, thus demonstrating how her agency and choices support hegemonic masculinity and patriarchy as the natural way to exist. In essence, the narrative depicts how powerful female-bodied characters will understand their true place in society. In the end, patriarchal social order is once again restored.

The Patriarchal Appropriation of Feminism

Katniss Everdeen ranges from a "game changer" to a "disappointment" (Manter & Francis, 2017, p. 287). Both make her a dangerous dame. As a postfeminist role model, she embodies girl power and simultaneously challenges and reaffirms gender norms. Drawing from third-wave feminism, girl power delineates the ability for a girl to be active, aggressive, and self-sufficient while adhering to a femme appearance (Newsom, 2004). This mentality "celebrates the fierce and aggressive potential of girls as well as reconstitution of girl culture as a positive force embracing self-expression through fashion, attitude, and a Do-It-Yourself (DIY) approach to cultural production" (Gonick, 2006, p. 7). Katniss engages in DIY activities coded more traditionally masculine (like hunting and trapping), acting in an aggressive, manly fashion. She offers images of femininity performed by a strong, non-passive female-bodied hero (Newsom, 2004).

Despite her hero status, she is regulated by her responsibility for the care of others. Aligned with Mother Nature and persistently functioning as a maternal figure, Katniss is constrained by gender scripts and ultimately by biological determinism. Although she is strong, secure, and self-sufficient, she appears content replacing her bow with a bassinet. In sum, she embodies the contradiction of postfeminist representation.

Scholars remain skeptical about girl power, identifying how patriarchal systems restrict, control, and govern agency (Bordo, 1993; Green-Barteet & Gilbert-Hickey, 2017; Palmieri, 2017). Girl power, therefore, offers a limited feminine and feminist empowerment, a false promise that depoliticizes the political (Bordo, 1993). That is, she can access the system, but she cannot be the boss for any extended time. Brown (2015) finds Katniss a "young action heroine [who] still grapples with discrimination, sexism, and gender expectations, but presents a fantasy of overcoming all these factors that try to limit her" (p. 11). The films are no exception; they depict an empowering feminine and feminist identity with Katniss, but she is restricted within patriarchal structures.

We posit that Katniss, and the films' audiences, are duped into false consciousness. As a pawn, this reluctant warrior (Rauwerda, 2016) was touted as a revolutionary symbol within the film and a symbol of feminine/feminist empowerment to audiences. Presenting a powerful protagonist constrained by patriarchal ideologies in this way appropriates Katniss, feminist politics, and girl power, twists them to reaffirm traditional scripts, and capitalizes upon them. As an industry, film has long appropriated feminism and girl power, converting it into iterations of postfeminism for profit (Lupold, 2014; Schilt, 2003). Katniss, unfortunately, is no different.

Notes

1. Normally, once a Tribute becomes a Victor, she or he is exempt from further competition.
2. We recognize that splitting the final films into two affords greater financial opportunity.
3. Although women held a broader range of roles, people of color remained largely absent (see Green-Barteet & Gilbert-Hickey, 2017; Moore & Coleman, 2015). Ultimately, the elected president is a black woman (Paylor, played by Patina Miller), and the commander of Katniss's unit in the second *Mockingjay* film is black (Boggs, played by Mahershala Ali). Despite this, very few other characters are people of color. A few Tributes (Enobaria, Beetee, Cedar, Chaff, Rue and Thresh), some extras (a trainer, victims at the District 8 hospital, a tech helping to run The Games, servants and entertainers at Snow's mansion, and a stylist), and Cressida's assistant are not white. Cinna (Katniss's stylist), and two Tributes, Rue and Thresh, are the only people of color given names in the first film.

Rue and Thresh hail from the same district, suggesting racial segregation in Panem. This District erupts in riots after Rue perishes, and the Peacekeepers use water hoses to quell the uprising. The parallels with 1960s race riots cannot be ignored. The text focuses on white, rural poverty, elevating class concerns above racial discord.

4. Rue is an herb or shrub baring small greenish-yellow flowers. It has a strong odor, has been used for medicinal purposes and is known as herb-of-grace (Miller, 2018). Katniss is a plant with arrow-shaped leaves and white three-petaled flowers that bloom along a long, upright stalk (Rhoades, 2018).

5. Blight is an infectious plant disease.

6. We acknowledge that Gale Hawthorne's name also connects with nature, although he is much more militant, which is related more to civilization. During the film, Katniss is associated with fire, and like a gust of wind, Gale can put out the fire. Also, Hawthorns are a variety of tree and Katniss climbs trees to hide and rest. Ultimately, Katniss selects Peeta Mellark as her mate, connecting cat and bird. Once Katniss transforms into The Mockingjay, the relationship is more simpatico, with the lark and the jay.

7. Greaghty (2016) explains that historically "children were idealized as primitive, either noble savages to be left alone or wild beasts needing training" (p. 203).

8. Drawing from famous Romans at the height of civilization mythology, many of the Capitol's citizenry have Latin names, such as Seneca, Claudius, Cato, Caesar, Flavia, Octavia, Brutus, Plutarch, and Portia.

9. The salute first appears when Katniss volunteers in lieu of Primm's selection to participate in The Games. Her district responds to her courage with this salute. She repeats it again after laying out Rue's body, saluting the camera, which launches the riots in District 11. The salute recurs throughout the series at moments of defiance or rebellious unity.

10. After leaving the Capitol during the revolution, Effie loses her external excesses. Instead, she aesthetically fits in with other District 13 citizens, wearing the same grey tones as they do, stripped of her outlandish cosmetics and wigs until she leaves District 13.

11. Earlier, Haymitch refers to Peeta and Katniss as "star-crossed lovers." This, combined with the potential double suicide, certainly hearkens Shakespeare's *Romeo and Juliet*.

12. Every couple portrayed in the films is heterosexual, further exemplifying heteronormativity.

References

Atkins, J. (2016, November/December). Saving sisters: *Little Women, The Hunger Games*, and *Frozen. The Horn Book Magazine*, 27–31.

Bignell, J. (2016). Representing violence, playing control: Warring constructions of masculinity in action man toys. In E. Wesseling (Ed.), *The child savage, 1890–2010: From comics to games* (pp. 189–202). Burlington, VT: Ashgate.

Boncori, I. (2017). Mission impossible: A reading of the after-death of the heroine. *Culture and Organizations, 23*(2), 95–107.

Bordo, S. (1993). *Unbearable weight: Feminism, Western culture, and the body*. Berkeley: University of California Press.

Brown, J. A. (2015). *Beyond bombshells: The new action heroine in popular culture*. Jackson: University Press of Mississippi.

Cain, M. (2001). *The childless revolution: What it means to be childless today*. New York, NY: Perseus.

Clover, C. J. (1992). *Men, women, and chain saws: Gender in the modern horror film*. Princeton, NJ: Princeton University Press.

Connors, S. P. (2014). The subjugation of nature and women in *The Hunger Games*. In *The politics of Panem* (pp. 137–156). Rotterdam, Netherlands: Sense Publishers.

Diamond, S. (1974). *In search of the primitive: A critique of civilization*. Brunswick, NJ: Transaction Books.

Douglass, S. J. (1994). *Where the girls are*. New York, NY: Times Books.

Dow, B. J. (2006). The traffic in men and the *Fatal Attraction* of postfeminist masculinity. *Women's Studies in Communication*, 29(1), 113–131. doi:10.1080/07491409.2006.10757630

Foucault, M. (1976). *The history of sexuality volume 1*. Paris, FR: Editions Gallimard.

Frankel, V. E. (2017). *Superheroines and the epic journey: Mystic themes in comics, film and television*. Jefferson, NC: McFarland & Company.

Gonick, M. (2006). Between 'girl power' and 'reviving Ophelia': Constituting the neoliberal girl subject. *NWSA Journal*, 18(2), 1–23. doi:10.2307/4317205

Greaghty, L. (2016). "Back to that special time": Nostalgia and the remediation of children's media in the adult world. In E. Wesseling (Ed.), *The child savage, 1890–2010: From comics to games* (pp. 203–220). Burlington, VT: Ashgate.

Green-Barteet, M. A., & Gilbert-Hickey, M. (2017). Black and brown boys in young adult dystopias: Racialized docility in *The Hunger Games* trilogy and *The Lunar Chronicles*. *Red Feather Journal*, 8(2), 1–22.

Guanio-Uluru, L. (2016). Female focalizers and masculine ideals: Gender as performance in *Twilight* and *The Hunger Games*. *Children's Literature in Education*, 47(3), 209–224.

Guanio-Uluru, L. (2017). Katniss Everdeen's posthuman identity in Suzanne Collins's *Hunger Games* series: Free as a mockingjay? *Jeunesse: Young People, Texts, Culture*, 9(1), 57–81.

Jacobson, N., & Kilik, J. (Producers), & Ross, G. (Director). (2012). *The hunger games* [Motion picture]. USA: Lionsgate.

Jacobson, N., & Kilik, J. (Producers), & Lawrence, F. (Director). (2013). *The hunger games: Catching fire*. [Motion picture]. USA: Lionsgate.

Jacobson, N., & Kilik, J. (Producers), & Lawrence, F. (Director). (2014). *The hunger games: Mockingjay – part 1* [Motion picture]. USA: Lionsgate.

Jacobson, N., & Kilik, J. (Producers), & Lawrence, F. (Director). (2015). *The hunger games: Mockingjay – part 2* [Motion picture]. USA: Lionsgate.

Jensen, D. (2006). *Endgame, volume 1: The problem of civilization*. New York, NY: Seven Stories Press.

Laird, E. E. (2017, May 13). Updating the final girl theory. *Medium: The Film Journal*. Retrieved from https://medium.com/@TheFilmJournal/updating-the-final-girl-theory-b37ec0b1acf4

Lashley, K. A. (2018). Girls on fire: Gender and disability in 'The Hunger Games' and 'Divergent.' *Dissertation Abstracts International*, 78(7). DAI0244049

Levithan, D. (2018, October 18). Suzanne Collins talks about 'The Hunger Games,' the books and the movies. Q & A. *The New York Times*. Retrieved from https://www.nytimes.com/2018/10/18/books/suzanne-collins-talks-about-the-hunger-games-the-books-and-the-movies.html

Lupold, E. (2014). Adolescence in action: Screening narratives of girl killers. *Girlhood Studies*, 7(2), 6–24.

Manter, L., & Francis, L. (2017). Katniss's oppositional romance: Survival queer and sororal desire in Suzanne Collins's *The Hunger Games* trilogy. *Children's Literature Association Quarterly*, 42(3), 285–307. doi:10.1353/chq.2017.0029

Mbembe, A. (2001). *On the postcolony*. Berkeley: University of California Press.

Miller, J. (2012). "She has no idea. The effect she can have.": Katniss and the politics of gender. In G. A. Dunn & N. Michaud (Eds.), The Hunger Games *and philosophy: A critique of pure reason* (pp. 145–161). Hoboken, NJ: Wiley.

Miller, R. (2018, December 15). What are rue plants used for? *SF Gate*. Retrieved from https://homeguides.sfgate.com/rue-plants-used-for-49380.html

Mitchell, J. (2012). Of queer necessity: Panem's Hunger Games as gender games. In M. F. Pharr & L. A. Clark (Eds.), *Of bread, blood and* The Hunger Games: *Critical essays on the Suzanne Collins trilogy* (pp. 128–137). Jefferson, NC: McFarland & Co.

Moore, E. E., & Coleman, C. (2015). Starving for diversity: Ideological implications of race representations in *The Hunger Games*. *The Journal of Popular Culture*, 48(5), 948–967.

Mumford, G. (2012, March 16). *The Hunger Games*: Jennifer Lawrence on Katniss, a 'futuristic Joan of Arc.' *The Guardian*, Culture section. Retrieved from https://www.theguardian.com/film/2012/mar/17/hunger-games-jennifer-lawrence-interview

Murphy, A. L. (1995). *Literature, nature, and other: Ecofeminist critiques*. Albany: State University of New York Press.

Newsom, V. A. (2004). Young females as super heroes: Super heroines in the animated *Sailor Moon*. *Femspec*, 5(2), 57–81.

Owen, A. S., Stein, S. R., & Vande Berg, L. R. (2007). *Bad girls: Cultural politics and media representations of transgressive women*. New York, NY: Peter Lang.

Palmieri, S. J. (2017). Assessing industry ideologies: Representations of gender, sexuality, and sexual violence in the book versions and film adaptations of *The Hunger Games* trilogy, the *Divergent* trilogy, and the *Vampire Academy* series. *Dissertation Abstracts International*, 78(5). DAI10240767

Quinn, D. (1999). *Beyond civilization: Humanity's next great adventure*. New York, NY: Harmony Books.

Rauwerda, A. M. (2016). Katniss, military bratness: Military culture in Suzanne Collins's *Hunger Games* trilogy. *Children's Literature*, 44, 172–191. doi:10.1353/chl.2016/0016

Rhoades, H. (2018, May 8). Growing katniss – Learn more about Katniss plant care. *Gardening Know How*. Retrieved from https://www.gardeningknowhow.com/ornamental/water-plants/katniss/growing-katniss-plant.htm

Romøren, R., & Stephens, J. (2009). Representing masculinities in Norwegian and Australian young adult fiction. In J. Stephens (Ed.), *Ways of being male: Representing masculinities in children's literature and film* (pp. 216–233). New York, NY: Routledge.

Schilt, K. (2003). 'A little too ironic': The appropriation and packaging of Riot Grrrl politics by mainstream female musicians. *Popular Music and Society, 26*(1), 5–16.

Scott, M. (2012, March 23). 'Hunger Games' movie review: Fans and newcomers alike will enjoy a brisk tale of survival. *The Times-Picayune*. Retrieved from https://www.nola.com/ entertainment_life/movies_tv/article_e4344a4d-51f6-5570-8d89-e5cc2213c91c.html

Box office revenue of *The Hunger Games* movie series in North America and worldwide as of 2018, by movie (in million U.S. dollars). (2019). *Statista: The Statistics Portal*. Retrieved from https://www.statista.com/statistics/608201/box-office-revenue-hunger-games/

The Hunger Games wiki. (n.d.). *Fandom*. Retrieved from http://thehungergames.wikia.com/ wiki/The_Hunger_Games_Wiki

Zerzan, J. (2015). *WHY HOPE? The stand against civilization*. Port Townsend, WA: Feral House.

· 3 ·

ASS-KICKING WOMEN AND
THE FIGHT FOR JUSTICE

Constructing a (White) Feminine/ist
Icon in *Wonder Woman*

Appearing on the big screen in a time of social unrest and divisions over issues of gender and sexual equality, race, immigration, and the nation under President Trump, *Wonder Woman* serves as a site of cultural and political negotiation. At the end of the day, "superheroes are more than fuel for fantasies or a means to escape from the humdrum world of everyday responsibilities. Superheroes symbolize societal attitudes regarding good and evil, right and wrong, altruism and greed, justice and fair play" (Nama, 2011, p. 9). *Wonder Woman* spoke to the issues of the day in U.S. society. Ranking seventh of the ten highest grossing movies in 2017, the movie was directed by a woman, Patty Jenkins, itself an important achievement when 96 % of Hollywood directors are men (Smith, Choueiti, & Pieper, 2018). The movie's opening drew women out in almost equal numbers to men—a rare accomplishment for a superhero film. Its audiences spanned generations, signifying Wonder Woman's long-standing cultural importance.[1] Sperling (2017) describes how "little girls took to theaters in gold tiaras and star-dusted shorts; older women watching the film spontaneously burst into tears when Diana pulled off her disguise and threw herself headfirst into No Man's Land" (p. 8). Deemed an inspiration for a new generation, the film's impacts extend beyond its still-growing profits.

Declared "a symbol of feminist revolt" in the same year *Roe v. Wade* changed the landscape of women's rights (Lepore, 2015, p. 287), Wonder Woman's reappearance in 2017 draws from her storied past as a feminist icon. Since her 1941 creation, the woman warrior with Amazonian origins has inspired the creation of other fictional female-bodied figures as well as the activism of real-life women (Yockey, 2012). In her history of the heroine's origins, Lepore (2015) calls Wonder Woman a "link in a chain of events that begins with the woman suffrage campaigns of the 1910s and ends with the troubled place of feminism fully a century later" (p. xiii). Although not the first, and obviously not the last, physically powerful woman to feature prominently on the pages of comic books and on the small and big screen, Wonder Woman's decades-spanning popularity relates to feminisms' complicated pasts and presents, including contemporary postfeminist media representations of dangerous dames.

Beginning in the early 21st century with Beatrix Kiddo (see Chapter 2) and, later, Katniss Everdeen (see Chapter 3), and continuing with all of the other female-bodied warriors, superheroes, spies, and assassins featured in increasing numbers in big-budget Hollywood action movies, the tough woman action niche owes some debt to Wonder Woman's cultural resonance and endurance. Conceived by William Moulton Marston as a feminine feminist hero (Lepore 2015), from the moment of her appearance Wonder Woman has simultaneously resisted and reinforced gender stereotypes by challenging male dominance while representing women's empowerment as rooted in femininity. Marston hoped that Wonder Woman would combat culturally entrenched ideas of women's inferiority in the 1940s, and, as a role model for children, offer a glimpse into a utopian future: a superior world ruled by women and guided by feminine virtues (Lepore, 2015). That world has not yet manifested, but the character of Wonder Woman finally, more than three quarters of a century after her creation, has ruled the screen in her own Hollywood blockbuster. Scholars have examined Wonder Woman's relationship to feminism, her changing portrayals in different historical contexts, and her influence on the female-bodied superheroes who follow her (Cocca, 2014; Darowski, 2014; DiPaolo, 2007; Robinson, 2004; Stuller, 2010; Zechowski & Neumann, 2014). We add a consideration of Wonder Woman's construction as a liberal white feminist par excellence.

This chapter briefly traces Wonder Woman's comic book roots and her ties to liberal (white) feminist imaginaries. We then turn to her contemporary filmic portrayal as it relates to her feminist potential, asking whether

Wonder Woman lives up to *Business Insider's* bold claim that the movie is a "beacon for the female empowerment movement going on in the country" (Guerrasio, 2017, para. 8). We find that, as a figure of women's empowerment, Wonder Woman's most recent big-screen iteration at times resists the male gaze. However, her construction as a "universal female hero" (Jenkins, 2016, para. 4) repeats many of the elisions that have characterized liberal white feminism, including its embrace of Republican Motherhood, alignment with heteronormative structures, and use of gendered rhetorics of heroism that uphold nationalist and imperialist endeavors.

Constructing a Historical (White) Feminine/ist Icon

"As lovely as Aphrodite—as wise as Athena—with the speed of Mercury and the strength of Hercules... she is known only as Wonder Woman!" (Marston, 1941). This description, which accompanied Wonder Woman's first public appearance nearly 80 years ago, ascribed Wonder Woman's power to a mixture of stereotypically feminine and masculine qualities. Designed to compete with popular male comic book superheroes including Superman, Batman, and Captain America, Wonder Woman was strong and fast, features associated with male gods and demi-gods. Her heroic "womanly" virtues, however, combined beauty with character. As such, Wonder Woman was capable of challenging physical feats, but, like her Greek goddess predecessors, played the role of a patron by also providing moral instruction to men. Even the ordering of these features in her comic-book introduction subordinates her "masculine" traits of strength and speed to her "feminine" traits of loveliness and peacefulness.

Wonder Woman emerges from a longer legacy of powerful women. Her origin story establishes that she descended from the god Zeus and Hippolyta, Queen of the Amazons.[2] The mythological Amazons typify the trope of the weapon-wielding warrior woman and the mystique of an essentialized vision of feminine power.[3] This trope has remained rhetorically significant in the contemporary era; it frequently has been tied to whiteness and employed for both feminist and anti-feminist purposes. The first figures of fierce femininity to appear in comic books were, in fact, not Wonder Woman, but Jungle Girl and Sheena, Queen of the Jungle, who both appeared on comic book covers a full five years prior to Wonder Woman. Like Wonder Woman, Sheena, the first heroine to have her own solo title, was simultaneously fierce and nurturing. She could tame the animals and defeat any threat she encountered from hunters, traders, and native peoples, all while wearing a leopard-print bikini with flowing, long blonde hair.[4] In constructing a vision of woman's power predicated on her femininity and ability to "tame" and civilize the native people and animals, the figure of the white jungle woman, which first rose to prominence in the 19th century, conveniently supported Anglo-European colonialism and empire.[5]

Wonder Woman's roots on the mysterious island of Themyscira reproduce this white-woman-in-the-jungle allure, and the "powerful woman vs. menaced-white-beauty dichotomy" on which it relies (Barnett, 2017, para. 11). The character was tied further to national and imperial histories by the racialized depictions of the enemy throughout the comic (Lepore, 2015). Wonder Woman's consistent ability to escape from or defeat her enemies did not negate her role as the menaced white beauty in her encounters with various Others. Instead, Wonder Woman's successes in breaking free from her comic-book captors allowed her to relive the narrative of (white) women's captivity and release, week after week, frame after frame. This rhetorical move ostensibly enabled Wonder Woman to fight patriarchy by giving her the bodily agency to break free from subordination to men, but in a manner compatible with the universalizing, imperial underpinnings of liberal feminism in which Anglo-European women's advancement was constructed in relation to racialized and/or non-national Others (see Amos & Parmar, 2001; Burton, 1991; Mohanty, 1988; Russo, 2006).

Wonder Woman was linked to U.S. American identity by her red bustier and star-spangled mini shorts—a costume modeled after Captain America's flag costume—and by her first mission: to contribute to the war effort of the allied forces in World War II (Fox, 1942). Although Wonder Woman opposed war on principle, it was essential that she "be willing to fight for democracy. In fact, she had to be superpatriotic" (Lepore, 2015, p. 196). By featuring a female-bodied democratic national hero, the Wonder Woman comics capitalized on Captain America's popularity and illustrated what creator Marston saw as "a great movement now underway" in the United States: "the growth in the power of women" (Lepore, 2015, p. 196). Proclaimed by Marston as "psychological propaganda for the new type of woman who should, I believe, rule the world" (Lepore, 2015, p. 202), the exceptional Wonder Woman was designed to challenge notions of women's inferiority while advancing U.S. American superiority and exceptionalism.

Because feminine/ist justice heroes "'trouble' genre conventions of heroism and nation," they are "at once disruptive and hegemonic" (Owen, Stein, & Vande Berg, 2007, p. 41). Wonder Woman's image simultaneously disrupts and reproduces patriarchy and nationalism. Marston issued explicit instructions regarding the illustration of Wonder Woman: she should be the most powerful woman the world had ever known but she should wear very little clothing (Lepore, 2015). In her most recent Hollywood appearance, Wonder Woman stayed true to this original vision.

Wonder Woman and Feminism on the Big Screen

Wonder Woman opens with a brief glimpse of Diana Prince (Gal Gadot) in present-day Paris holding a photograph. The action really begins on the idyllic island of Themyscira, where her flashback unfolds. Here, audiences see Wonder Woman as young Amazon princess Diana, a child growing up surrounded by natural and feminine beauty. In Amazon history, passed on to Diana by her mother Hippolyta (Connie Nielsen), Ares, the god of war, sought to destroy humanity, but Zeus, before dying, bequeathed the Amazons an island and the "Godkiller" sword so that they might defeat Ares should he return. Trained as a warrior by her aunt, General Antiope (Robin Wright), the young adult Diana has only begun to discover her superpowers when she witnesses the offshore crash of U.S. American pilot and spy Steve Trevor (Chris Pine). She rescues Steve, who is enamored with her from the moment he opens his eyes. When the German soldiers who have been hunting him arrive, the Amazons defeat them in battle.

Believing World War I to be the work of Ares, Diana decides she must leave her home in paradise to help save the world. She tells her mother Hippolyta, "I cannot stand by while innocent lives are lost. I have to go." She travels to London with Steve, who, upon her insistence, takes her with him to the front. He plans to locate and stop the unleashing of a very dangerous gas; Diana intends to find and kill Ares to end the war. On their way, Diana vanguards crossing the treacherous No Man's Land, thereby liberating a long-suffering village. In the midst of the warmth of the villagers' celebration, her romance with Steve begins. As the plot proceeds, Diana finally finds Ares (David Thewlis), who attempts to convince her to join forces with him, while Steve destroys the lethal gas laboratory, sacrificing himself and dying a martyred hero. Diana, now fully embodying her powers as Wonder Woman, kills Ares. At the close of the film, present-day Diana's trip down memory lane ends with her emailing Bruce Wayne to thank him for the photograph. A century later, the character has not aged; Wonder Woman is an immortal hero who continues to dedicate herself to fighting for good.

The film's reception was overwhelmingly positive, with Rotten Tomatoes (2020) naming it number four on their list of the "72 Best Superhero Movies of All Time." James Cameron, who is known for writing and directing strong female-bodied characters in movies including *Aliens* (1986), *The Terminator* (1984), and *Terminator 2: Judgment Day* (1991), did not view *Wonder Woman* as a success for women, proclaiming, "She's an objectified icon, and it's just male Hollywood doing the same old thing" (Couch, 2017, para. 1). Clearly, Marston's vision of Wonder Woman's beauty is realized with the casting of the conventionally stunning Gadot in the starring role and the form-fitting leather armor she wears.

Despite the film's superficial adherence to Hollywood's objectification of women, there are overt feminist critiques embedded within the movie. Wonder Woman's entrance into European society as a foreigner allows her to remark naively upon the norms of patriarchal society. For example, on the boat to London, Diana quotes her extensive research about sex to Steve, saying the Amazons had concluded "that men are essential for procreation, but when it comes to pleasure, unnecessary." This rejects the cultural script of women engaging in sexual activity only for procreation and embraces women's pleasure. Through this comment, Wonder Woman offers a mild challenge to constructions of masculine sexuality as dominant as well as ostensibly undoing what Rich (1980) calls "compulsory heterosexuality" (p. 631). After arriving in London, in keeping with Marston's original assertion that the society ruled by women would provide the only path toward peace (Lepore, 2015), Wonder Woman expresses curiosity about war meetings attended entirely by men. She launches a classic second-wave critique of the subordination of women in the workplace, wryly responding to Etta Candy's job title of secretary by observing, "where I'm from, that's called slavery." In another scene, several men in a bar make sexist comments to her, and she effortlessly defeats them in a fight. In terms of the movie's feminist gains, Gadot's character is a fully developed female-bodied hero and a powerful figure. Critics and viewers alike praised the film's feminism on social media, celebrating its emotional impact and its portrayal of Wonder Woman as an agentic, powerful subject rather than an object.

Resisting the Male Gaze

Cameron's critique was based largely on Wonder Woman's being played by Gadot, a former model and Miss Israel. Casting an "absolutely drop-dead gorgeous" actor in the role was, according to Cameron, a step backward for Hollywood (Masters, 2017, para. 6). However, Wonder Woman is not overtly sexualized in the film. Despite her iconic, tight, and revealing red, white, and blue leather armor, the camera does not further objectify the character. Throughout the two-and-a-half-hour movie, viewers do not have the voyeuristic pleasure of seeing Wonder Woman naked, having sex, or getting dressed, activities often associated with leading ladies in film (see Chapter 4). In Mulvey's (1975) theorization of the male gaze, she notes that scopophilic pleasure, pleasure derived from seeing something private or forbidden, is part of cinema's intrigue. Although this pleasure frequently is satisfied by watching women in the nude, Jenkins instead directs the camera to disrupt the male gaze, positioning Wonder Woman as a subject by focusing on action and avoiding lingering gazes on parts of Gadot's body.[6]

Mulvey (1975) regarded cinema as an "advanced representation system" structured by a series of looks originating from the camera, the audience, and the characters "within the screen illusion" (p. 7, 17). Narrative film, she argued, conventionally denies the first two ways of looking by subordinating them to the third. In doing so, it positions the audience to act as voyeurs who experience pleasure by looking through the eyes of the film's protagonist. Because film largely has been produced for men by men—a problem that remains true over 40 years after Mulvey's essay, despite increased attention to this inequity (Smith, Choueiti, & Pieper, 2018)—narrative film routinely centers male heroes. Women, on the other hand, have often been portrayed as Others through whom the hero's subjectivity is realized, with women frequently playing supporting characters in hero films. Both men and women learn to identify with the main character, with the identification in turn gendering subject status as male and positioning female characters' bodies as objects of the subject's gaze. In this manner, as viewers learn to see from a masculine standpoint, they subject women to objectification.

In *Wonder Woman*, the camera gaze follows convention to encourage identification with the protagonist but placing a female body in this position disrupts the maleness of the gaze, with production techniques typically reserved for male heroes extended to this female-bodied hero. What Watercutter (2017) describes as "the hero shot," a slow-motion shot depicting a hero in battle, recurs throughout *Wonder Woman*. From the scene in Themyscira where the Amazon warriors jump off the cliff to battle incoming war ships to Wonder Woman taking all the fire in order to cross No Man's Land and vanquish the enemy, over 20 epic moments feature female-bodied heroes as acting subjects. Given that "the hero shot is a staple of superhero movies, and action movies in general... the impact of those shots is hard to ignore" (Watercutter, 2017, para. 3). Indeed, "aesthetic elements in film function rhetorically to elicit identifiable sensual and affective experiences" (Ott & Keeling, 2011, p. 378). In this case, the camera angles, close-up shots that focus on Wonder Woman's face (rather than her body parts), slow motion shots in battle, epic music, dramatic lighting, and special effects combine to produce Wonder Woman aesthetically as a formidable hero. Engaging audiences' senses to propel connection with the protagonist and her abilities has the potential to create surprising, and memorable, experiences and affects for viewers. As Watercutter (2017) puts it: "When you don't expect to see yourself as the hero, you don't easily forget what it looks like" (para. 1).

The film's promotional materials highlight the rhetorical power of the hero shot. In one movie poster, Wonder Woman holds her arm aloft as a shield as she runs into battle, her eyes fierce as her powerful glowing bracelets protect her from bullets. In contrast to the long-standing sexualization of tough or athletic women through passive objectification (Shugart, 2003), Wonder Woman's body is portrayed as active and agentic. In a welcome change from the sexy pout frequently donned by feminine characters, her arm hides her mouth, directing focus instead to her superhuman speed, indicated by her streaming hair and the blurring of the scene behind her juxtaposed with the crispness of her forward-moving body.

In a different close-up image, Wonder Woman wields a sword, light glinting off her headpiece. The focus splits between her rippling arm muscles and, again, her fierce gaze, dark eyebrows drawn, mouth mostly obscured. On this image appears a single word: "Wonder." One of a set of three, the other two posters in this series feature Wonder Woman in heroic action and are captioned with "Power" and "Courage." These posters do not entirely disrupt the feminine beauty standards central to the image of Wonder Woman; indeed, they maintain emblems of femininity, including Wonder Woman's flowing hair, tiara, and costume. However, they do cast Wonder Woman in the role of the heroic subject rather than the sexualized object, emphasizing Wonder Woman's strength and character rather than her looks.

Of course, despite these depictions, Wonder Woman does not entirely escape sexualization over the course of the movie. Most obviously, she is conventionally beautiful and dressed in a revealing costume, even during her most heroic moments. Furthermore, her powers are connected to her sex appeal. In the bar scene, when she throws one of the men across the room, another man remarks, "I'm both frightened and aroused." This perpetuates the mythological construction of the Amazon figure who, according to Adams (2010), "occupies an unusual place in the ranks of feminine archetypes. She is hypersexualized, but her sexual prowess is figured as part of her extraordinary and indomitable political and martial power" (para. 8). Reinscribing this archetype, Wonder Woman fails to transcend the eroticization of the fighting female body. The male character's comments instruct viewers how to interpret her, suggesting that strong women are sexually desirable. Even as Wonder Woman acts as subject, other characters place her back into the object position, reasserting the male gaze. With her glamorous look, revealing outfit, and sexualized Amazonian strength, Wonder Woman, despite her power, thus remains within the norms of white supremacist patriarchy (hooks, 1994).

Questions regarding the character's sex appeal have been at the forefront of critics' debates about whether the film is feminist (Cauterucci, 2017; Killian, 2017; Rios, 2017). However, we believe several other issues constrain Wonder Woman's feminist potential, or, rather, make the title character an exemplar of liberal white feminism rather than a truly progressive feminist figure. One of the movie's most memorable and symbolic battle scenes, addressed in the next section, identifies how Wonder Woman's construction as a female-bodied justice hero aligns with imperial feminism.

Crossing No Man's Land and Becoming a Female-Bodied Justice Hero

One of the most definitive scenes of Wonder Woman opens with an establishing shot of a desolate terrain. Periodic explosions appear as specks of light across a bleak landscape. Diana, Steve, and their team have just arrived at the war front. As they make their way through a trench, Steve shields Diana from the fallout of a strike. Horrified by the suffering surrounding them, Diana wants to stop to help, but Steve plans to bypass this treacherous warzone. Down in the trench, as the men attempt to push forward, a woman stops Diana. Her head covered by a scarf, she taps into visual rhetorics of refugee women of war-torn countries in need of U.S. aid (see Kozol, 2004). The woman begs Diana, "Help, please help, they've taken everything." The German soldiers have seized her village and enslaved the people. Diana tells Steve they have to help; women and children are dying. Steve explains that this is "No Man's Land," terrain that "no man can cross." The entire battalion of men has been unable to gain an inch, he elaborates. "This is not something you can cross. It's not possible. We can't save everyone in this war. This is not what we came here to do." Diana turns from him, her frustration and despair giving way to determination. She takes her hair down, dons her warrior headband, and responds, "No, but it's what *I'm* going to do."

Discarding her coat, she emerges from the bunker into the bleak expanse in slow motion, glowing in her red, white, and blue battle armor. Steve, panic in his voice, yells, "Diana!" She walks out slowly and deflects the first bullet that comes at her with her golden cuff; it explodes into glittering pieces. The next bullet comes, and she deflects it, too. As she proceeds, the bullets come faster, the German army focusing fire on her. She begins to run toward the enemy, batting the bullets away as quickly as they arrive. The soldiers behind her are able to climb out of the trench as Diana fields all of the fire. As the gunfire intensifies, she blocks it with her shield, a deter-mined grimace on her face as she digs her heels into the demolished gray earth, unwilling to be deterred. As the mythical scene unfolds with Wonder Woman leading the way in her national colors with the troops behind her, it invokes the iconic image of Lady Liberty found in Eugène Delacroix's *Liberty Leading the People*, which features a woman or goddess leading men to revolution.[7]

As the soldiers continue to advance with Diana at the helm, she catapults into one of the trenches and crushes enemy soldiers' weapons with her super-human strength while the troops clear the other trenches. She leaps into the top story room of a building where she handily defeats all her male enemies in a slow-motion battle scene that uses visual effects including digital doubles and bullet time. Increasingly confident in her power with each move, Diana jumps high into the air to stop a cannon ball with her shield. She overturns a truck. She swings the golden lasso, alternating between lassoing and kicking to launch the men rushing her far into the distance.[8] Duplicating an Amazon warrior move employed during the earlier battle on the island of Themyscira, the men launch Diana into a tower so she can neutralize a sniper. The force from Diana's impenetrable body smashing into the building crumbles the brick. As the villagers come out of hiding, Diana appears amidst the debris atop the building, like a goddess standing over her people with the dusky clouds behind her. As she looks down benevolently, they cheer.

This pivotal scene, much celebrated by audiences for its emotional impact (Abad-Santos, 2017; Skye, 2017), transforms Diana into Wonder Woman. She emerges as a leader, and the scene synecdochally symbolizes the larger battle she fights for freedom and equality. Told, in so many words, to keep her head down and trudge through the trench—the only way to cross the field alive—Diana refuses. She defies men's authority to stand up for what she knows is right. She focuses not on slaying enemies, but on dismantling their weapons to eliminate the danger. Where no man could cross, Diana did. And when no man could save the village, Diana did. The scene is poignant; the histories and myths it invokes, as well as the careful cinematography and layers of effects, offer audiences a critical message about women's empowerment. However, this scene relies on a construction of Wonder Woman's powers in ways that draw upon long-standing liberal white feminist tropes including Republican Motherhood, heteronormativity, and the (white) savior.

Reproducing Republican Motherhood

In a world of male superheroes, Wonder Woman stands out as a figure of classic femininity, coupling beauty with virtue. Although her superhuman strength equips her to emerge victorious from battle, the No Man's Land scene focuses on the extraordinary depths of her compassion, even extending to her enemies. The ideology of Republican Motherhood, which emphasized that women's loving and angelic natures made them especially worthy of political participation, fueled the nineteenth-century rhetorics of women's suffrage and influenced Marston's original vision of Wonder Woman (Lepore, 2015). This ideology allowed women to fight for rights through their societal roles as mothers, claiming their empowerment would enable them to guide their men in virtuous action (Kerber, 1976; Zagarri, 1992).

Women have long been envisioned as central to the nation and its (re)production due to their roles as biological reproducers and symbolic position as the bastions of national traditions, values, and culture (Chatterjee, 1990; Kaplan, Alarcón, & Moallem, 1999; Sinha, 2006; Stoler, 2002; Yuval-Davis, 1997). Given that Diana originates on the remote fictional island of Themyscira, a matriarchy (governed by mothers), her Amazonian roots position her as a matronly figure and a kind of national mother even as she escapes the confines of traditional motherhood, family, and marriage.[9] As a feminine/

ist superhero, Wonder Woman's power is "not just in physicality but also in love, empathy, sisterhood, families, perseverance, and forgiveness" (Cocca, 2016, p. 215). Through caring for others, Wonder Woman thus destroys evil and brings people, and nations, together.

In the No Man's Land scene, Wonder Woman's ability to empathize with the refugee woman's suffering invokes her desire to end the entrenched violence that the men accept. In other words, Wonder Woman is not powerful simply because she measures up to (and exceeds) men physically and on the battlefield; she is powerful because her womanhood guides her virtues, so she sees from a different, morally elevated, vantage point. The cinematic construction of this battle scene reinforces her elevation. Wonder Woman literally rises above the men as she leaves the trenches to forge forward; she rises further above them in her climactic leap to the top of the building to take down the sniper, positioning her so the villagers look up to her as she steps from the ruins.

Instead of relegating tough women to assume the masculine façade deemed more fitting for an action hero (Gilpatric, 2010), a superhero whose powers come from her compassion constructs new models for what emotions heroes can experience and express. However, Wonder Woman (in both the comic books and the film) relies upon the rhetorically sticky depiction of women's moral superiority. The idyllic island society of the Amazons epitomizes this construction, suggesting that without the folly of men, women would construct a more perfect, peaceful world. In this manner, Wonder Woman dramatizes stereotypical gender differences by presenting women as innately caring and nurturing.

Marston spoke to the concerns we have with this feminine/ist archetype, noting Wonder Woman was created as a hero with "all the strength of Superman plus *all the allure of a good and beautiful woman*" (as cited in Lepore, 2015, p. 187, emphasis added). Diana is good. She is beautiful. She is most certainly a superhero and a woman, which is refreshing. But does re-presenting myths grounded in stereotypical, dated, maternal, and essentialist constructions of femininity make the work feminist? We have doubts.

Performing Heteronormativity

Despite the queer potentiality embedded within Wonder Woman's background on an island populated only with women, the film follows a formula, crafting a heteronormative love story between Diana and Steve. Within this narrative, Wonder Woman occupies a subject (rather than object) position occasionally. In the first flirty scene, when she gazes upon a naked Steve and asks him about his body as he steps out of the hot springs on Themyscira, dominant scripts are briefly reversed as he is objectified by her, the audience's, and the camera's gazes. A casual critique of marriage and support for feminine pleasure springs from their conversation on the boat. With the power she commands on the battlefield and her assertive willpower, Wonder Woman is not subordinate to Steve. Nevertheless, their developing romance follows a standard progression due primarily to Steve's behaviors.

Steve does not initially believe Diana about Ares, but he brings her along because he is enamored. He engages in protective masculine gestures throughout the movie, ranging from adjusting her clothing when they first walk through London to draping her with his coat when they sit around a campfire on their way to the front to shielding her from shrapnel in the trench to attempting to stop her from entering the range of enemy fire. As Wonder Woman's "guide" in an unfamiliar world, Steve functions as the resident expert juxtaposed with Wonder Woman's naïve, foreign innocence.

When Steve and the men see what Wonder Woman can accomplish in battle, their attitudes change, but the heteronormative script persists. Following this transformative scene, Steve and Diana dance, and she asks, "Is this what people do when there are no wars to fight?" After he responds, "This and other things," they go upstairs to consummate their relationship. Despite her character having once been derided by psychologists and conservative crusaders as a lesbian who would damage young children (Lepore, 2015), in the 2017 film, Wonder Woman emerges as unquestionably heterosexual. In fact, Steve's death overwhelms her, and her love and grief motivate her and boost her strength as she fights Ares. As a strong, powerful woman, Wonder Woman remains a sexual object available to men, a fantasy fueled further by the implication of heterosexual virginity accompanying her Amazon origins.

The film's heteronormative story instructs women to love men, rely upon them for protection, and be (sexually) available to them. The ostensibly empowering message of the "No Man's Land" scene is limited by a heternormative suggestion: by believing in yourself you can attain anything— read: any man—you desire. Immediately following her battle win, Wonder Woman returns to the more stereotypically feminine context of the heterosexual relationship where Steve, once again, serves as her guide, thus taming her progressive potential.

Saving Women and Children

Evidenced in the No Man's Land scene, and repeated throughout the film, is a not-so-subtle storyline upholding nationalism, militarism, and empire. Wonder Woman steps into the role of the (white) savior in a manner that draws upon the construction of women's maternal virtues while reinforcing the paternalistic nation-state. As an Amazon, it is Diana's "sacred duty to defend the world," she argues before leaving Themyscira. In her position as a matronly goddess, all the world's citizens become her children. This parallels the paternal duty the U.S. claims for itself in its role as global police, which reproduces (neo)colonial and imperial relationships. In fact, representations of Amazons have aligned with the colonial mission and its purported aegis to spread democracy and civilization for a long time (Adams, 2010).

Diana's repeated insistence that they must save the innocent women and children and that she is "willing to fight for those who cannot fight for themselves" plays into patriarchal narratives of rescue, reflecting what Young (2003) terms the logic of masculinist protection. This logic rhetorically configures the U.S. nation-state as protector of vulnerable populations, including its own citizens and the "womenandchildren" of the world (Enloe, 1990).[10] Despite her female body, Wonder Woman steps into this national and imperial role, which is not "self-consciously dominative" but based on the ideal of the chivalrous and caring masculine man who "faces the world's difficulties and dangers in order to shield women from harm" (Young, 2003, p. 4). Wonder Woman's shield symbolizes her special role as protector; the rhetoric of protecting the innocent while advancing the military's cause enables any casualties to be forgiven as necessary and just, in contrast to the actions of the senselessly violent and uncaring enemy.

The suffering of women and children and, specifically, the woman in the trenches who begs for help, enables Wonder Woman to advance masculinist protection even while embodying feminine virtue. As a maternal figure, she is permitted to defend children, and as a feminine/ist hero she is permitted to fight for women. She does not trumpet men's need for protection, nor is she positioned as a soldier upholding a particular national banner; instead, she comes from outside the nation as a white savior, reinforcing an imperialist uptake. Despite Wonder Woman's positioning as a foreigner visiting a strange land, however, U.S. American audiences are encouraged to read Wonder Woman as aligned with the United States. Steve, her love interest and the person who takes her to the war and fights the Germans alongside her, is U.S. American. Through their efforts, the United States wins the war, fights evil, and extends its national compassion to the global community through military strength.

Combined, the film's engagement with Republican Motherhood, heteronormativity, and saving "womenandchildren" limit the scope of the film's feminist possibilities. As a national superhero, Wonder Woman's godly abilities reinforce myths of U.S. superiority and manifest destiny along with stereotypical gender roles. Wonder Woman's extensive training by a feminist and female-bodied community, mastery of powerful weaponry, and ability to defend the world, subtly reinforce the imperialistic militarism that her maternally virtuous character attempts to undo.

Tales of Empowerment

Wonder Woman was celebrated as a feminist movie for (finally) portraying a female-bodied superhero who was neither a villain nor merely an eroticized ass-kicking sidekick. The plot of Wonder Woman follows the classic structure of a hero tale: an "American monomyth" (Jewett & Lawrence, 1979). The film begins by identifying an evil enemy within the global or national community—in this case, World War I. Because the existing community and institutions are unable to resolve this evil alone, enter the hero, Wonder Woman, who "arrives, resists temptation, and copes with evil" (p. 312). Wonder Woman's heroism is unique because her compassion is central to her character and fighting style. Wonder Woman's beauty, likewise, is presented as an inherent virtue, and her bodily strengths are undergirded by her "feminine" virtues of love and kindness.

In a media landscape where women continue to be underrepresented, Wonder Woman's Hollywood success expands the possibilities for more inclusive representation and offers pleasures to viewers who have not always been able to recognize themselves in the heroes on screen. However, the film also relies on a series of erasures. By examining the configuration of Wonder Woman as a feminine/ist icon, we have argued that Wonder Woman is constrained by liberal white feminist assumptions.

In the 2017 movie, despite the multicultural Amazon tribe, few scenes feature a woman of color prominently—or even speaking. The wondrous female-bodied hero is "predicated on a particular set of effacements or repressions: of those women whom [she] cannot represent" (Thornham, 2007,

p. 29). Wonder Woman's long-standing legibility as a feminist icon serves to sublimate race in order to construct an empowered white womanhood. This "becomes something of a standard for how female superheroes are written" (Cocca, 2016, p. 17). To promote the film as a feminist film and as a universalized construction of women's empowerment therefore reinforces limiting, racist, and imperial discourses within mainstream feminisms.

The success of another superhero film that hit the box office at the same time, *Black Panther*, cements this division of race and gender, illustrating a familiar pattern in which mainstream feminist agendas have centered white women while mainstream civil rights agendas have centered men of color. From the fights for the franchise to civil rights, to Barack Obama defeating Hillary Clinton in the 2008 Democratic primary, to the first big-screen appearances of a female-bodied superhero and black superhero, the false division of race and gender oppression and empowerment persists. Even though strong black women appear in *Black Panther*, the characters feature in an Afro-futurist story about black masculinity. The titles of the films confirm the construction of gender without race and race without gender, phenomena documented by black feminist scholars in the collection *All the Women Are White, All the Blacks Are Men, But Some of Us Are Brave* (Hull, Scott & Smith, 1982). Although *Wonder Woman* does offer indices for women's empowerment through its expansion of the superhero genre and its partial resistance to the male gaze, we are concerned by the extent to which it erases race, and other vectors of identity, in order to perpetuate myths of equality that do not exist.

As of 2019 we question the myth of the American Dream when immigrants are being blocked at the U.S.-Mexico border. We see that the sonnet associated with the Statue of Liberty is more of an U.S. American ideal rather than a reality. Although some people believe we are in a post-racist society, more black and Hispanic families live in poverty compared to white families (de Brey et al., 2019), and a disproportionate number of black men are incarcerated (Bureau of Justice Statistics, 2019). Likewise, women continue in their quest for justice. Despite the 1964 Civil Rights Act and various gender discrimination laws, the average gender pay gap in the United States is about 19 %, and "black and Hispanic women are most affected by the wage gap" (Sheth, Gal, & Kiersz, 2019, para. 14). Based on the 2017 U.S. Census, "white women earn 79 % of what white men do, while black women earn 67 % and Hispanic women earn 58 %" (Sheth, Gal, & Kiersz, 2019, para. 15).

Clearly, battles on the screen inform and reflect battles off the screen, in which women of different sexualities, races, gender identities, socioeconomic statuses, abilities, and nationalities continue to struggle for rights, access, and equality. Films offer frameworks for audiences to understand themselves, and others, and the ways feminisms have evolved is tied intimately to these mediated constructions. Before we declare every ass-kicking woman to appear on the big screen a feminist achievement, we must remember that the hero myths we construct also construct us.

Notes

1. The non-italicized "Wonder Woman" is used when referring to the character, as opposed to the italicized title of the film. For a more complete history of the character of Wonder Woman see Berlatsky (2015), Daniels (2004) and Lepore (2015).
2. Although in some versions of the Wonder Woman story she is crafted from clay by Hippolyta, in the movie version she is not crafted of clay—though this is the story her mother tells her—instead, she is the result of an affair between Hippolyta and Zeus (Robinson, 2017).
3. Some evidence points to the historical existence of Amazons (Mayor, 2014). The use of the word "myth" here is not intended to deny this history but to point to the portrayal of Amazons in Greek mythology, which was drawn upon by U.S. suffragists, and served as a source of inspiration for Wonder Woman's creator William Moulton Marston (Lepore, 2015).
4. The term "native" is used here rather than Indigenous in order to encapsulate the racist, colonial depictions, stereotypes, and language utilized in the comics. Comic book representations of the female-bodied jungle hero drew upon the success of Tarzan, an inherently colonialist figure reflecting Anglo-European fascinations with taming the wilderness and civilizing the "dark continent" of Africa.
5. Take, for example, the novel *She: A History of Adventure* (Haggard, 1887), in which a jungle queen named Ayesha fulfilled the image of a white woman "either dominating or at perpetual risk from 'uncivilized' black African men" (Barnett, 2017, para. 5).
6. We are aware that this is an imperfectly realized vision. Although Gadot's character resists objectification, she does not avoid it entirely, and there are occasional body scans, including from her boot-clad legs up her body as she emerges from the trench in the No Man's Land scene. These scans, however, occur with far less frequency than shots of her body in action.
7. Lady Liberty is a comic by Soleil as well as a fictional character in DC comics whose special abilities include the projection of energy beams from her torch.
8. The image of the Amazon warrior, lasso in hand, is also one replicated from ancient art.
9. Prior to the creation of Wonder Woman, the connection between Amazons, women's virtues, and women's rights within the context of the nation-state had already been drawn

by U.S. suffragists, who deployed the representational power of the Amazons to assist in their fight (Lepore, 2015).

10. Enloe (1990) utilizes the term "womenandchildren" to describe how women and children perform a rhetorical function in international politics wherein individual subjects are discursively transformed into a single, helpless, victimized entity in need of rescue and/or pity (p. 29).

References

Abad-Santos, A. (2017, December 15). *Wonder Woman's* "no man's land" scene was the best superhero moment of 2017. *Vox Magazine*. Retrieved from https://www.vox.com/2017-in-review/2017/12/15/16767902/wonder-womans-no-mans-land-scene

Adams, M. E. (2010). The Amazon warrior woman and the de/construction of gendered imperial authority in nineteenth-century colonial literature. *Nineteenth-Century Gender Studies*, 6(1). Retrieved from http://m.ncgsjournal.com/issue61/New%20PDFs/NCGS%20Journal%20Issue%206.1%20-%20The%20Amazon%20Warrior%20Woman%20-%20Maeve%20E.%20Adams.pdf

Amos, V., & Parmar, P. (2001). Challenging imperial feminism. In K. Bhavnani (Ed.), *Feminism and 'race'* (pp. 17–32). New York, NY: Oxford University Press.

Barnett, D. (2017, July 6). From she to Sheena: Can modern audiences ignore the jungle queen's racist roots? *The Guardian*. Retrieved from https://www.theguardian.com/books/2017/jul/06/she-sheena-jungle-queens-enduring-ambiguous-allure-h-rider-haggard

Berlatsky, N. (2015). *Wonder Woman: Bondage and feminism in the Marston/Peter comics, 1941–1948*. New Brunswick, NJ: Rutgers University Press.

Bureau of Justice Statistics. (2019). Table 381: Jail inmates by sex, race, and Hispanic origin: 2000 to 2016 [selected years, as of June 30]. ProQuest Statistical Abstract of the U.S. 2019 Online Edition. Retrieved from https://statabs-proquest-com.ezproxy.mtsu.edu/sa/docview.html?table-no=381&acc-no=C7095-1.5&year=2019&z=0A37C438AD41C0A9392E2C3F6DE2B192951D3212&rc=1&seq=8&y=current

Burton, A. (1991). The feminist quest for identity: British imperial suffragism and "global sisterhood" 1900-1915. *Journal of Women's History*, 3(2), 46–81. doi:10.1353/jowh.2010.0098

Cauterucci, C. (2017, June 2). I wish *Wonder Woman* were as feminist as it thinks it is. *Slate Magazine*. Retrieved from https://slate.com/human-interest/2017/06/i-wish-wonder-woman-were-as-feminist-as-it-thinks-it-is.html

Chaterjee, P. (1990). The nationalist resolution of the women's question. In K. Sangari & S. Vaid (Eds.), *Recasting women: Essays in Indian colonial history* (pp. 233–253). New Brunswick, NJ: Rutgers University Press.

Cocca, C. (2014). Negotiating the third wave of feminism in *Wonder Woman*. [Symposium: The politics of the superhero]. *American Political Science Association*, 47(1), 98–103. doi:10.1017/S1049096513001662

Cocca, C. (2016). *Superwomen: Gender, power, and representation*. New York, NY: Bloomsbury.

Couch, A. (2017, August 24). James Cameron calls 'Wonder Woman' "a step backwards." *The Hollywood Reporter*. Retrieved from https://www.hollywoodreporter.com/heat-vision/james-cameron-calls-wonder-woman-a-step-backwards-1032433

Daniels, L. (2004). *Wonder Woman: The complete history*. San Francisco, CA: Chronicle Books.

Darowski, J. J. (2014). *The ages of Wonder Woman: Essays on the Amazon princess in changing times*. Jefferson, NC: McFarland & Company.

de Brey, C., Musu, L., McFarland, J., Wilkinson-Flicker, S., Diliberti, M., Zhang, A., …Wang, X. (2019, February). Status and trends in the education of racial and ethnic groups. *National Center for Education Statistics: Institute for Education Sciences*. Washington DC: U.S. Department of Education.

DiPaolo, M. E. (2007). Wonder Woman as World War II veteran, camp feminist icon, and male sex fantasy. In T. R. Wandtke (Ed.), *The amazing transforming superhero! Essays on the revision of characters in comic books, film and television* (pp. 151–173). Jefferson, NC: McFarland & Company.

Enloe, C. (1990, September 25). Womenandchildren: Making feminist sense of the Persian Gulf Crisis. *The Village Voice*, pp. 29 ff.

Fox, G. (1942, June-July). The Justice Society joins the war on Japan. *All-Star Comics #11*. New York, NY: All-American Publications.

Gilpatric, K. (2010). Violent female action characters in contemporary American cinema. *Sex Roles*, 62, 734–746. doi:10.1007/s11199-010-9757-7

Guerrasio, J. (2017, December 19). The 10 highest-grossing movies of 2017 that ruled the box office. *Business Insider*. Retrieved from https://www.businessinsider.com/highest-grossing-movies-of-2017-list-2017-12

Haggard, H. R. (1887). *She: A history of adventure*. London, United Kingdom: Longmans, Green, & Company.

hooks, b. (1994). *Outlaw culture: Resisting representations*. New York, NY: Routledge.

Hull, G. T., Scott, P. B., & Smith, B. (Eds.). (1982). *All the women are white, all the men are black, but some of us are brave*. New York: The Feminist Press at the City University of New York.

Jenkins, P. (2016, December 9). Interview with Rebecca Ford. 'Wonder Woman' director Patty Jenkins: How to make a female heroine "vulnerable," but not "lesser in any way." *The Hollywood Reporter*. Retrieved from https://www.hollywoodreporter.com/heat-vision/wonder-woman-director-patty-jenkins-how-make-a-female-heroine-vulnerable-but-not-lesser-any-w

Jenkins, P. (Director), Roven, C., Synder, D., Snyder, Z., & Suckle, R. (Producers). (2017). *Wonder Woman*. [Motion picture]. United States: Warner Brothers Pictures.

Jewett, R., & Lawrence, J. S. (1979). The problem of mythic imperialism. *American Culture*, 2(2), 309–320. doi:10.1111/j.1542-734X.1979.0202_309.x

Kaplan, C., Alarcón, N., & Moallem, M. (Eds.) (1999). *Between woman and nation: Nationalisms, transnational feminisms, and the state*. Durham, NC: Duke University Press.

Kerber, L. (1976). The Republican mother: Women and the enlightenment—an American perspective. *American Quarterly*, 28(2), 187–205.

Killian, K. D. (2017, June 19). How *Wonder Woman* is and isn't a feminist superheroine movie. *Psychology Today*. Retrieved from https://www.psychologytoday.com/us/blog/intersections/201706/how-wonder-woman-is-and-isnt-feminist-superheroine-movie

Kozol, W. (2004). Domesticating NATO's war in Kosovo/a: (In)visible bodies and the dilemma of photojournalism. *Meridians, 4*(2), 1–38.

Lepore, J. (2015). *The secret history of Wonder Woman*. New York, NY: Vintage Books.

Marston, W. M. (1941 December-1942 January). Introducing Wonder Woman. *All-Star Comics* #8. New York, NY: All-American Publications.

Masters, K. (2017, September 27). James Cameron doubles down on the 'Wonder Woman' critique, details the 'Avatar' sequels. *The Hollywood Reporter*. Retrieved from https://www.hollywoodreporter.com/features/james-cameron-doubles-down-wonder-woman-critique-details-avatar-sequels-1043026

Mayor, A. (2014). *The Amazons: Lives & legends of warrior women across the ancient world*. Princeton, NJ: Princeton University Press.

Mohanty, C. T. (1988). Under western eyes: Feminist scholarship and colonial discourses. *Feminist Review, 30*, 61–88.

Mulvey, L. (1975). Visual pleasure and narrative cinema. *Screen, 16*(3), 6–18. doi:10.1093/screen/16.3.6

Nama, A. (2011). *Super black: American pop culture and black superheroes*. Austin: University of Texas Press.

Ott, B., & Keeling, D. (2011). Cinema and choric connection: *Lost in Translation* as sensual experience. *Quarterly Journal of Speech, 97*(4), 363–386. doi:10.1080/00335630.2011.608704

Owen, A. S., Stein, S. R., & Vande Berg, L. R. (2007). *Bad girls: Cultural politics and media representations of transgressive women*. New York, NY: Peter Lang.

Rich, A. (1980). Compulsory heterosexuality and lesbian existence. *Signs, 5*(4), 631–660.

Rios, C. (2017, June 6). Feminists respond to *Wonder Woman*. *Ms. Magazine blog*. http://msmagazine.com/blog/2017/06/06/feminists-respond-wonder-woman/

Robinson, J. (2017, June 1). The subtle genius of *Wonder Woman's* cinematic origins. *Vanity Fair*. Retrieved from https://www.vanityfair.com/hollywood/2017/06/wonder-woman-movie-easter-egg-father-zeus-clay-bondage

Robinson, L. (2004). *Wonder women: Feminisms and superheroes*. New York, NY: Routledge.

Rotten Tomatoes. (2020). 72 best superhero movies of all time. *Fandango*. Retrieved from https://editorial.rottentomatoes.com/guide/best-superhero-movies-of-all-time/2/

Russo, A. (2006). The Feminist Majority Foundation's campaign to stop gender apartheid: The intersections of feminism and imperialism in the United States. *International Feminist Journal of Politics, 8*(4), 557–580. doi:10.1080/14616740600945149

Sheth, S., Gal, S., & Kiersz, A. (2019, April 2). 6 charts that show the glaring gap between men and women's salaries. *Business Insider*. Retrieved from https://www.businessinsider.com/gender-wage-pay-gap-charts-2017-3

Shugart, H. A. (2003). She shoots, she scores: Mediated constructions of contemporary female athletes in coverage of the 1999 US Women's soccer team. *Western Journal of Communication, 67*(1), 1–31. doi:10.1080/10570310309374756

Sinha, M. (2006). *Gender and nation*. Washington, DC: American Historical Association.

Skye, L. (2017, November 29). Why *Wonder Woman*'s no man's land scene is 2017's best film moment. *Digital Fox Media*. Retrieved from https://www.digitalfox.media/explained/why-wonder-womans-no-mans-land-scene-is-2017s-best-film-moment/

Smith, S. L., Choueiti, M., & Pieper, K. (2018). Inclusion in the director's chair?: Gender, race, & age of directors across 1,100 films from 2007–2017. *USC Annenberg Inclusion Initiative*. [White paper]. Retrieved from http://assets.uscannenberg.org/docs/inclusion-in-the-directors-chair-2007-2017.pdf

Sperling, N. (2017, June 16). *Wonder Woman* wins. *Entertainment Weekly*, pp. 8–9.

Stoler, A. L. (2002). *Carnal knowledge and imperial power: Race and the intimate in colonial rule*. Berkeley: University of California Press.

Stuller, J. K. (2010). *Ink-stained Amazons and cinematic warriors: Superwomen in modern mythology*. New York, NY: I.B. Tauris and Company.

Thornham, S. (2007). *Women, feminism, and media*. Edinburgh, United Kingdom: Edinburgh University Press.

Watercutter, A. (2017, June 6). *Wonder Woman* and the importance of the female hero moment. *Wired*. Retrieved from https://www.wired.com/2017/06/wonder-woman-hero-moment/

Yockey, M. (2012). *Wonder Woman* for a day: Affect, agency, and Amazons. *Transformative Works and Cultures, 10*. doi:10.3983/twc.2012.0318.

Young, I. M. (2003). The logic of masculinist protection: Reflections on the current security state. *Signs, 29*(1), 1–25.

Yuval-Davis, N. (1997). *Gender and nation*. London, United Kingdom: Sage.

Zagarri, R. (1992). Morals, manners, and the Republican mother. *American Quarterly, 44*(2), 192–215.

Zechowski, S., & Neumann, C. E. (2014). The mother of all superheroes: Idealizations of femininity in *Wonder Woman*. In M. Bajac-Carter, N. Jones, & B. Batchelor (Eds.), *Heroines of comic books and literature: Portrayals in popular culture* (pp. 133–144). Lanham, MD: Rowman & Littlefield.

· 4 ·

VISUALIZING VIOLENT FEMININITY: RACE, SEX AND FEMMES FATALES IN *ATOMIC BLONDE* AND *PROUD MARY*

Wonder Woman (2017) may have shattered one of Hollywood's glass ceilings by centering a female-bodied superhero who was not a villain. However, violent, heroic women were not lacking in Hollywood that year. Women starred in blockbusters including *Alien: Covenant* (2017), *Star Wars: The Last Jedi* (2017), *Ghost in the Shell* (2017), *Red Sparrow* (2018), and *Tomb Raider* (2018), and performed supporting roles in *Kong: Skull Island* (2017), *Guardians of the Galaxy 2* (2017), *Valerian and the City of a Thousand Planets* (2017), *Thor: Ragnarok* (2017), and *Black Panther* (2018). With the exception of the Afrocentric *Black Panther*, the preponderance of these films featured white women who are young, thin, and conform to stereotypical standardized notions of beauty. This limited visual representation of violent femininity normalizes a narrow definition of dangerous dames.

To further explore intersections of gender, race, and sexuality in the construction of dangerous dames in media, this chapter examines two films featuring fighting femmes appearing months after *Wonder Woman*. In *Atomic Blonde*, Charlize Theron plays Lorraine Broughton, a ruthless M16 agent. In *Proud Mary*, Taraji P. Henson plays Mary, an assassin for a major crime ring. Contrasting the construction of these two protagonists and their on-screen enactments of violence, we find that both characters transgress as well as reproduce feminine scripts. Although the films encompass differences in the races, sexualities, motives, and skills of their central characters, both operate in accordance with a postfeminist visual style in which beautiful women literally kick ass. The cinematography of *Atomic Blonde* and *Proud Mary* is replete with body scans and lingering foci on body parts that typify the male gaze and the fetishization of women's bodies as sexual objects (Mulvey, 1975, 1996). The films further sexualize the women through the femme fatale figure: the mysterious, well-coiffed woman who leads to men's destruction through her sexuality.[1]

These films offer productive sites for interrogating contemporary representations of women's power. Each movie was, to some extent, promoted and received as feminist (Brown, 2018; Lee, 2018; Mazziotta, 2017). Theron was featured on the cover of *Variety* and described as "fierce and fearless" in her starring role (Setoodeh, 2017). Henson was described in her role as "kick ass," a "queen," and "a feminist icon" (*Glitter Magazine*, 2018; Jutton, 2018; Madison, 2018). In an interview about the movie, Henson asserted, "Fuck that. If men can do it, why can't we?" (Lee, 2018, para. 2). Marketing materials celebrated the ass-kicking the films' heroes promised to deliver, as well. For instance, a promotional video for *Atomic Blonde* titled "Fight Like a Girl" features Theron's behind-the-scenes training (Universal Pictures, 2017). Analyzing how these Hollywood depictions simultaneously fetishize and celebrate these dangerous dames for their fighting and firearm skills offers insight into the commodification of feminist messages by postfeminist media.

As traced by our previous chapters, women in leading roles in action movies have proliferated over the last quarter of a century. Beginning in the late 1970s, a constellation of forces, including shifting gender roles and an increase in women's social, political, and economic power, led to an expansion of fierce, fighting female-bodied figures in film, in turn challenging stereotypical depictions of women as passive objects. However, in the highly masculinized arena of Hollywood blockbusters, women's entrance into the cinematic "space of the justice hero narrative" has taken place "through highly conventional masculine portals" (Owen, Stein, & Vande Berg, 2007, p. 44). Active leading ladies appear in westerns, detective tales, sci-fi stories, superhero movies, and spy/assassin films. In action/adventure movies starring women, leading ladies' gender performances in many ways align with masculine norms: they are strong, they are warriors, they are fighting.

Dangerous Dames in *Atomic Blonde* and *Proud Mary*

Released in May 2017 and directed by David Leitch, Atomic Blonde centers on M16 spy Lorraine Broughton who is one of two female-bodied characters in the film. Set in Germany during the end of the Cold War, the film features Lorraine fighting her way through a series of hurdles in her efforts to find a list of double agents. Along the way, she becomes romantically involved with agent Delphine Lasalle (Sofia Boutella), who is later murdered by MI6 double agent David Percival (James McAvoy). Arriving moments after Delphine's death, Lorraine murders David and acquires the list. In her MI6 debriefing, however, she denies knowing the list's whereabouts. As the movie closes, her true loyalties are revealed as she boards a plane to the United States with the list and CIA Agent Emmett Kurzfeld (John Goodman). A story of deception and action, in which no one is what they appear to be and dangers await around every corner, the film grossed $100 million worldwide and received largely positive acclaim, drawing especially high praise for the action sequences one critic labeled "insane" (Sperling, 2017; also see Brayson, 2017; Debruge, 2017; Mazziotta, 2017).

In Proud Mary, Mary is the lone female-bodied assassin in a crime gang. Released in January 2018 and directed by Babak Najafi, Proud Mary stars Henson in the title role. Set in Boston, Mary seeks to save a young boy, Danny (Jahi Di'Allo Winston). Mary sees Danny playing video games in the other room right after she shoots her target, his father, point blank. Guilt ridden, she follows and watches over the boy. When he appears to be in danger from "Uncle" (Xander Berkeley), his employer, she rescues the boy by killing Uncle, initiating a war between her crime family and their rivals. Mary tells her crime family she wants out, but her father figure Benny (Danny Glover) and his son and her ex-lover Tom (Billy Brown) assert that she will never leave. They order her to train Danny to work for the family. When Danny confronts Benny, a conflicted Mary shoots Benny. In the final scene, Mary kills all the men who work for Benny, and Tom, to save Danny. With a much smaller budget and less promotion than Atomic Blonde, Proud Mary grossed only $21 million and received fewer positive reviews (Collins, 2018; Jutton, 2018; Madison, 2018).

In the analyses of Kill Bill, The Hunger Games, and Wonder Woman offered in preceding chapters, we have seen how the transgressions of dangerous dames can be contained by their sexualization. Even when featured as a tough protagonist, or placed within more stereotypically masculine contexts, women's sexually desirable appearance is emphasized. Thornham (2007) establishes that the category of "woman" has been "naturalized *as* image, a fetishized object to be looked at, a 'mask of beauty'" (p. 29). This expands in postfeminist media, in which the visual positioning of women as sexual objects is paired with an appropriated feminist celebration of strong female bodies. Owen et al. (2007) deem such representations as still structured by the male gaze. For example, they characterize Lara Croft (Angelina Jolie), as "a comic book dominatrix marked by eroticized violence, phallic weapon play, and gratuitous thigh and ass shots" (p. 240). Like their predecessors, the transgressive protagonists in *Atomic Blonde* and *Proud Mary* invoke this postfeminist aesthetic by sexualizing and fetishizing women's strong bodies in their roles as femmes fatales.

Gender Performativity and Femmes Fatales

Gender performativity entails the constitution of gender through banal, repeated performances (Butler, 1988, 1990, 1993). Although visual presentation is an aspect of gender performance, we do not merely don gender like a pair of pants, dress, mascara, or a hairstyle. Instead, repeating various everyday acts related to gender roles and identities reproduces gender as a reality. Classifying the gendered body as a "historical situation," Butler (1988) compares gender to a theatrical performance rehearsed and repeated over time (p. 520). In this manner, people (unconsciously) take up a received script for performing gender and, in enacting it, make it real. In turn, this creates and perpetuates gender norms, "much as a script survives the particular actors who make use of it" but nonetheless "requires individual actors in order to be actualized" (p. 526). Paradoxically, the performative "doing" of gender produces the cultural fiction of stable gender identities that preexist their enactment.

Race can similarly be understood as performative: an "effect of discourse" through which bodies are brought into "a system of racialized meanings" that is socially and historically constituted (Inda, 2000, p. 87).[2] As a theory of subjectivity, performativity addresses how identities are produced within and subject to ideologies and regimes of social control. Serving as sites of cultural reproduction, media offer insights into the sedimentation of—and sometimes challenges to—dominant scripts that serve these disciplinary functions. Thus, this chapter seeks to identify how bodies are disciplined into particular gendered and racialized performances.

Although Lorraine and Mary are sexualized and racialized differently, these films present their characters using a similar aesthetic. These two leads join the tradition of the femme fatale—an iconic storytelling technique depicting a seductive woman as a man's foil. Although the mythological construction of the beautiful but deadly femme fatale figure can be traced as far back as Eve, Lilith, and Pandora, cinematically it was popularized by film noir, in the mid-twentieth century (Grossman, 2007; Hales, 2007; Place, 1980). Featuring actresses like Lana Turner, Veronica Lake, and Joan Bennett, classic film noir stories centered on cynical or disillusioned male characters who frequently faced fatal choices propelled by a seductive, double-dealing woman.

Visually, *Atomic Blonde* is characterized by shadows, chiaroscuro lighting, use of black and white sequences, and silhouettes, which together set a dark, urban mood suited to a story of suspicion, sex, and violence. Its complicated plot, grim settings, and deceptive characters further hearken back to film noir style. The striking cinematography, in which Lorraine is frequently foregrounded in crisp detail against the background of bleak Eastern European Cold War locations, makes it a stunning site to examine Theron's visual embodiments of feminine power.

A mysterious spy of few words with a penetrating gaze from her steely blue eyes and the ability to unremorsefully execute her male foes, Lorraine is cold, decisive, and distant. In the beginning of the film, her physical and mental toughness is immediately revealed when she emerges from an ice bath, and the camera zooms in on her bare back, rippling muscles, and bruised body. Emotionless, she downs vodka on ice while perched naked on the side of the tub with the cityscape visible out the window. This visual is revisited throughout the film, her healing ice baths revealing her wounded body even as her icy eyes resist revealing any emotions roiling beneath her hardened exterior. Even her drink, a clear liquor easily mistaken for water, deceives with its appearance.[3] In this black and white opening scene, her powerful but bruised body on display, Lorraine proceeds to dress and moves to the mirror. Audiences watch her apply layers of foundation, black eye makeup, and darkened lipstick that cover her bruises and transform her into the iconic 1940s version of the femme fatale. This scene reveals how Lorraine's constructed and high-maintenance appearance as a culturally desirable feminine woman conceals both the dangers posed by her strong body and her human fragility. Throughout the film, Lorraine's various black and white haute couture styles reinforce the noir connection further, and her signature large-framed dark sunglasses mask her identity and thwart, or reflect, the attempted male gaze.

Like Lorraine, Mary exhibits many of the noir femme fatale characteristics. Her involvement in a crime ring requires her to hide her true identity; her urban world thus emphasizes deception and disguise. The title credits for *Proud Mary* draw from blaxploitation themes;[4] bright red and yellow 1970s-style lettering gives way to an image of Mary staring at the camera while performing military-style push-ups, hands gripping dumbbells as she raises and lowers herself. As the credits roll, Mary showers, her naked silhouette clouded by the shower door. Out of the shower, she applies makeup, the camera zooming in on her lips and lashes as audiences watch her, like Lorraine, mold herself into a polished femme. The camera focuses in on her legs as she pulls on high-heeled stiletto boots. As the opening credits end, and after finishing her outfit with a pair of leather gloves, Mary opens a door inside her closet to reveal an extensive cabinet of guns, and carefully selects one. She looks in the mirror at her black hair before reaching for a platinum blonde wig. At the close of this first scene, audiences watch a transformed Mary walk down the hall. In her black leather trench coat and blonde wig, the visual resemblance to *Atomic Blonde*'s Lorraine is striking. Their gendered performance as iconic femmes becomes fatal as they wield weapons—their prowess presenting a formidable challenge to their male foes.

Framing Women Action Heroes

Stuller (2010) establishes that a superwoman "can be a spy, a secret agent, an assassin, a detective, a witch, a reporter, or a superhero. She becomes super by surpassing the limits of the human body and mind" (p. 5). As contemporary feminine/ist action heroes, Lorraine and Mary's skills, strengths, and abilities to avoid fatal injury surpass human, as well as gendered, limits. Similar to Beatrix Kiddo's performance of hegemonic masculinity in a feminine body in *Kill Bill* (see Chapter 1), both Lorraine and Mary embody many "masculine" characteristics: they act "tough," they engage in physical violence, and they take their alcohol straight. In contrast to the extension of Wonder Woman's superhuman powers through "feminine" objects, including her magic bracelets and tiara, the female-bodied heroes in *Atomic Blonde* and *Proud Mary* use guns, the ultimate phallic signifier.[5] And yet, although Lorraine and Mary present a more sinister version of fierce femininity than Wonder Woman's heroic compassion, the films both subtly reference the superhero genre in their framing. However, unlike Wonder Woman's construction as a universal hero able to (finally) stand toe-to-toe with the male superheroes despite her feminine fighting style, Lorraine and Mary are constructed with raced and gendered particularity despite—or perhaps because of—their use of more masculine weapons and violence.

Based on the graphic novel *The Coldest City* (Johnston, 2012), *Atomic Blonde* constructs its protagonist through the same naming convention as *Wonder Woman* and many other superhero movies. The adjective "atomic" here suggests the explosive power of the main character, who, rather than "woman," receives a more racially specific noun: "blonde."[6] Blonde is a hair color associated with whiteness,[7] and, specifically, with a universalizing construction of ideal white femininity that came into fashion in the mid-twentieth century United States (Dyer, 1993).[8] The development of the "blonde bombshell" character as epitomizing women's desirability is clearly evidenced by Marilyn Monroe's iconic rise through feature roles in Hollywood films such as *Gentlemen Prefer Blondes* (1953) (Banner, 2008; Dyer, 1986).

Juxtaposing Theron's blonde bombshell status with the femme fatale's dangerous power, *Atomic Blonde*'s two main promotional posters both feature a pale, platinum-locked Theron holding a gun. In one poster, her body is visible down to the top of her thigh-high boots. She wears a little black dress and black trench coat, one boot-clad leg bent in a classic model pose, gun in hand, and eyes hidden behind fashionable black sunglasses. In the other black-and-white promotional image, she appears to be naked, turned to the side with her alabaster skin exposed on her shoulder and back silhouetted against a sea of black, her finger on the trigger of her cocked gun. Her heavily made-up smoky eyes are nearly covered by her bangs, and her cheekbones are prominent as she averts her gaze from the camera. Her platinum hair and flawless skin glow. The word "Atomic" is set in light blue against the otherwise black and white image over "Blonde," which appears in comic book style block letters.

Proud Mary follows the same naming convention, constructing its hero as tough, capable, and feminine gendered. However, in contrast to the more universalizing "woman," or "blonde," the title character here is identified by name, "Mary." The adjective "proud" qualifies the character as fierce and accomplished but also arrogant or excessive in her power, characteristics associated with black womanhood.[9] The title "Proud Mary" also specifically invokes legendary black icon Tina Turner, known both for her accomplishments in the male-dominated music industry, and for bringing black women's sexuality center stage.[10]

The most prominent *Proud Mary* promotional posters draw upon racialized particularity through their direct references to blaxploitation films. In one, Henson—dressed almost exactly like Theron in tall black stiletto boots, short black dress, and black leather jacket—stands silhouetted against a 1970s-era light yellow and orange background. Gun drawn and pointed toward the camera, she appears to step out of the poster from the circle at the center of the image. "Proud Mary" is emblazoned in the same font as the title of the blaxploitation film *Foxy Brown* (1974), which featured the sexy, gun-wielding character Foxy (Pam Grier). These visual references place *Proud Mary* within the hero realm given that blaxploitation film characters drew upon the appearance of black superheroes, sharing stylistic cues and "the same signifiers of a superhuman status" (Nama, 2011, p. 6). In *Proud Mary*, these signifiers include Mary's ability to outsmart, outrun, and outfight her foes, all while dressed in a tightly fitted all-black wardrobe similar to Catwoman's catsuit.

In another poster, the movie title, in the same font, this time in red, appears atop a black and white image. A black queen, Henson's perfectly made-up face, with long lashes, darkened cheekbones, and heavily lined lips, is flanked by an "afro" composed of a collage of images from the film. Henson does not wear her hair in an afro in the film; this image again elicits Foxy Brown. The afro images offer a militarized, and masculinized, Black Power medley: the cityscape and the projects; male co-stars Danny Glover, Billy Brown, and Jahi Di'Allo Winston; silencers and gun chambers; piles of money; bottles of booze; and Mary, dressed in black, in multiple poses with her gun drawn. In one of these smaller images, Mary wears a platinum blond wig, and she confronts the gaze by pointing her revolver directly toward the camera. In the only pose where a gun is not featured, Mary is pulling on her thigh-high stiletto boots. These framings enable the fetishizing of the powerful female body and, in turn, contain its threatening power and transgressive potential.

Fetishizing the Female Body

Femme fatales are dangerous because they are sexy, seductive, and deadly, illustrating the precarity of the (hetero)sexual relationship (Hallissy, 1987). However, if, in her role as femme fatale, Theron embodies woman's disturbing power, she also embodies "ideal" femininity. She is beautiful, dressed to the nines, and "impossibly thin, long legged, and big breasted" (Carter & Steiner, 2004, p. 13). Even when she is alone in her hotel room, she is shown in styled hair and beautifully applied makeup, poised on the edge of a table or counter and wearing only a bodysuit or tee shirt complemented by thigh-high fishnets. These stylized seductive poses prop Lorraine up almost as an *objet d'art* for the camera's—and thus the viewers'—gaze.[11] This voyeuristic invitation serves to contain Lorraine's gendered transgressions as a hardened agent willing to kill at any time by placing her back in an object position.

From *Proud Mary*'s opening scene's focus on Mary's body parts through close-up shots, to the fight scenes where she is dressed in body-hugging black clothing and frequently fighting alongside a man with her gun drawn, Mary's body is fetishized as an object for the gaze through its positioning and camera angles, as well. Mulvey (1996) describes the fetishizing of the female body as "born out of a refusal to see" (p. 64). The close-ups on Mary's and Lorraine's body parts are thus also a turning away, "not of the eyes but of understanding, of fixating on a substitute object to hold the gaze" (p. 64). Put differently, the fragmenting and objectifying focus on women's bodies limits the characters' agency while constraining the audiences' ability to identify with the characters as subjects.

Sexualizing representations of physically powerful women and feminine anger through the gaze, and then placing violent femme protagonists into scenes that leave them bruised and bloody portends fetishizing the battered woman, making her wounds a visual commodity and badge of her toughness. Similar to the revealing of Lorraine's bruised body, a scene in *Proud Mary* features Mary at home nursing an injury. Lifting her shirt before the bathroom mirror, Mary exposes, cleans, and bandages her wounds before falling into bed. By withstanding extreme violence, Lorraine and Mary both surpass typical human limits. Although this attests to their super-heroic strength, it threatens to sexualize gendered violence (Brown, 2014). As the characters expose and attend to their bodies, audience members may fetishize the bruised female form. In addition, the violence inflicted upon their bodies serves as a reminder of their weakness, entrenching "disparate power relations" (Meger, 2016, p. 149).

Toward the end of one of *Atomic Blonde*'s epic fight scenes, Lorraine's face is drenched in blood, resembling a pornographic "money shot," in which a man ejaculates onto a woman's body, face, or mouth. The money shot itself is a fetish, fulfilling a pornographic promise to deliver the goods, and illustrating "how commodity culture, sexual pleasure, and phallic subjectivity interpenetrate" (Williams, 1999, p. 106). Lorraine's dishevelment is doubly striking given that she remains impeccable, even in the midst of violence, throughout most of the film. While the blood in this scene may be more realistic than her immaculate appearance in other fight scenes, it also draws from an image repertoire that combines male dominance and women's degradation, denying women's subjectivity as well as sexual pleasure.

Sexual Excess in *Atomic Blonde*

Lorraine's sexuality is portrayed as dangerous, indicated by her first fight scene taking place in the back seat of a car, in which she kills a man by jabbing her red stiletto into his throat. The use of a fetish object as a weapon appeals to the femme fatale iconography in which the evil seductress "tempts man and brings about his destruction" (Place, 1980, p. 35). While the agent David desires Lorraine during their encounter, he acknowledges the inherent danger of his passion, sneering, "I trust you about as far as I can throw you." Despite his distrust, he tells her, "my God I think I fucking love you," to which she responds, simply, "that's too bad." She deflects his desire in the same casual manner she flicks her ever-present cigarette; her cool composure remains unmoved.

Although she rejects David, Lorraine deploys her sexuality as a potential weapon against other men, and she winds up in a sexual relationship with another woman, Delphine. In the celebrated sex scene between actresses Theron and Boutella, which was featured in the trailer and fixated on by the press (Dry, 2017; McCarthy, 2017; Porrecca, 2017), Lorraine wears a black dress with eyeholes and lacing reminiscent of a dominatrix. Lorraine forcefully pushes Delphine against a restroom wall as she begins kissing her, pulls a gun on her, and continues to dominate her as the scene unfolds. This invokes a fetishized, depoliticized version of dangerous queer sexuality.[12] Tracing the proliferation of portrayals of bisexual women as sexy but deadly femmes fatales in movies like *Femme Fatale* (2002), *Wild Things* (1998), *Cruel Intentions* (1999), and *Pretty Persuasion* (2005), Farrimond (2012) critiques this trend for echoing depictions found in mainstream pornography. She argues that the bisexual femme fatale is "the perfect fantasy figure in a culture where the conventionally attractive, behaviorally bisexual woman who is still predominantly more interested in men is presented as the dream woman" (p. 140). As the gazes of cameras, presses, mainstream marketing materials, and audiences fixate on Lorraine's (and Theron's) sexual involvement with another woman, declaring it "steamy," and "hot" (Dry, 2017, para. 2), they shape the character's sex appeal in accordance with heterosexual fantasies. In this manner, queer women's sexuality is appropriated for the male gaze.

Lorraine's duplicity and illegibility further contributes to this construction because her sexual loyalties are never fully clear. Some moments suggest a "real" romantic alliance with Delphine. During an intimate moment when Lorraine briefly lets down her guard, Delphine observes aloud to Lorraine, while stroking her hair, "you look different when you tell the truth." Lorraine looks away, responding, "I'd better not do that again. It's going to get me killed one day." Although the film, and this scene, have queer potential, as a femme fatale, Lorraine's actions and motives for having sex with women are suspect. Even as the unfixability of Lorraine's sexuality challenges heteropatriarchy and transgresses norms of gender performance, it also threatens to glamorize same-sex attraction and convert it into just another weapon in the femme fatale arsenal. In such portrayals, "the mark of the lesbian ceases to be her sexual outlaw status in heterosexual society and becomes her gender outlaw status in a patriarchal society" (Calhoun, 1995, p. 18). For this reason, heterosexual women can claim outlaw status and, in so doing, perform queer erasures.

In the case of Lorraine and Delphine, their first kiss takes place in a night club—a setting already associated with straight-identified women kissing for male audiences. The ambiguity of their sexual attraction, combined with their bad-girl fashion styles, deviant occupations, and use of "masculine" force subsumes queer sexuality to gender transgressions. This scene thus exemplifies Calhoun's (1995) claim that feminist frames can serve "to closet lesbians" (p. 8). In fact, even in media coverage of the film, Theron gets to play the figurative lesbian, as she is questioned about filming the sex scene with Boutella. "It was really easy," she explains, "she's gorgeous!" (McCarthy, 2017, para. 6). Much as Lorraine's gender transgressions are contained by fetishizing her appearance, same sex desire is thus encased within (hetero)sex appeal.

Controlling Images of Black Womanhood in *Proud Mary*

As a black female-bodied action hero, Mary resists gender stereotypes while navigating their racial containment. O'Grady (1992) describes the signification of the female body as constituted by what it is not: "white is what woman is; not-white (and the stereotypes not-white gathers in) is what she had better not be" (p. 174). Black female bodies already reside outside the confines of ideal femininity, their signifiers shaped by "crosscurrents of racism and sexism" (Crenshaw, 1989, p. 155). Black women are thus positioned ontologically as "double-transgressors" (Owen et al., 2007, p. 3).

Although *Proud Mary* fills a surface void given the underrepresentation of black women on the big screen, it fails to escape the stereotype of the overly sexualized female body. Saunders (2018) notes, "seemingly an ode to black female physical and mental strength, *Proud Mary* subversively sexualizes the black female form" (para. 18) with "a heightened sexuality intertwined with an underscored masculinity" (para. 2). The female-bodied action hero of blaxploitation films is "a sexy, aggressive, and cool super bitch, a bad mama who dishe[s] out violence in its most extreme forms" (Schubart, 2007, p. 41). Despite the undeniable strength and independence of women in blaxploitation films, however, subjecting such characters and stars to the heterosexist, white supremacist male gaze presents the black female body as simultaneously an enigma and a threat.[13]

In *Proud Mary*, this threat is tamed by reinscribing Mary's body within a maternal and familial context. As we saw with Beatrix Kiddo in *Kill Bill* and Katniss Everdeen in *The Hunger Games*, Mary is motivated to save a child, a distinction emphasized by her name, which invites a comparison to the archetypes of the virgin, mother, and mammy (Hill Collins, 2000; West, 1995, 2012). Simultaneously, Mary is portrayed as the long-suffering, dutiful daughter in her crime family. Unlike Lorraine, Mary does not use her sexuality for gain. Her ex-boyfriend Tom is still in love with her, but she rejects his advances (much as the asexual mammy figure must) and instead focuses on saving the child. The rhetorical construction of her character as an asexual mother figure to a child she did not conceive robs her of the sexual agency Lorraine wields. The black female body thus functions as the object of sexual desire rather than a desiring sexual subject. In this sense, the potentially dangerous sexuality Mary inhabits through the visual construction of the femme fatale is negated even in its presence.

Mary is not just any mother, however. In her interactions with Danny, she epitomizes the tough-love style of the black matriarch. The matriarch figure presents a strong black womanhood more positive than other long-standing "controlling images" like the jezebel, welfare queen, or mammy (Hill Collins, 2000, p. 5; also see Davis, 1973; Sewell, 2013).[14] However, this image emasculates black men, removing them from the role of familial patriarch, while portraying black women as failing to perform appropriate gender behavior. As Mary the assassin attempts to step into the role of Mother Mary, Tom critiques her "failure" to embody the role fully, telling her, "you ain't the mothering type." Her defiance of his judgment is emphasized by the soundtrack's use of Turner's "Proud Mary" during her final killing spree, which saves Danny.[15] This juxtaposition invokes stereotypes of black womanhood as aggressively assertive and, in particular, aligns Mary with the damaging undercurrents of the controlling image of the black matriarch. In its most degrading aspects, this stereotype attributes the problems black people face not to structural and systemic racial and economic oppression but rather to the failure of the black family (Gadsden, 1999; Raspberry, 2005). Portraying black women's power as inappropriate thus functions to contain the threat it poses to the patriarchal family structure and to white society (Hill Collins, 2000).

At the end of the film, Mary saves Danny, finds her own redemption, and secures release from her life of crime through her path to motherhood. Mary is thus, in some ways, the one "saved." She presents a somewhat empowering figure but is nonetheless constrained by dangerous stereotypes. With the plethora of tough women movies coming out of Hollywood, limiting the lone black woman's motives to her impulse to save a child reveals some of the restrictions on the types of heroism available to black women in the cultural imaginary.

Proud Mary's narrative demonstrates how contemporary figurations of postfeminist empowerment resubstantiate whiteness. Mary is portrayed through the racial stereotypes of the matriarch and mammy, and her toughness is constructed at the expense of the black men in the film and her own racial identity. When Mary tries to leave the crime gang, she pleads to Benny, "If you love me, let me go." Benny replies, "I own you and you're not going anywhere. You're going to stay in the family and work for me...If you leave, we will find you." Benny's assertion that he owns her, and she will never be free, constructs the black man "as desiring to possess the black female form—a sentiment that mirrors the oppositional perception and use of black bodies against one another" (Saunders, 2018, para. 9). Tom's inability to let go of his romantic past with Mary further emasculates him but Mary does not need him and eventually kills him.

Mary kills all of the adult black men in her life to find freedom. As black men thus become disposable bodies along Mary's journey to empowerment, her story illustrates how race and gender scripts work together to construct, and delimit, pop culture portrayals of feminine/ist strength.[16] As a black female-bodied action hero, Mary is unique among the leading characters discussed so far, and her characterization pits gender against race. The film's cast is black aside from the rival, white crime family. When a "war" between the crime families erupts, it is ostensibly a race war. Whereas Lorraine fights for the U.S. in the Cold War, amidst a white cast, Mary fights to be released from the racialized environment in which she lives. Put differently, to fulfill her journey from assassin to hero Mary must choose her gender over her race, leaving blackness and violence to the criminal men in the film. Her access to "masculine" strength, and to independence as a woman, thus comes at a cost; she must "free herself from 'blackness' via her supplementary phallus to emerge as woman" (Saunders, 2018, para. 12).[17] In this manner, Mary, despite her own black skin, reinforces whiteness as a system. Like the trope of the (white) jungle queen at risk from black (savage) men (see Chapter 3), Mary dominates the black men in her life in order to rise above them. When she kills Danny, and then Tom, she is released from their patriarchal control as well as from the racialized criminality they embody. Her power thus comes at the cost of reinforcing "the deathly production of anti-blackness" (Walcott, 2014, p. 93).[18]

Nevertheless, the film received acclaim from some black critics and audiences, for reasons similar to the praise given *Wonder Woman*: black women finally could see themselves reflected on the screen as the star rather than the sidekick (Brown, 2018; *Glitter Magazine*, 2018; Jutton, 2018). In this respect, the movie succeeds, because seeing different kinds of bodies fulfill the role of hero remains important. "It's impossible to overstate the satisfaction that comes with seeing a 47-year-old woman of color show the Hollywood hero fraternity that anything they can do, she can do better," one critic noted (Jutton, 2018, para. 5). Another pointed out the actors who typically would be cast, including "Theron, Milla Jovovich, Angelina Jolie, or Scarlett Johansson," proclaiming "a Black woman on the screen allowed me to see myself in this story in a way that the likes of *Atomic Blonde* never could. I identified with her. I understood her. I connected with her" (Brown, 2018, para. 2, 9). Black women *felt* something while watching *Proud Mary*: "Powerful, affirmed, seen, and of course proud" (para. 13). Yet, the film was a far more modest production than the films featuring white leads produced in the same time period, leading audiences and Henson to speculate whether the film was being deliberately downplayed (Brown, 2018). For black women to be celebrated on the big screen, they must transgress both gender and race barriers.

Violent Femmes and Gender Transgressions

The portrayals of women's strength in *Atomic Blonde* and *Proud Mary* offer insight into the constellation of gender, race, sexuality, and power that defines dominant versions of feminine fierceness in the postfeminist media environment. Lorraine and Mary, like other dangerous dames in this book, defy as well as reproduce stereotypical containments. Both resist disrespect from men, fight for survival in a world of masculine violence, and utilize their deadly capacities to overpower the men who threaten them. Although their heroism is more morally ambiguous than Wonder Woman's godly virtuosity (see Chapter 3) or Katniss's grassroots activism (see Chapter 2), they are guided by notions of justice—protecting U.S. national security and escaping a life of crime. Finally, they both transgress masculine authority at times; however, their ability to do so relies on powers cultivated through their seductive appeal. As a gender transgression, their enactment of violence and strength is balanced by their beauty. Without it, the characters would be deemed "unfeminine and more symbolically threatening" (Zechowski & Neumann, 2014, p. 140). Although the embodied power of the characters does create the possibility for rhetorical agency, their bodies are fetishized. Both characters offer moments of potential resistance and departure, but they still exist within a media landscape that disciplines gendered bodies.

Stereotypes of gender, sexuality, and race orient around a familiar dichotomy—virgins and whores, or the (hetero)sexualized construction and desirability of "good" and "bad" women. In this dichotomy, good women willingly subject themselves to men. The "bad" woman, on the other hand, is one who does not have "a man willing to protect her, or who refuses such protection by claiming the right to run her own life. In either case, the woman without a male protector is fair game for any man to dominate" (Young, 2003, p. 14). Lorraine and Mary resist this gendered logic, but they do not dismantle it. They choose to participate in the "man's world" of violence, espionage, and crime, placing their bodies at risk. Thus, their bodily resistance is more out of necessity than an act of feminist empowerment.

However, Atomic Blonde and Proud Mary, beyond simply expanding women's representation on the big screen, do offer kernels of transformation rooted in gender-deviant portrayals. Even if not fully realized, the films' progressive potentialities reside in the performative disruption of gendered essences through the simultaneous transgression of stereotypical femininity juxtaposed with the hyperfeminine femme self-presentation. Rather than depicting beauty as an inherent womanly virtue, cameras capture Lorraine's and Mary's "made up" appearance that presents their beauty as a symbolic weapon, highlighting its performative nature. Their constructed femme image is not who they are; it is ammunition. In this reading, Lorraine and Mary signify not only the sexualized female body but also reveal "its production as elaborate spectacle" (Bernheimer, 1989, p. 96). This is both a strength and limitation of the femme fatale figure.

The femme fatale's appeal results from "a play of intriguing signs and changing masks" (Bernheimer, 1989, p. 96). As the bearer of the gaze, the weaponized body of the femme fatale manipulates the fates of those who catch her in their fields of vision (Bronfen, 2004). The mirror in which she applies her image thus reflects the complexities of resisting without fully reversing gendered frames. In performing the simulacrum of a copy of a copy of femininity, the femme fatale reveals the production of gender's value through pure exteriority (Baudrillard, 1975, 1994). To the less critical viewer, however, the femme fatale risks merely reproducing sexualized femininity.

Violent femmes placed within stereotypically masculine contexts are marked by their gendered and racialized particularities. Adding women to action arenas and roles propagates a vision of ostensible equality devoid of political and social context. Nonetheless, we resist "the temptation to dismiss the development of popular, consumer-led versions of feminism as simply more of the (patriarchal) same" (Tasker & Negra, 2005, p. 108). The commodification of feminist messages within postfeminist media texts such as Atomic Blonde and Proud Mary produces contradictory configurations of beauty, race, and power that are not always empowering. However, by depicting female-bodied heroes acting in ways previously associated with masculinity while calling attention to the visual construction of femininity, these films also productively highlight the artifice of gendered performance. Finally, given that representations offer audiences equipment for living, the dangerous dames in this chapter expand the possibilities for "livable lives" within oppressive systems where—despite their constructedness—gender, race, and sexuality have real, material impacts (Butler, 2007, p. 39). Acting in a "masculine" way changes "the very meaning of what it is to be a woman" (Butler, 1989, p. 260). In a world where women's bodies are subject to policing and vulnerable to violence, expanding the possibilities for women's embodied agency and portraying women as able to fight back against these systems remains a necessary, and revolutionary, act.

Notes

1. For further discussion of femmes fatales in film, see Doane (1991), Grossman (2007, 2009), and Hales (2007).
2. For further discussion of race as performative, see Bell (1999), Inda (2000), Moreman & McIntosh (2010), and Muñoz (1999).
3. Since vodka is a staple of Russian culture (Kott, 2014), Lorraine's consumption of this beverage can also be seen to contribute to her double identity, as it suggests that she is on the Russians' side.

4. The blaxploitation subgenre, popular in the 1970s, was unique in its centering of black heroes and their communities. The films often perpetuated stereotypes of hypersexual black women and violent, hypermasculine black men who were pimps and drug lords, but were emblematic of the Black Power movement in featuring characters fighting against their oppression by "The Man."

5. In terms of the phallocentrism of guns, King (2007) notes that not only do "men dominate gun cultures and gun cultures extend male domination" but also "guns amplify sexualized power, projecting masculinity and violence, which encourages dehumanization and degradation while also allowing the possibility for subversion and negotiation" (p. 87).

6. The use of "atomic" in the title also associates the main character with the Cold-War era fear of the bomb's use. After the atomic bomb was set off in Japan in 1945, the world knew its capabilities. Through this simile, Lorraine is constructed as having the same capacities as the bomb: power, domination, and devastation.

7. See Dyer (1997) on how the power of whiteness is reproduced through the visual centering and reproduction of white bodies.

8. We recognize that the valuation of blonde hair has led people of many races to bleach their hair, which allows blonde to also take on new meanings; it is nonetheless tied to a signifying system privileging whiteness. As Simpson (1996) explains, "blonde hair on non-white skin is a marker of difference, appropriation, or deviation. Gender displaces race in the consumption of the image of the blonde, yet the ideology that fuels that elision still binds the two together" (p. 113).

9. Unlike the rest of the dangerous dames discussed in this book, Mary is known only by her first name in the film, which further supports our argument that the character is differently constructed than her white peers.

10. Tina Turner, a legendary black female-bodied pop singer, performed/recorded a cover of the song "Proud Mary," originally by Creedence Clearwater Revival, with Ike Turner in 1970. This version of the popular hit came to be widely recognized as one of Turner's signature songs. It reached #4 on the pop charts in 1971 and won a Grammy Award for best R&B Vocal Performance in 1972 (for further discussion see Turner, 2018, pp. 76–77). Similarly to the dangerous dames in this book, Turner's use of her sexuality onstage has been considered both transgressive and exploitative by feminist scholars. See, for example, hooks' (1997) critique, and Roberts' (1990) praise.

11. Steele (2004), in her discussion of femmes fatales as they related to the construction of the modern, fashionable and elite Parisiènne describes how "woman, in general, was fetishized as an art object" (p. 319).

12. Different interpretations of this scene are possible given debates over whether lesbian sadomasochism reproduces "male dominance over and violence against women," and the heteropatriarchal eroticization of violence (Calhoun, 1995, p. 16; also see Reti, 1993).

13. In her analysis of how cinema is shaped by the systems of white supremacy, capitalism, and patriarchy, hooks (1996) argues that "a distinction must be made between oppositional representations and romantically glorifying and valorizing images of blackness," given that visibility is not in itself "inherently radical or progressive" (p. 48).

14. Hill Collins's (2000) discussion of "controlling images" identifies stereotypes of black women originating during slavery that continue to have power today.

15. Tina Turner was famously in an abusive relationship with Ike Turner, with whom she performed this song. The use of this song in the film's title, and its placement as the signature song on the soundtrack during Mary's final action sequence when she finally frees herself by killing all the black men in her life, further support our claims that Mary's emergence as a strong woman reinforces negative stereotypes of black men and requires that Mary negate/transcend race to be liberated from gendered oppression.

16. Numerous scholars have addressed the gendered, racialized, sexualized systems through which certain bodies are marked as "human," and worthy of life, while other bodies are rendered inhuman, animalistic, Other, unintelligible, and/or ungrievable (see, for example, Puar, 2007; Butler, 2006, 2007). Cacho (2012) argues that liberal notions of personhood are themselves premised on the devaluation, or what she calls "social death," of criminalized populations of color (p. 4). The process of fragmenting persons "into disposable bodies and human subjects" within U.S. citizenship discourses, and specifically, the anti-Black logics associated with this phenomenon, has roots in slavery and colonialism, and continues in the contemporary era (Brace, 2014, p. 488; see also Fanon, 1967; Walcott, 2014).

17. In Saunders' (2018) reading, "Mary's espousal to a big black gun" throughout the duration of the film simultaneously sexualizes and masculinizes her, painting "the black female form as not a lady with a gun but a female with a supplemental phallus" (para. 6). When she kills Tom and Benny, Mary thus emerges as a strong woman who frees herself from gendered oppression through the gun while simultaneously breaking away from "blackness as embodied through black males Benny and Tom" (para. 12).

18. Anti-blackness, or the discursive articulation of Black and African peoples with inferiority, violence, barbarism, criminality, and subhumanity, was a key element of the Anglo-European colonial project and continues to shape contemporary constructions of race, including the production of whiteness (Allen, 2012; Fanon, 1967).

References

Allen, T. W. (2012). *The invention of the white race: Volume I: Racial oppression and social control* (2nd ed.). Brooklyn, NY: Verso.

Banner, L. W. (2008). The creature from the black lagoon: Marilyn Monroe and whiteness. *Cinema Journal, 47*(4), 4–29.

Baudrillard, J. (1975). *The mirror of production.* St. Louis, MO: Telos Press.

Baudrillard, J. (1994). *Simulacra and simulation.* Ann Arbor: University of Michigan Press.

Bell, V. (1999). Mimesis as cultural survival: Judith Butler and anti-Semitism. *Theory, Culture, & Society, 2,* 133–161. doi:10.1177/02632769922050584

Bernheimer, C. (1989). *Figures of ill repute: Representing prostitution in nineteenth-century France.* Cambridge, MA: Harvard University Press.

Brace, L. (2014). Bodies in abolition: Broken hearts and open wounds. *Citizenship Studies, 18*(5), 485–498. doi:10.1080/13621025.2014.923701

Brayson, J. (2017, July 26). Was the 'Atomic Blonde' staircase fight scene done in one shot? It's the best action sequence of the year. *Bustle.* Retrieved from https://www.bustle.com/p/

was-the-atomic-blonde-staircase-fight-scene-done-in-one-shot-its-the-best-action-sequence-of-the-year-72286

Bronfen, E. (2004). Femme fatale: Negotiations of tragic desire. *New Literary History, 35*(1), 103–116.

Brown, J. A. (2014). Torture, rape, action heroines, and *The Girl with the Dragon Tattoo*. In N. Jones, M. Bajac-Carter, & B. Batchelor (Eds.), *Heroines of film and television: Portrayals in popular culture* (pp. 47–64). Lanham, MD: Rowman & Littlefield.

Brown, S. J. (2018, January 15). 'Proud Mary' deserved more than Sony Entertainment gave it. *Intersectional feminist media*. Retrieved from https://wearyourvoicemag.com/more/entertainment/proud-mary-deserved-far-sony-entertainment-gave

Butler, J. (1988). Performative acts and gender constitution: An essay in phenomenology and feminist theory. *Theatre Journal, 40*(4), 519–531.

Butler, J. (1989). Gendering the body: Beauvoir's philosophical contribution. In A. Garry & M. Pearsall (Eds.), *Women, knowledge, and reality: Explorations in feminist philosophy* (pp. 253–262). Boston, MA: Unwin Hyman.

Butler, J. (1990). *Gender trouble: Feminism and the subversion of identity*. New York, NY: Routledge.

Butler, J. (1993). *Bodies that matter: On the discursive limits of "sex."* New York, NY: Routledge.

Butler, J. (2006). *Precarious life: The Powers of mourning and violence*. New York, NY: Verso.

Butler, J. (2007). *Undoing gender*. New York, NY: Routledge.

Cacho, L. M. (2012). *Social death: Racialized rightlessness and the criminalization of the unprotected*. New York: New York University Press.

Calhoun, C. (1995). The gender closet: Lesbian disappearance under the sign "women." *Feminist Studies, 21*(1), 7–34. doi:10.2307/3178313

Carter, C., & Steiner, L. (2004). *Critical readings: Media and gender*. Maidenhead, United Kingdom: Open University Press.

Collins, K. A. (2018, January 13). 'Proud Mary' makes less sense as a movie than as a Taraji P. Henson role. *The Ringer*. Retrieved from https://www.theringer.com/movies/2018/1/13/16888556/proud-mary-film-review-taraji-p-henson

Crenshaw, K. (1989). Demarginalizing the intersection of race and sex: A black feminist critique of antidiscrimination doctrine, feminist theory and antiracist politics. *University of Chicago Legal Forum*, 139–167.

Davis, A. (1973). The myth of the black matriarch. *The first Ms. Reader*. New York, NY: Warner Paperback Library.

Debruge, P. (2017, August 3). How the 'Atomic Blonde' team pulled off the incredible 10-minute, 'one-take' action sequence. *Variety*. Retrieved from https://variety.com/2017/artisans/production/atomic-blonde-10-minute-action-scene-charlize-theron-1202512814/

Doane, M. A. (1991). *Femmes fatales: Feminism, film theory, psychoanalysis*. New York, NY: Routledge.

Dry, J. (2017, July 28). Why "Atomic Blonde' earns its steamy Charlize Theron lesbian sex scene. *IndieWire*. Retrieved from https://www.indiewire.com/2017/07/atomic-blonde-charlize-theron-lesbian-sex-scene-lgbt-1201860628/

Dyer, R. (1986). *Heavenly bodies: Film stars and society*. Oxford, United Kingdom: Macmillan Education.

Dyer, R. (1993). The colour of virtue: Lillian Gish, whiteness, and femininity. In P. Cook & P. Dodd (Eds.), *Women and film: A sight and sound reader* (pp. 1–9). Philadelphia, PA: Temple University Press.

Dyer, R. (1997). *White: Essays on race and culture.* London, United Kingdom: Routledge.

Fanon, F. (1967). *Black skin, white masks.* New York, NY: Grove.

Farrimond, K. (2012). 'Stay still so we can see who you are': Anxiety and bisexual activity in the contemporary femme fatale film. *Journal of Bisexuality, 12*(1), 138-154. doi:10.1080/15299716.2012.645725

Gadsden, V. L. (1999). Black families in intergenerational and cultural perspective. In M. E. Lamb (Ed.) *Parenting and child development in nontraditional families* (pp. 221–246). New York, NY: Lawrence Erlbaum.

Glitter Magazine. (2018, January 15). Golden Globe winner & Oscar nominee Taraji P. Henson slays as 'Proud Mary' in theaters now. Retrieved from http://glittermagrocks.com/connect/2018/01/15/why-proud-mary-is-the-feminist-movie-weve-all-been-wanting/

Grossman, J. (2007). Film noir's "femme fatales" hard-boiled women: Moving beyond gender fantasies. *Quarterly Review of Film and Video, 24*, 19–30. doi:10.1080/10509200500-48983

Grossman, J. (2009). *Rethinking the femme fatale: Ready for her close-up.* New York, NY: Palgrave-Macmillan.

Hales, B. (2007). Projecting trauma: The femme fatale in Weimar and Hollywood film noir. *Women in German Yearbook, 23*, 224–243.

Hallissy, M. (1987). *Venomous women: Fear of the female in literature.* Westport, CT: Greenwood Press.

Hill Collins, P. (2000). *Black feminist thought: Knowledge, consciousness, and the politics of empowerment.* New York, NY: Routledge.

hooks, b. (1996). *Reel to real: Race, class and sex at the movies.* New York, NY: Routledge.

hooks, b. (1997). Selling hot pussy: Representations of black female sexuality in the cultural marketplace. In K. Conboy, N. Medina, & S. Stanbury (Eds.), *Writing on the body: Female embodiment and feminist theory* (pp. 112–128). New York, NY: Columbia University Press.

Inda, J. X. (2000). Performativity, materiality, and the racial body. *Latino Studies Journal, 11*(3), 74–99.

Johnston, A. (2012). *The coldest city.* Portland, OR: Oni Press.

Jutton, L. (2018). Proud Mary: Bow down before queen Taraji. *Film Inquiry.* Retrieved from https://www.filminquiry.com/proud-mary-2018-review/

King, C. R. (2007). Arming desire: The sexual force of guns in the United States. In C. F. Springwood (Ed.), *Open fire: Understanding global gun cultures* (pp. 87–97). New York, NY: Berg.

Kott, T. (2014, February 12). Russians and their vodka: A brief history. *Canada.Com NewsWorld.* Retrieved from https://o.canada.com/news/world/russians-and-their-vodka-a-brief-history

Lee, A. (2018, January 5). Taraji P. Henson on taking action in 'Proud Mary' and (not) selling "black culture" overseas. *The Hollywood Reporter.* Retrieved from https://www.hollywoodreporter.com/heat-vision/taraji-p-henson-taking-action-proud-mary-not-selling-black-culture-overseas-1071185

Leitch, D. (Director), Theron, C., Kono, B., Dix, A. J., McCormick, K., Glitter, E., & Schwerin, P. (Producers). (2017). *Atomic blonde.* [Motion picture.] United States: Focus Features.

Madison, I. (2018, January 12). 'Proud Mary' and why Hollywood won't let black women kick ass. *Daily Beast.* Retrieved from https://www.thedailybeast.com/why-proud-mary-and-hollywood-wont-let-black-women-kick-ass

Mazziotta, J. (2017, July 25). How Charlize Theron prepared for the intense fight scenes in *Atomic Blonde:* 'Her ability was incredible.' *People.* Retrieved from https://people.com/bodies/charlize-theron-fight-scenes-atomic-blonde/

McCarthy, T. (2017, July 20). Charlize Theron on 'Atomic Blonde' sex scene with a woman: 'It was really easy.' *Fox News.* Retrieved from https://www.foxnews.com/entertainment/charlize-theron-on-atomic-blonde-sex-scene-with-a-woman-it-was-really-easy

Meger, S. (2016). The fetishization of sexual violence in international society. *International Studies Quarterly, 60,* 149–159.

Moreman. S. T., & McIntosh, D. (2010). Brown scriptings and rescriptings: A critical performance ethnography of Latina drag queens. *Communication and Critical/Cultural Studies, 7*(2), 115–135. doi:10.1080/14791421003767912

Mulvey, L. (1975). Visual pleasure and narrative cinema. *Screen, 16*(3), 6–18. doi:10.1093/screen/16.3.6

Mulvey, L. (1996). *Fetishism and curiosity.* London, United Kingdom: BFI.

Muñoz, J. E. (1999). *Disidentifications: Queers of color and the performance of politics.* Minneapolis: University of Minnesota Press.

Najafi, B. (Director), Duncan, T., Schiff, P., Ajemain, A., & Henson, T. P. (Producers). (2018). *Proud Mary* [Motion picture]. United States: Sony Pictures.

Nama, A. (2011). *Super black: American pop culture and black superheroes.* Austin: University of Texas Press.

O'Grady, L. (2003). Olympia's maid: Reclaiming black female subjectivity. In A. Jones (Ed.), *The feminism and visual culture reader* (pp. 174–187). New York, NY: Routledge

Owen, A. S., Stein, S. R., & Vande Berg, L. R. (2007). *Bad girls: Cultural politics and media representations of transgressive women.* New York, NY: Peter Lang.

Place, J. (1980). Women in film noir. In E. A. Kaplan (Ed.), *Women in film noir* (pp. 35–67). London, United Kingdom: BFI Publishing.

Porrecca, B. (2017, July 28). Why 'Atomic Blonde' sex scenes almost didn't happen. *The Hollywood Reporter.* Retrieved from https://www.hollywoodreporter.com/heat-vision/atomic-blonde-sex-scenes-charlize-theron-sofia-boutella-almost-didnt-happen-1024754

Puar, J. (2007). *Terrorist assemblages: Homonationalism in queer times.* Durham, NC: Duke University Press.

Raspberry, W. (2005, July 25). Why our black families are failing. *The Washington Post.* Retrieved from https://www.washingtonpost.com/wp-dyn/content/article/2005/07/24/AR2005072401115.html?noredirect=on

Reti, I. (Ed.). (1993). *Unleashing feminism: Critiquing lesbian sadomasochism in the gay nineties.* Santa Cruz, CA: Herbooks.

Roberts, R. (1990). "Sex as a weapon": Feminist rock music videos. *NWSA Journal, 2*(1), 1–15.

Saunders, C. C. (2018, January 16). Proud Mary, a review: The strong black woman as super-hero/assassin medley. *Whispers of a womanist: A black female perspective*. Retrieved from https://whispersofawomanist.com/2018/01/16/proud-mary-a-review-the-strong-black-woman-as-superhero-assassin-medley/

Schubart, R. (2007). *Super bitches and action babes: The female hero in popular cinema, 1970-2006*. Jefferson, NC: McFarland.

Setoodeh, R. (2017, July 11). How Charlize Theron got ripped, bruised (and naked) for 'Atomic Blonde.' *Variety*. Retrieved from https://variety.com/2017/film/features/charlize-theron-atomic-blonde-female-action-stars-1202489664/

Sewell, C. J. P. (2013). Mammies and matriarchs: Tracing images of the black female in popular culture 1950s to present. *Journal of African American Studies, 17*(3), 308–326. doi:10.1007/s12111-012-9238-x

Simpson, A. (1996). Black on blonde: The Africanist presence in Dorothy Parker's "Big Blonde." *College Literature, 23*(3), 105–116.

Sperling, N. (2017, August 1). How *Atomic Blonde* got its most insane action sequence. *GQ Magazine*. Retrieved from https://www.gq.com/story/atomic-blonde-david-leitch

Steele, V. (2004). *Femme fatale:* Fashion and visual culture in fin-de-siècle Paris. *Fashion Theory, 8*(3), 315–328. doi:10.2752/136270404778051663

Stuller, J. K. (2010). *Ink-stained Amazons and cinematic warriors: Superwomen in modern mythology*. New York, NY: I.B. Tauris and Company.

Tasker, Y., & Negra, D. (2005). In focus: Postfeminism and contemporary media studies. *Cinema Journal, 44*(2), 107–110.

Thornham, S. (2007). *Women, feminism and media*. Edinburgh, United Kingdom: Edinburgh University Press.

Turner, T. (2018). *My love story*. New York, NY: Atria books.

Universal Pictures (2017, July 11). *Atomic blonde – Fight like a girl* [Video File]. Retrieved from https://www.youtube.com/watch?v=GdB1XP8rpx8

Walcott, R. (2014). The problem of the human: Black ontologies and "the coloniality of our being." In S. Broeck, & C. Junker (Eds.), *Postcoloniality – decoloniality – black critique: Joints and fissures* (pp. 93–107). Frankfurt, Germany: Campus Verlag.

West, C. (1995). Mammy, sapphire, and jezebel: Historical images of black women and their implications for psychotherapy. *Psychotherapy, 32*(3), 458–466.

West, C. (2012). Mammy, jezebel, sapphire, and their homegirls: Developing an "oppositional gaze" toward the images of black women. In J. C. Chrisler, C. Golden, & P. D. Rozee (Eds.), *Lectures on the psychology of women* (pp. 286–299). Long Grove, IL: Waveland Press.

Williams, L. (1999). *Hard core: Power, pleasure, and the "frenzy of the visible."* Berkeley: University of California Press.

Young, I. M. (2003). The logic of masculinist protection: Reflections on the current security state. *Signs, 29*(1), 1–25.

Zechowski, S., & Neumann, C. E. (2014). The mother of all superheroes: Idealizations of femininity in *Wonder Woman*. In M. Bajac-Carter, N. Jones, & B. Batchelor (Eds.), *Heroines of comic books and literature: Portrayals in popular culture* (pp. 133–144). Lanham, MD: Rowman & Littlefield.

· 5 ·

HYBRIDIZING AND NETWORKING BEYOND BINARIES: CYBORGS AND COGNISPHERES IN THE *BIONIC WOMAN* AND *DARK MATTER*

Up to this point, we have examined how dangerous dames who kick ass have been featured in films in the contemporary postfeminist media landscape. Our final two chapters extend to incorporate episodic media: television and video games. Science fiction television and games provide a robust space for exploring how gender articulates in posthuman contexts. Posthumanism complicates long-standing binaries, dualisms, and dialectics that undergirded Enlightenment humanism. Thus, like science fiction, posthumanism has the capacity to expand the horizon of possibilities for feminism.

From the ensemble of skilled assassins in *Kill Bill* to Mary's fierce mother-hood, the women we have analyzed so far all employ advanced, and violent, skills. Although each of these protagonists employs fierce fighting abilities that extend beyond typical human limits, of the characters discussed thus far, only Wonder Woman possesses actual superhuman powers. Our final case studies build on our consideration of how expanding ability affects the representation of gender in postfeminist media. Thus, we turn our attention to dangerous dames who have been enhanced mechanically. These added abilities emerge from technological innovation rather than superpowers or magic. We cannot all hail from Krypton, but we all have the capacity to become cyborgian or distributed throughout digital spaces.

In this chapter, we consider characters in two science fiction television shows: the *Bionic Woman* reboot and *Dark Matter*. These women find themselves with superhuman abilities due to technological augmentations imposed upon them without their explicit knowledge or consent. Thus, the ways they navigate technological modification differ dramatically from women who choose to alter themselves (see Chapter 6). By tracing the responses of the non-consenting cyborgs and women connected to the cognisphere in these two series, we illuminate how two humanist dialectics (mind/body and human/machine) are revivified and revised. These dangerous dames navigate the posthuman condition by reinstantiating, revising, and rising above the lines between mind and body, human and machine.

Becoming More Than Human

From the reimagination of the iconic Bionic Woman, a cyborg from 1970s television, to a prototype superhuman captaining a spaceship in *Dark Matter*, these mechanically modified dangerous dames must come to terms with becoming partially machine and the possibilities and limitations of their alterations.

Cyborgs and Cognispheres

The cyborg is "a hybrid of machine and organism, a creature of social reality as well as a creature of fiction" (Haraway, 1991, p. 149). Haraway's manifesto popularized the cyborg in academia, generating robust inquiry (Balsamo, 1996; Clark, 2003; Gray, 2000; Gray, Figueroa-Sarriera, & Mentor, 1995; Hughes, 2004; Kirkup, Hovenden, Janes, & Woodward, 2000; McCracken, 1997; Zylinska, 2002). Like Haraway's conception of the cyborg as both material and metaphorical, science fiction visions of the cyborg combine the futuristic with the contemporary to link mind, body, human, and machine. Augmentation might range from a cochlear implant or pacemaker to a prosthetic body part to a technology that alters neurological or socioemotional abilities to an assemblage of theoretical constructs.

These changes can even be purely code, affecting the virtual body (Hayles, 1999). As our bodies inhabit more and more virtual spaces, the cyborg's limitations become increasingly clear. Hayles (2006), for example, points out that the cyborg requires the notion of a subject that remains unified and therefore fails to adapt to the distributed, fragmentary nature of our techno-logical landscape. She proposes Whalen's (2000) concept of the cognisphere instead: "Incorporation of intelligent machines into everyday practices cre-ates distributed cognitive systems that include human and non-human actors; distributed cognition in turn is linked to a dispersed sense of self, with human awareness acting as the limited resource that artificial cognitive systems help to preserve and extend" (Hayles, 2006, p. 162). The cognisphere addresses distributed subjectivity and cognition, complementing the cyborg's hybridity.

Although Hayles identifies a key change in how cognition functions amidst technological dispersion, some subjects do still center on a unified self, even when the self integrates with machines. Furthermore, the cognisphere's overwhelming alliance with mind (erasing, or sublimating, the body in the digital) reinforces an Enlightenment binary (mind/body) that has been used to oppress and diminish many people. Therefore, both the cyborg and the cognisphere help us to adopt a posthuman analytical framework to explore the possibilities and constraints presented by uniting human with machine.

Philosophical Posthumanism

Braidotti (2006) notes that Haraway's cyborg "deliberately blurs categorical distinctions (human/machine; nature/culture; male/female; oedipal/non-oe-dipal)" (p. 200). Posthumanism challenges dualisms, and it positions humans among others as part of a larger ecology. One might think of it as homologous to a Copernican shift, placing the Earth within the solar system rather than viewing it as the center of that system. Hayles (1999) notes, "the posthuman does not really mean the end of humanity. It signals instead the end of a cer-tain conception of the human" (p. 286). This shift includes contextualizing humans in relation to digital spaces and technologies, complex sociopolitical and economic systems, and the natural world.

Posthumanism spans disciplines, but several key terms organize the schol-arly conversation (Braidotti & Hlavajova, 2018). Due to its expansive scope, Braidotti (2006, 2013a, 2013b) divides posthumanism into clusters. For example, one cluster includes digital phenomena (e.g., AI, algorithms, digital citizenship, hypersociality, neocybernetics, and robophilosophy). Similarly, studies of the transhuman and post-human (indicating after humanity) emphasize the role of machines and technology. Some scholars chart ecologies that engage with the natural world, nonhumanity (e.g., ahumans, animals, and multispecies), and those treated as less-than-human or inhuman. Others take up changing sociopolitics and economics, including cosmopolitics, eco-materialism, necropolitics, geo-hydro-solar-bio-techno-politics, peer-to-peer economies, and surveillance. Responses to the posthuman condition include artistic and new, or repurposed, theoretical apparati like Afrofuturism, camp, Monster/the Unhuman, nomadic sensibilities, resilience, and socially just pedagogies. Finally, some scholars adopt a more abstract approach, engaging in projects that re-theorize the ontological nature of humanity or decenter the unified human subject (along with other Enlightenment projects). We follow Braidotti's philosophical posthuman perspective and add a rhetorical one, considering how strong women refashion, or reaffirm, two long-standing binaries (mind/body and human/machine).

Challenging Binaries

Since the ancient Greeks (and reaching its apex in Descartes's cogito), the mind has been viewed as distinct from the body (Lakoff & Johnson, 1999; Spelman, 2017).[1] The mind/body binary is gendered, as well, with the mind aligned with masculinity and the body with femininity, and it has been used to justify exclusion and oppression. Feminist philosophers have challenged this by theorizing embodied epistemologies (Price & Shildrick, 2017; Tuana, 2004, 2006, 2018). Despite these interventions, the binary persists.

Similarly, human has been divided from machine. Machines are not recognized as agents. Even when they displace human workers, are made in the image of humans, cannot be distinguished from humans (e.g., bots online), or replace parts of the human body, machines are classified as separate from and in service to humanity. As our world has become increasingly technologically dense and converged, however, more and more people, and stories, are cyborgian and dispersed throughout the cognisphere. As a result, the line between human and machine has become increasingly difficult to draw.

Across numerous contemporary philosophers, posthuman thought establishes "the need to overcome binaries and to state that matter, the world, and humans themselves are not dualistic entities structured according to dialectical principles of internal or external opposition, but rather materially embedded subjects-in-process circulating within webs of relation with forces, entities, and encounters" (Braidotti & Hlavajova, 2018, pp. 7–8). These divisive binaries rely upon a dialectical epistemology that has animated philosophical work ranging from Plato to Hegel to Marx (Cudworth & Hobden, 2014). They are trenchant and entrenched.

By taking a posthuman approach to analyze the dangerous dames in *Bionic Woman* and *Dark Matter*, we consider how the mind/body and human/machine binaries are evolving and intersecting ability with gender in contemporary science fiction television. Some of the cyborgs uphold the binaries, keeping human distinct from machine and mind distinct from body with augmentations boosting either mental skills or physical prowess. However, the introduction of mechanical modifications can complicate the binaries, reversing their gendering or switching their valences, blurring or merging the poles together, or transcending them altogether. We begin our inquiry with an iconic televisual cyborg: the Bionic Woman.

The Bionic Woman

Viewers first met the Bionic Woman (Lindsay Wagner) when she graced televisions in the mid-1970s. The 2007 reboot of the series *Bionic Woman* stars two: a reluctant cyborg and an earlier prototype. Cast into a good/evil dichotomy, these two women reinforce the split of mind from body. Similarly, they blur the division of human from machine, but they consistently elevate the human over the machine. These characters, changed against their will, reveal some of the limitations that constrain the promise of the cyborg for feminist politics.

Rebooting the *Bionic Woman*

The original series, *The Bionic Woman*, ran three seasons from 1976 through 1978. Joining many rebooted series from the 1960s and 1970s, the new *Bionic Woman* aired on Wednesday nights on NBC. Like many series that year, it fell victim to industry issues that culminated in the strike by the Writer's Guild of America, and it was cancelled midseason. The main character, Jaime Sommers (Michelle Ryan), is outfitted with a "bionic" arm, eye, ear, and legs after a life-threatening car crash. Both the original and the rebooted Bionic Woman work as field agents after their transformation. In the reboot, Jaime goes to work for The Berkut Group, "a private clandestine group dedicated to stopping rogue organizations from ending civilization as we know it," which they present as "saving the world" (Ep. 2). Her liaison with the organization clarifies: "We do what the military, CIA, and FBI can't" (Ep. 5).

In the original, Jaime is a famed tennis player injured while skydiving with her fiancé. The U.S. government replaces her body parts, and she becomes a spy and cares for a bionic dog (Sherrard, 1998). In the reboot, Jaime, like the Bride (see Chapter 1), Katniss (see Chapter 2), and Mary (see Chapter 4), provides primary care for a minor: her adolescent sister Becca (Lucy Hale). A college dropout working as a bartender, Jaime lacks direction and maturity; one of her colleagues notes, "you're smart, you're honest, but you don't quite know who you are yet" (Ep. 2). Although her injuries are inflicted during an outing with her fiancé, the car accident occurs due to malice perpetrated by another cyborg, Sarah Corvus (Katee Sackhoff). Jaime's fiancé works for Berkut Group, the secret organization that transformed Sarah. In the accident's aftermath, he rushes the unconscious Jaime to his laboratory, where he repairs her extensively damaged body without her consent and against his superiors' wishes. The rebooted Bionic Woman begins her new life as a rescued (albeit angry) damsel in distress, with no career and little family to bind her to her previous life. Thus, unlike the original Bionic Woman, who had an established career and suffered harm due to an adventurous accident, the new Bionic Woman performs a service job that hypersexualizes her and her injury comes at the hands of another powerful, spiteful woman. These differences manifest many of the characteristics of postfeminist media: women working a job rather than excelling in a career, pitting women against one another, isolating women from systems of support, and hypersexualizing strong women.

Although women wrote half of the reboot's episodes, men directed and produced every one. Some early reviews were receptive, but the show did not fare well overall. Some critics lamented the tonal shift from the campy original to a darker, conspiracy theme (Goodman, 2007). Metacritic's aggregate scoring, across 28 critics, yielded 57 out of 100, and a 5.2 out of 10 across 93 viewer reviews. On IMDB, the show settled at a 6.0 mean; the highest ratings (mean = 6.2) came from women 18-29 and the lowest (mean = 5.3) from women over 45. One reviewer pointed out the persistent insecurity and neediness expressed by the characters, and lambasted the postfeminist adaptation:

> Viewers don't need to be feminists to yearn to turn the clock back 30 years to when Ms. magazine had half a million readers, the Equal Rights Amendment seemed on the brink of ratification, and Ms. Wagner played an accomplished professional who was courteous, well balanced, and actually seemed to like herself. (Stanley, 2017, para. 12)

Rumors of a new showrunner coming aboard to save the series never had a chance to come to fruition. The writers went on strike, the series was paused, and it never returned. Despite the show's commercial failure, it provides a productive petri dish for tracing the ways strong feminine figures in contemporary science fiction television navigate the mind/body and human/machine binaries.

Feminine Bionic Bodies
Divided from Masculine Minds

Jaime works as a field agent for Berkut Group; Sarah initially did but is estranged from them. Both women demonstrate extraordinary bodily strength, but others strategize the missions. Analysts issue orders; field agents execute them. This division of labor typifies media portrayals of intelligence agency work, with analysts functioning as the agency's mind and field agents as its body. The Bionic Woman's technologically modified body enhances her abilities in the field, but she does not receive strategic, linguistic, or intelligence boosts. Limiting her ability and assignments to the physical reinforces the mind/body binary and its gendering.

Bionic Speed, Strength, Senses, and Recuperation

Jaime uses her newfound super-speed to run, with extreme speed shown via blurring, and to jump exceedingly far or high. Her trainer Jae Kim (Will Yun Lee) estimates she can run approximately 60 miles per hour (Ep. 2).[2] When a little girl in a car sees Jaime running, keeping pace with the car, she remarks to her mother, "I just thought it's cool that a girl could do that" (Ep. 1). Moments like this suggest feminist aspirations, with the writers wanting to provide a role model, like we saw with *Kill Bill* (see Chapter 1) and *Wonder Woman* (see Chapter 3).

In addition to super-speed, Jaime gains extraordinary strength. Before learning to control this power, she casually tosses her fiancé across the room and breaks his arm. Her trainer explains that she can "bend steel" and "shatter brick" (Ep. 2). Another character remarks, "What doesn't kill you makes you stronger," and she responds, "You don't know how true that is" (Ep. 2). Indeed, the trainer assures her, "You can become one of the most powerful weapons ever developed" (Ep. 2). Sarah boasts similar bodily enhancement and strengths.[3] She tells Jaime, "I'm cutting away all the parts of me that are weak" (Ep. 1), equating increased strength with decreased size. When someone Jaime saves asks how she was able to do so, she blithely lies, "Pilates"

(Ep. 2). Later in the season, Jaime's boyfriend asks, "What do you weigh? A buck ten?" (Ep. 6). The cyborgs have strength, but they do not gain bulk; they adhere to beauty norms that prize slender, toned bodies. These moments combine to perpetuate a dangerous, postfeminist narrative suggesting their super-strength derives from exercise, "cutting away" human parts to become more bionic, and maintaining a low body weight.

In addition, the cyborgs' senses are heightened. Super-hearing, depicted via a computer graphic (CG) effect zooming into a speaker-like eardrum or with concentric waves, enables Jaime to hear sounds up to two miles away. Her supervisors reprimand her repeatedly for eavesdropping, but she employs this ability to help people, as well. After hearing someone contemplating jumping off a building, for example, she intervenes. Her enhanced sight empowers her to see through two-way glass and up to 2000 feet away, shown using a quick zoom. For example, after hearing a gun cock, she looks for the source, helping her to locate distant snipers on more than one occasion.

The cyborgs can recuperate from injuries rapidly, as well. Tiny machines ("anthricites") provide scar-free healing for injuries ranging from major surgery to minor burns (Eps. 1, 4). Furthermore, they filter impurities, demonstrated using CG of muscle fibers; Sarah shows Jaime she can smoke, for example, without any ill effect (Ep. 1). Their super-abilities allow them to engage in risky behavior without consequence. Jaime challenges her trainer, "What risk? I'm bionic," and he replies, "Bionic. Not immortal" (Ep. 7). Despite their mortality, however, Sarah and Jaime face few physical limits; they are more than human.

Don't Think, Just Do

All of the bionic augmentations enhance the women's bodies, not their minds or the mind-body connection, thereby reinforcing the mind/body binary. Because the analysts are primarily male, it reinforces the binary's gendering by aligning female field agents with the body and male intelligence analysts with the mind. Moreover, Jaime's body becomes an asset directed by Berkut Group, extending their control and diminishing hers. Even as her body becomes more than human, Jaime becomes less—not even possessing her own body.

Jaime's body is appropriated; her life-saving operation converts her into an expensive weapon owned and operated by Berkut Group. One of the analysts describes her as a "$50 million weapon living a double life" (Ep. 4). Aware of the cost incurred, Jaime asks, "You think because I'm worth $50 million that my life is worth more than his?" (Ep. 4). She remarks, "You know, I find your whole proprietary attitude about my body to be deeply inappropriate" (Ep. 4). Such exchanges reflect Jaime's awareness that placing a dollar value on her body serves to dehumanize and diminish her agency, but no change occurs. Jaime's comments function as jest more than protest, undermining the political possibility raised by her assertions.

Neither cyborg has her intelligence enhanced. When Jaime discloses, "guess I'm not used to thinking of myself as artificially intelligent," her trainer stresses, "that's not what I said" (Ep. 2). One of her supervisors designates her "my muscle," and when Jaime observes, "I'm a lot faster than you are," the supervisor quips, "only at running" (Ep. 3). Indeed, Jaime's lack of intelligence serves as a running joke throughout the show's short run. An analyst suggests she try wearing glasses, teasing, "then you'd *look* smarter" (Ep. 5). Reduced to performing an artifice of intelligence, Jaime's containment to bodily strength is presented as attractive. Her love interest observes, "clearly you can kick some ass," and when she demurs, he insists, "You can," and concludes, "God, you're beautiful" (Ep. 6). Jaime retorts, without rancor, "Oh, so I'm your trophy spy?" (Ep. 6). Her moments of resistance become comic relief, appropriating her agency as much as her body.

Computer chips implanted in the cerebral cortex monitor Jaime's location with GPS, stream visual content, and assist with her combat training. This suggests she could have had her mind enhanced. Instead, Jaime is reduced to her body alone. It is strong and agile, but others own and control it. The strict mind/body division positions her as an object directed rather than a subject capable of independent thought or action.

Humans, Not Machines

Applying a posthuman lens to human/machine in the *Bionic Woman*, we discover that, despite increased physical abilities, the cyborgs' humanity remains central; the machine is always secondary to, even impinging upon, the human. "Technology's at the point where science fiction isn't fiction anymore," discloses Will Anthros (Chris Bowers), who is Jaime's fiancé, a surgeon, bioethics professor, and scientist developing bionics for Berkut Group (Ep. 1). During a lecture, he asks his class, "When is it okay to intervene in God's work?" (Ep. 1). The series never answers his question, but it explores some of the risks of augmenting the human with machines and consistently re-centers the human.

Fearing rejection, Jaime never entrusts her sister with the knowledge that she has been altered. Her initial reaction to the bionics separates what she perceives as her human self from the mechanical additions to her body. She tells Will that her bionic hand "isn't even me" (Ep. 1), and she protests, "You turned me into a half-robotic freak" (Ep. 2). Although she learns to take advantage of the augmentations, Jaime never fully integrates her humanity with the imposed machinery. She accepts her new cyborg body as inevitable, but she never joins human with machine in her self-concept. Describing her body as "a science experiment" (Ep. 7), Jaime thinks of herself as a human with machines tacked on, not as an integrated cyborg.

In contrast, Sarah embraces the machines, but the technology going awry becomes her undoing. Her bionic components make her vulnerable to external hacking, leading her to kill 14 agents before anyone can contain her. After escaping from Berkut, Sarah, like Frankenstein's monster, seeks her creator (Jaime's fiancé's father). The Berkut Group tries, over and over, to kill or recapture her. Ultimately, she capitulates and returns to try to obtain a cure, to prevent the failing machines from killing her. Viewers last see her being wheeled away, in restraints, a prisoner of Berkut Group and her manipulated, mechanized body.

Surprisingly, two women partially comprised of machines do not challenge the human/machine dichotomy much. Their trainer remarks, "the machine is nothing without the woman" (Ep. 2). More accurately, the machines are forced upon these women, and they both become less human, not more, due to the alterations. They learn to live with the technological imposition by viewing themselves as humans with machine elements rather than as cyborgs. Jaime rejects incorporating the machine into her definition of self; Sarah's body rejects the machines and leads to her imprisonment. Both tales re-center the human, and therefore uphold the binary.

Dark Matter

In contrast to the metaphysical angst endured by the cyborgs in *Bionic Woman*, our second text offers a rosier picture. *Dark Matter* aired on Syfy (U.S.) and Space (Canada) from 2015 to 2017. The cyborgian protagonist combines enormous physical resilience with expertise as a skilled hand-to-hand fighter, and she transcends the mind/body and human/machine binaries. Her willpower, visionary leadership, diplomatic skill, and quick strategic thinking connect with her physical prowess and fluid, unapologetic sexuality to present a cyborg who integrates mind and body as well as human and machine. Furthermore, two other characters (Android and Nyx) demonstrate visions of women deriving strength from connecting with the cognisphere. Together, these dangerous dames unmake the binaries in ways that reveal the promise of the embodied cyborg and the distributed cognisphere for feminisms.

Matters in the Dark

Mallozzi and Mullie, the showrunners, adapted *Dark Matter* from their comic book series (also titled *Dark Matter*). Although the series received middling critical reviews, it was nominated for production, sound, visual effects, and acting awards.[4] Users on IMDB rate it a mean of 8 out of 10 (across 34,036 ratings). Women wrote a little over a third of the episodes and directed six of the 39 total episodes. The array of strong female-bodied characters engaging with technological, mechanical enhancement makes this series worth our consideration. As one of the most recent texts we examine, it also comes closest to realizing the feminist promise of posthuman/transhuman science fiction.

Dark Matter begins when six people aboard a spaceship awaken from stasis with amnesia. The characters adopt numbers as names and retain these monikers for most of the series.[5] Of the seven central characters, three are women. Two (Melissa O'Neil) is the primary protagonist. Created as a prototype by Dwarf Star Technologies, she is an ambiguously raced cyborg with tiny machines (nanites) in her body.[6] These enable her to recuperate from remarkable harm and accomplish feats that would kill an ordinary human, ranging from recovering from incurable diseases to walking in space without a protective suit. Five (Jodelle Ferland) initially joins the crew as a stowaway; a white teen girl with a talent for technology, she sports blue/green hair and serves as the heart of the crew. The group is accompanied by a robotic android with a white, female physical form. Referred to simply as Android (Zoie Palmer), she integrates wirelessly with the *Raza* (their ship and home). With her connections across distributed digital networks, Android presents an example of a subject completely enmeshed in the cognisphere.

The other four core characters are male humans. One (Marc Bendavid), a white male, dies very early in season two. Three (Anthony Lemke), also white and male, provides an example of hegemonic masculinity, complete with posturing and machismo, that softens over time. Four (Alex Mallari, Jr.), an Asian male, eventually leaves the crew to assume his birthright as Emperor of Zairon.[7] Finally, Six (Roger Cross), a black male, is a compassionate veteran who ultimately departs to help alleviate suffering in the galaxy.

Like *The Hunger Games*, the series features numerous strong women as minor characters, but it reflects greater racial diversity. *Dark Matter* includes many physically formidable women, including Solara (Ayisha Issa), a warrior who works as a bodyguard and proves a valuable ally, and Tash (Jessica Sipos), a mercenary the crew encounters repeatedly. Others derive authority from their positions, such as Commander Delaney Truffault (Torri Higginson), Chief Inspector Shaddick (Franka Potente), and Empress Ishida (Mung-Ling Tsui). Some, like Misaki Han-Shereikan (Ellen Wong), who commands the Ishida Royal Guard, wield numerous forms of power; she provides counsel, friendly rivalry, and physical protection to Four.

Several of the minor characters gain power from technology, either as machines or via digital connections. For example, Wendy (Ruby Rose), an "entertainment" android turns out to be an assassin and fierce fighter (the actor is a trained boxer). Among the humans, Nyx Harper (Melanie Liburd) rivals Two in hand-to-hand combat. Nyx's greatest strength comes from her connection with a cognisphere; she had many people's minds connected with hers, against her consent. Others start out human and become virtual. For example, after Three's partner Sarah (Natalie Brown) perishes from a terminal disease, Five uploads Sarah's memories into a virtual space that she inhabits in later episodes (much like Zoe in *Caprica* in Chapter 6). All of these women derive power from technology in some fashion.

The array of strong women in the series includes cyborgs, androids, military commanders, royals, and corporate tycoons. They command power through their willpower, physical skills, careers, and technological enhancements. Together, they present numerous ways for women to progress in posthuman contexts. As we detail below, some uphold the mind/body and human/machine binary. However, others reveal the fluidity and fragility of the binaries, and some transcend them altogether.

Mind and Body Separated, Blended, Expanded, and Transcended

Some of the characters in *Dark Matter* uphold the mind/body binary. Five derives her strength from technological skill, which requires thought and dexterity, but she lacks physical strength. Truffault, a brilliant corporate strategist, similarly has little muscle bodily. In contrast, Solara boasts great physical power, but she leaves strategizing to others. None of these characters alter the binary; indeed, by relying so fully on either their minds or bodies, they implicitly reinforce it.

At first glance, strong "female" androids (Wendy and Android) seem more promising; they possess both mental and physical strength. However, their bodies are divorced from their minds. After disabling the traitorous Wendy, the crew disposes of her (mechanical) body and plugs her head into a computer, thereby locating all aspects of her "mind" in her hard drives, with no processing capability provided by the robotic body. Although Android differs from other androids, her divergent characteristics blur the human/machine binary more than the division of mind from body. Both androids' minds are programmed code, and their bodies are robotic tools. Mind and body are not unified, leaving the binary intact.

Similarly, transfer transit clones allow people to travel great distances by copying their mind into a blank clone body. The clone body deteriorates within a couple of days, and the traveler must re-enter a pod to upload memories back to their original body or risk losing the new experiences. Designed for travel, this technology strictly divides mind from body, with the body emerging as an interchangeable vessel and the mind containing the true self.

The binary is fluid, however. Sarah's stories early in the series focus on the body: nursing Marcus Boone back to health, uniting with him after he has become Three, and suffering and dying from an illness. After her digital resurrection, Sarah exists disembodied, fully as mind. She learns to control her surroundings in the virtual world, but she is isolated and lonely, connecting to others only when they visit her virtual space. Unlike the characters we turn to in Chapter 6, however, Sarah does not choose this virtual life. Although she demonstrates the fluidity of body and mind, this move never challenges the underlying binary.

In contrast, Two provides a potent example of imploding this binary. She assumes leadership of the crew almost immediately, besting some of the muscled males in hand-to-hand combat and wielding incomparable will. Others on the team are stronger or quicker physically, including the fully mechanical Android and Four, who is an expert martial artist. Some, such as tech-savvy Five and Android, who is literally a computer, process information more rapidly. But Two displays both mental and physical strength. The real root of her strength, like Wonder Woman's, comes from her character, willpower, and emotional intelligence. Her integration of mind/body, drawing strength from both as well as adding sources that do not fall within the binary, troubles the dichotomy.

Two's strength of mind manifests as situational awareness, strategic think-ing, and emotional intelligence. For example, early in the season, she must leave half of the crew behind, creating a ruse that makes it seem as though she abandoned them. However, she left to save the crew by forming a new corpo-rate alliance and double-crossing the corporation that had hired them. When Ferrous Corp's representative protests, "We had a deal," she shrugs and replies, "I got a better offer" (Ep. 2). Two adapts well to hazardous circumstances, and she navigates complex political and social situations with facility. She works hard to unite the crew and instill trust, episode after episode, repeatedly show-ing extensive emotional intelligence. Her ability to maintain harmony among people who make their living as smugglers and criminals, and who repeatedly discover traitors in their midst, attests to Two's strength as a leader.

Two draws upon her ability to command and, more importantly, lead the crew. Three initially calls her "boss lady" (Ep. 1, 2). Her leadership style involves discussion, delegating, voting, and compromise. For example, after a prolonged debate, she steps in, prompting, "Alright, enough. So we know the situation. What can we do?" Despite this egalitarian style, Two does not hes-itate to take charge. After One wonders who made her the leader, she states, "I did. By stepping up. And so did all of you by not challenging me when I did. Unless you've had a change of heart. You think you could do a better job? Didn't think so" (Ep. 2). She follows up with One privately, disclosing reason-ing for her position and cementing his support. Two frequently pairs decisive decision-making with explanation. In short, she unites situational savvy with emotional intelligence, expanding a narrow definition of mind to encompass adaptability and emotions.

Two combines her mental strength with a physically powerful body. She wears clothing and armor that complements, but does not overemphasize, her body. Her clothing is practical; it is usually black, with tees, armor, boots, and holsters for her weapons. The macho Three wears a similar outfit. Although it rarely calls attention to itself, her clothing shows off her figure well, with-out sexualizing her overtly. This is no Lara Croft, Lorraine Broughton (see Chapter 4), or Catwoman. Her inclusive, unapologetic sexuality does not serve as the root of her power.

However, Two's body does not completely escape the male gaze. In the pilot, an extended tracking shot positions viewers to follow her down a hall-way. Apart from showcasing her swagger, this shot emphasizes her attractive derrière. Such shots, while uncommon, appear throughout the series. More frequently, viewers see Two behaving as a woman who recognizes that she is attractive and cares for her appearance, without drawing on it as a source of power for her leadership or relationships. Indeed, she acknowledges this gaze, directing One to "stop staring at my ass" (Ep. 2). Her assertion scolds the viewers, as well, and audiences learn to regard her as a whole person rather than sexualized or fetishized body parts.

In a confrontation between Two and the gruff (male) head of an external crew, Two's physical strength and self-confidence are reinforced. In response to his reprimand, "Barking orders at me, I gotta tell you, it's not very attractive" (Ep. 10), Two scoffs, "You think I give a shit whether or not you find me attractive?" He tries a different tactic, acknowledging, "You're clearly the brains of your operation." He continues, "Smart, beautiful. You intimidate men in order to maintain control. What you really need, deep down, is a man to step up and take control of you." She orders him to remove his hands (which he places on her throat), and he taunts, "Tell me you don't enjoy this." She responds, "No, you're right. I'm going to enjoy this quite a bit," and takes him down, leading to two broken ribs, a broken wrist, and bruised testicles. In scenes like this, Two's physical strength, her ownership of her body, and her confidence combine to refute masculine power, violence, and presumptive access to female bodies. She does not regard her body as an object, and she does not permit others to do so, either. Two roots her strength in her will-power and self-confidence, not in her strong mind or body, which diminishes the significance of the binary.

Like Two, Nyx displaces this binary, as well. Unlike Two, she does not merge mind and body as a cyborg; instead, she connects with the cognisphere. Across nearly a third of the series, viewers see a strong black woman challenging the binary. Nyx demonstrates extraordinary physical strength, rivaling both Four and Two when they spar, and easily beating the hegemonically masculine Three. Her mental strength derives from her ability to integrate with other minds, providing a tangible vision of the cognisphere.

Nyx allies with the crew of the *Raza* to escape imprisonment and rescue her brother. The group who holds her brother hostage, and who altered her, assimilates enhanced brains to collate data, treating each person plugged in as nodes in a network. Allegorically, this network represents major social media platforms, who engage in similar data mining and predictive algorithmic work. Eventually, her brother returns to the group to protect Nyx, but he ends up killing himself to escape rejoining the exploitative system. The way Nyx connects with a literal cognisphere with figurative import for viewers introduces new ways of thinking about the mind.

By amplifying people's ability to connect with and decode other nodes, the people plugged into this cognisphere amass data, parse it, and predict probable outcomes. Nyx retains these enhanced processing abilities even when disconnected from the network. She can process information so quickly she can predict people's actions, which enables her to spar with the mechanically enhanced Two and expertly trained Four. For Nyx, the mind/body binary becomes passé; she combines the two to the point they cannot be teased apart.

Although not all of *Dark Matter*'s powerful female-bodied characters overcome this binary, those who do demonstrate multiple ways to complicate it. Sarah moves between the poles, revealing the binary's fluidity. Two expands what counts as mind, and she implodes the binary by merging the concepts. She also transcends it by drawing most of her strength from willpower and self-confidence. Nyx, a powerful node in the cognisphere, troubles the division by deriving her power from connections to the network and between her mind and body. This disperses power, decenters the unified human subject, and treats mind and body as inextricably interwoven. Together, the cyborg and the woman connected to the cognisphere illuminate ways strong women can challenge the mind/body binary and the ways it limits feminist progress.

Human and Machine Integrated, Blurred, and Entangled

Dark Matter challenges the human/machine binary by integrating the two poles, blurring the line between them, and entangling the relations between the concepts to the point that they no longer have epistemological utility. The initial hints that Two may be more than human emerge from cryptic comments from Android (Ep. 3 & 8), and a scene in which Two defeats a group of guards, by herself, frightening Five with her lethal efficiency (Ep. 4). The mystery comes to a climax late in the first season. After a hijacker flushes Two out of an airlock, she reboards the ship after surviving an extended period in space without a suit. From there, she disables a pod of armed soldiers, frees her crew (with Five's help), kills the hijacker, and reclaims her ship.

The confirmation of her superhuman power prompts everyone to come to terms with her hybridity. The crew wonders, "What the hell is she?" She acknowledges, "After today, I don't know what I am." Android determines that Two has a human body with "heart, lungs, kidneys, fluids" but is "an advanced biosynthetic organism," noting, "you weren't born; you were engineered" (Ep. 11). At first, the group worries about this revelation, but every member of the crew has multiple identities, blended and fragmented. They are metaphorical cyborgs; she is a literal one. This multiplicity and decentering of the unified subject hastens the normalizing of Two's new identity.

Two experiences a brief existential crisis, leading her to ponder: "I have thoughts and emotions: anger, sadness, happiness. But I'm starting to wonder how real are they?" She continues, "If part of me was designed and manufactured, including my brain, then are my thoughts my own or are they just what somebody else wants me to think? And who is that somebody else? Who constructed me and for what purpose?" (Ep. 12). Later in the episode, she meets her maker, Alexander Rook (Wil Wheaton). She learns her origins, including multiple iterations that involved mapping a consciousness onto an inert body. Like Sarah Corvus in *Bionic Woman*, she escaped her makers violently, killing 43 scientists. Having returned to this facility as Two, she must escape again. Rook tries to hold her hostage with a dampening field to neutralize her abilities. Despite this handicap, she escapes by using strategy, resourcefulness, and her diminished fighting skill to eliminate the guards and scientists standing in her way. Demonstrating her efficacy without the enhancements confirms that her strength exceeds the abilities granted by the nanites. Two integrates human with machine so seamlessly that, like Nyx, even she cannot differentiate between the two.

Although she is robotic, Android blurs the lines between human and machine, as well. Six notes, "Ours [android] is a little different," and Five responds, "she's just like the rest of us [humans]" (Ep. 3). Indeed, Android develops relationships with the crew, to the point that she begins to question whether her programming is flawed. She generates a simulated version of herself as a diagnostic, and this simulation critiques Android for illogical, emotional decisions that defy her programming and make her more like a human. Later, Android obtains a chip that enhances her ability to pass as human. By developing her own agency and crossing from machine toward human, she blurs the binary.

Two and Android together tangle human with machine in such a complicated fashion that the divide ceases to make any sense. All of the crew are fond of Android, but Two discovers her affinity arises from Android's body being modeled after a woman Two loved before joining the *Raza* and before her amnesia. Their mutual regard, and Android's resemblance to this deceased woman, challenge heteronormativity and normalize queer and feminist potentialities in posthuman contexts. The machine, made in the image of a beloved human, and her humanity, and the chimeric cyborg, part human and part machine, share an emotional attachment that significantly complicates the divide between human and machine.

Hybridizing and Networking
Beyond Binaries

Across these two texts, the mind/body and human/machine binaries are renewed, refashioned, and rejected. The *Bionic Woman* reinstantiates the mind/body division and its gendering. The men work as analysts using minds; the cyborgian women work as field agents using bodies. The show reiterates a norm of slender and fit female bodies, and positions Jaime's body as property owned and directed by Berkut Group. These cyborgs may be strong and agile, but they reinforce the mind/body binary. Furthermore, the machine impinges upon the human. Jaime never integrates her bionic parts into her self-concept, and she sees herself as an aberration. Failing technology ruins Sarah. Even as strong cyborgs, these dangerous dames uphold the human/machine binary and re-center the human. Similarly, some characters in *Dark Matter* reinforce the mind/body binary by either having strong minds (Five, Truffault) or bodies (Solara). The androids have both, but mind and body remain discrete. The transfer transit clones make bodies interchangeable and locate the self in the mind. Sarah moves from body to mind, demonstrating the binary's fluidity, but even she does not alter it fundamentally.

In *Dark Matter*, however, the binaries are complicated. Two and Nyx implode the distinction between mind and body. Their strong bodies and minds provide means, not sources, of strength, thereby de-essentializing humanist divisions. Two's true strength comes from emotional intelligence, willpower, and self-confidence. She owns her body and her sexuality. Although she is subject to the gaze, she is not oversexualized, and her body and sexuality do not serve as the root of her power. Nyx derives her strength from connections between her mind/body and to the cognisphere, blurring the mind/body divide and diminishing its importance. Two and Android further blur the human/machine binary. Although Two experiences some existential angst, she quickly embraces her hybrid, cyborgian identity. Android wishes to become more like a human, and she blurs the boundaries in her pursuit of this goal. The mutual affection and complex history between these characters further complicates the relationship between human and machine by introducing queer and feminist potential.

Altogether, the *Bionic Woman* proffers a postfeminist reworking of an iconic figure. Despite their strength, these dames are dangerous primarily because they reaffirm the binaries, present outdated and sexist ideas as normal, and absorb, repackage, and tame feminist politics. In the era of #MeToo, Jaime has a right to object to her body being treated as property in the workplace. The little girl inspired by a woman who can run as fast as a car deserves far better.

In contrast, *Dark Matter* endangers the status quo. It unsettles both binaries and their gendered associations. It presents strong women in a range of roles, with a rainbow of forms of strength. Smart and strategic, physically powerful and agile, emotionally intelligent, sexy, confident, and connected, these women provide actual role models. They also demonstrate how unmaking Enlightenment binaries could yield progressive politics for feminisms in posthumanity. They are dangerous, indeed.

Notes

1. In his second meditation, Descartes (1641/2003) posited the cogito as the firm foundation for knowledge in the face of radical skepticism. That is, we can doubt everything except that we think. Descartes emerges from his abyss of doubt with the conclusion "cogito, ergo sum," which translates to "I think, therefore I am."

2. Lee is cast stereotypically as an Asian martial arts trainer. However, the actor was a competitive Taekwondo competitor for the University of California, Berkeley. In 2002, he was among *People*'s Most Beautiful People, and in 2007 included as one of their sexiest men alive. Positioning him as a love interest counters the typical de-sexualization of Asian men in mainstream media. Those interested in exploring this issue more would do well to begin with Ono and Pham (2009).

3. Despite the series featuring two cyborgs with similar enhancements, the series retains "Woman" in the title.

4. Specifically, *Dark Matter* was nominated for best production design in 2016 (Director's Guild of Canada and Canadian Screen Awards), Visual Effects in 2017 (Leo Awards and Prix Aurora Awards), sound in 2017 (Canadian Screen Awards), and Visual Effects again in 2018 (Canadian Screen Awards). In 2016, Jodelle Ferland was nominated for an acting award by the Academy of Science Fiction, Fantasy, and Horror Films.

5. The characters all have multiple names. The crew all have at least three; some have even more, due to working undercover, assuming aliases, or starting over. For ease of reference, we use their numbered names unless referring to an alternate version of the character.

6. The actor is Canadian, and her maternal grandfather is Chinese.

7. The Empire clearly is modeled after Imperial Japan, but the characters are portrayed by actors of pan-Asian descent, hailing from China, Hong Kong, and the Philippines. This presents a visual that melds people with diverse geopolitical histories, ethnic relations, and cultures into a single group, suppressing difference and reiterating racist flattening of diversity among the peoples of east, south, and central Asia and Polynesia.

References

Balsamo, A. M. (1996). *Technologies of the gendered body: Reading cyborg women*. Durham, NC: Duke University Press.

Braidotti, R. (2006). Posthuman, all too human: Towards a new process ontology. *Theory, Culture & Society, 23*(7–8), 197–208.

Braidotti, R. (2013a). Feminist epistemology after postmodernism: Critiquing science, technology and globalisation. *Interdisciplinary Science Reviews, 32*(1), 65–74.

Braidotti, R. (2013b). *The posthuman*. Cambridge, United Kingdom: Polity.

Braidotti, R., & Hlavajova, M. (Eds.). (2018). *Posthuman glossary*. London, United Kingdom: Bloomsbury.

Clark, A. (2003). *Natural-born cyborgs: Minds, technologies and the future of human intelligence*. New York, NY: Oxford University Press.

Cudworth, E., & Hobden, S. (2014). Analysing change: Complex rather than dialectical? *Globalizations, 11*(5), 627–642.

Descartes, R. (1641/2003). *Discourse on method; and, Meditations on first philosophy* (E. S. Haldane & G. R. T. Ross, Trans.). Mineola, NY: Dover.

Goodman, T. (2007, September 23). Tim Goodman reviews: 'Journeyman,' 'Chuck' and 'Bionic Woman'. *SFGate*. Retrieved from https://www.sfgate.com/news/article/Tim-Goodman-Reviews-Journeyman-Chuck-and-2501475.php

Gray, C. H. (2000). *Cyborg citizen: Politics in the posthuman age*. New York, NY: Routledge.

Gray, C. H., Figueroa-Sarriera, H. J., & Mentor, S. (1995). *The cyborg handbook*. New York, NY: Routledge.

Haraway, D. (1991). *Simians, cyborgs, and women: The reinvention of nature*. New York, NY: Routledge.

Hayles, N. K. (1999). *How we became posthuman: Virtual bodies in cybernetics, literature, and informatics*. Chicago: University of Chicago Press.

Hayles, N. K. (2006). Unfinished work: From cyborg to cognisphere. *Theory, Culture & Society, 23*(7–8), 159–166.

Hughes, J. (2004). *Citizen cyborg: Why democratic societies must respond to the redesigned human of the future*. New York, NY: Westview Press.

IMDB. (2018). *Bionic Woman* (2007): User ratings. IMDB.com, Inc. Retrieved from https://www.imdb.com/title/tt0880557/ratings?ref_=tt_ql_op_4

Johnson, K. (2007). *Bionic Woman* [Television series]. New York, NY: NBC Universal Television.

Kirkup, G., Hovenden, F., Janes, L., & Woodward, K. (Eds.). (2000). *The gendered cyborg: A reader*. London, United Kingdom: Routledge.

Lakoff, G., & Johnson, M. (1999). *Philosophy in the flesh: The embodied mind and its challenge to Western thought*. New York, NY: Basic.

Mallozzi, J., & Mullie, P. (2015–2017). *Dark matter* [Television series]. New York, NY: Syfy.

McCracken, S. (1997). Cyborg fictions: The cultural logic of posthumanism. *Socialist Register 33*, 288–301.

Metacritic. (2018). *Bionic Woman*: Season 1. CBS Interactive, Inc. Retrieved from https://www.metacritic.com/tv/bionic-woman

Ono, K. A., & Pham, V. (2009). *Asian Americans and the media*. Malden, MA: Polity.

Price, J., & Shildrick, M. (Eds.). (2017). *Feminist theory and the body*. New York, NY: Routledge.

Sherrard, J. (1998, March). Jaime's story. *Bionic Woman files*. Retrieved from http://www.bionicwomanfiles.com/

Spelman, E. V. (2017). Woman as body: Ancient and contemporary views. In J. Price & M. Shildrick (Eds.), *Feminist theory and the body* (pp. 32–41). New York, NY: Routledge.

Stanley, A. (2017, September 26). *Bionic Woman - Private Practice - TV - Review. Nytimes.com*. Retrieved from https://www.nytimes.com/2007/09/26/arts/television/26priv.html

Tuana, N. (2004). Coming to understand: Orgasm and the epistemology of ignorance. *Hypatia, 19*(1), 194–232.

Tuana, N. (2006). The speculum of ignorance: The women's health movement and epistemologies of ignorance. *Hypatia, 21*(3), 1–19.

Tuana, N. (2018). *Feminism and philosophy: Essential readings in theory, reinterpretation, and application*. New York, NY: Routledge.

Whalen, T. (2000, 23 September). Data navigation: Architectures of knowledge. Paper presented at Banff Summit on Living Architectures: Designing for Immersion and Interaction conference, Banff New Media Institute. Retrieved from http://philipbeesleyarchitect.com/publications/BNMI/EupohoriaDystopia_sample.pdf

Zylinska, J. (Ed.). (2002). *The cyborg experiments: The extensions of the body in the media age*. New York, NY: Continuum.

· 6 ·

TRANSCENDING BOUNDARIES: POSTHUMANISM AND TRANSHUMANISM IN *CAPRICA* AND *DEUS EX*

Unlike those discussed in Chapter 5, the women in this chapter actively choose transhuman augmentation. Transhumanism draws upon scientific and technological advances to improve humanity (Bostrom, 2005; Dvorsky, 2008; Fukuyama, 2002). These types of advances, including purposeful technological augmentation, appear routinely in science fiction across media (e.g., *Gattaca, Limitless, Avatar, Helix, Stargate, Babylon 5, Westworld, Half-Life, Halo, BioShock*). Thus, in this chapter, we consider how mechanical manipulations, both material and metaphorical, complicate the mind/body, us/them, and human/machine binaries for dangerous dames who actively choose augmentation in the television series *Caprica* and in the *Deus Ex* series of video games.

The figures featured in this chapter, like those in the previous one, all have undergone some form of purposeful modification. These women respond in a range of ways to their transhuman alterations, sometimes embracing their mechanical mods, sometimes coming to cope with them, sometimes resisting, and sometimes transcending the binaries altogether. At points, they fall victim to leaky hegemony, like Katniss (see Chapter 2) and the Bionic Women (see Chapter 5). At other points, they find creative ways to apply their technological enhancements in new ways, like Two and Android in *Dark Matter* (see

Chapter 5). Throughout, they illuminate and challenge Enlightenment binaries that constrain women in postfeminist media. In both *Caprica* and *Deus
Ex*, the characters' mechanical modifications concretize the limits and promise of the cyborg and the cognisphere for feminisms. In other words, they can
teach us about feminist politics, possibilities, and perimeters in posthumanity.

Creating Cyborgs in *Caprica*

Caprica aired on Syfy (U.S.), Space (Canada), and Sky1 (U.K.) starting in
2010. Its protagonist, the prodigy and zealot Zoe Graystone (Alessandra
Torresani), perishes in a martyr bombing during the first episode. The viewers
follow a virtual reality version of Zoe that she programmed prior to her death;
this version eventually inhabits a physical robot, creating a literal ghost in
the machine.[1] Zoe becomes a metaphorical cyborg who first interacts with
a copy of herself in a virtual digital platform, then exists on that platform
exclusively after her body dies, and later re-embodies herself by appropriating
and inhabiting a robotic body. She transforms from a tech-savvy human to a
virtual intelligence to an embodied artificial intelligence (AI) entangled with
the cognisphere. The various versions of her trouble the notion of a single
self bounded by flesh. Who is self? Who is other? What is human? Machine?
Will the real Zoe please stand up? This dangerous dame reveals the increasing
difficulty of relying on Enlightenment binaries to make sense of, or improve,
life in a posthuman society.

Preceding *Battlestar Galactica*

Caprica was a spin-off prequel to the enormously popular reboot of the 1970s
science fiction series *Battlestar Galactica* (BSG). Created by Aubuchon and
Moore (one of the BSG reboot creators), *Caprica* was directed and written mostly by men; women directed a single episode and wrote two.[2] Like
its predecessor, the show garnered fairly positive reviews from critics, and it
was nominated for numerous visual effects and sound awards (IMDB, 2018;
Metacritic, 2018a).

Set 58 years prior to the fall of the colonies that launches BSG, *Caprica*
tells the tale of three primary groups: the Graystones, the Church of the One,
and the Adamas. The Graystones, white and wealthy, live in the eponymous
capital city of the planet Caprica. Daniel Graystone (Eric Stoltz) made a

fortune inventing a virtual reality space known as V-World, and his technology firm creates robot centurions for the Caprican government.

Clarice Willow (Polly Walker) is a prominent member of The Church of the One. Members of the Church worship a single god, rather than a pantheon like most people in the show's universe. These monotheists revere the same deity as the Cylons in BSG, and Caprica reveals the origins of this faith. Clarice and her cronies attempt to orchestrate a massive terrorist attack to inaugurate thousands of deceased people into a virtual heaven as a form of marketing. Instead, Zoe's coconspirator and best friend, Lacy Rand (Magda Apanowicz) thwarts Clarice's dream of creating an afterlife in V-World and ascends to become Mother Superior of the Church of the One. As Mother Superior, Lucy indoctrinates the new race of Cylons, with Zoe at the vanguard.

Finally, viewers follow a third group: the Adamas. This working-class family, ancestors to two of the main characters in BSG, is portrayed primarily by Latinx actors. The main character from this family, Joseph Adama (Esai Morales), loses his daughter, Tamara (Genevieve Buechner), in the terrorist attack. Daniel Graystone convinces Joseph to create a virtual version of her. After a traumatic meeting with the frightened virtual version of Tamara, however, Joseph slowly deteriorates as he regrets trapping her consciousness in V-World. Tamara lives the afterlife Clarice envisions, but she resents it. Her inability to die gives her time to mature from a timid, trapped avatar to a reigning virtual queen, but her strength accumulates while walking a path rife with suffering.

The tale moves between the "real" world and V-World. Within V-World, a dedicated area hosts a game: New Cap City. In this space, visitors who "die" can never log in again. However, the two girls, purely code, cannot be killed and thus accumulate notoriety and power through their ability to survive and thrive in this cognisphere. Together, the characters in Caprica teach us a lot about how mind/body, us/them, and human/machine are evolving in posthuman science fiction.

Merging Mind, Body, and Cognisphere Connections

Zoe begins as a girl, mind and body integrated and unquestioned in a single, reified subject. She creates a virtual version of herself that is fully mind with no physical body, separating the two elements. After she and Tamara die and become only virtual, their minds cohere around avatars that mirror human bodies, and both lament the lack of a material body. The newly awakened Tamara, for example, worries that she cannot feel her heart beat, and she resents her father for consigning her to a perpetual virtual life. Similarly, Zoe's avatar, wishing to experience the "real" world, discovers how to inhabit the centurion robot. Zoe's father suspects a virtual version of Zoe has entered the robot, and he tries to force her to divulge this to him by torturing the centurion. Thus, Zoe and Tamara's desires for embodiment appear as adolescent willfulness and struggles between daddy and daughter, rather than women claiming bodies for themselves and using those bodies to create descendants, knowledge, or mobility.

However, as the characters mature, Zoe and Tamara come to revel in their ability to move freely in V-World, embracing the possibilities that come from being unencumbered by bodily constraints. Nevertheless, Zoe views embodiment as more genuine. She hides her virtual limits from the boy she meets in V-World, the lab technician who cares for the centurion. When she enters the centurion's robot body, Zoe downloads not as a copy of the mind of her "original," embodied self; instead, she enlivens the mechanical body with her more developed AI and connections with the cognisphere. In this iteration, Zoe's mind thus precedes and enriches her body.

Ultimately, Zoe's awakening of the centurion creates the Cylons, who are born like Athena springing from the mind of Zeus. Although this restores creation and birth to a female figure, rather than Zoe's father, the Cylons emerge from her mind rather than her body, thereby suppressing the productive power of the female body. The robot is all machine body; the virtual Zoe is all virtual mind. Combined, however, Zoe becomes the consummate cyborg.

Self as Other, Us as Them

In all, Zoe exists in four forms: embodied human, avatar vessel, self-directed avatar, and embodied centurion. As a result, she lives liminally, and her multiplicity blurs the threshold between us and them. Zoe begins as an embodied teenage girl. In this form, she, like Katniss (see Chapter 2), demonstrates a form of "girl power" (Newsom, 2004). Zoe wears a flowing purple Grecian-style dress and a braided headband. With long, straight hair and a thick blunt-cut fringe of bangs, she appears youthful, feminine, and innocent. However, working with Clarice and the Church of the One, Zoe and her friends become pawns and perpetrate a terrorist attack. She may look innocent, but Zoe is a dangerous dame, both serious and deadly. This first iteration is firmly human, embodied, and adolescent, and "us" for her includes the radical sect of the Church.

The second iteration of Zoe is the avatar that the embodied Zoe created to enter V-World. For most people, their virtual avatar has no sense of self or persistence of being. It exists as a shell that the human entering V-World can pilot, and when the human logs out it ceases to exist. Although V-World has a culture (primarily vice clubs), participants cannot affect the environment, and they cannot perish unless they enter a special space, like the game *New Cap City*. Zoe's avatar is special; she moves fluidly in this space. Newsom (2004) notes that characters with "girl power" balance "fantastic systems" with "the victim role that the characters constantly resist," which functions to "confine these images" (p. 58). Zoe's avatar looks like the original Zoe, and she lives in a world of pure fantasy. She actively resists being a victim or a mere vessel. She possesses coding skills of her own, and she enhances and changes her avatar to please herself, such that versions of her late in the season sport new outfits more suited to the maturing virtual-Zoe. Unlike other avatars, she can affect the environment around her, and she exists apart from the embodied Zoe. Although initially she feels a strong desire to please embodied Zoe and realize her plans, the virtual Zoe grows after the enfleshed Zoe dies and develops a sense of self apart from her creator. Eventually, she and Tamara come to rule in *New Cap City*, transforming from talented teens into virtual powerhouses. Virtual Zoe is no victim.

Eventually, overcome by her desire for a body outside of V-World, Zoe downloads herself into one of the centurion bodies. She inadvertently becomes trapped in this body, unable to return to V-World or *New Cap City*. Embodiment becomes victimhood. To escape her father and secure her freedom, she coordinates with Lacy to arrange transport of her new centurion body to the Church of the One headquarters. Hence, the two girls combined re-empower Zoe and create the Cylons.

As this story grows into *BSG*, the machines develop more advanced versions who pass as human, a technological affordance they employ to infiltrate society and to promote their monotheistic religion. Although many look identical, their multiplicity and complexity blurs the us/them binary. The Cylons come in different forms, and, within a form, begin with the same infrastructure, programming, and skins. The same origin and appearance does not lead them to become the same individual, however, and the same Cylons out of the box mature into very distinct people. Code provides a point of origin from which avatars and Cylons learn and evolve based on experiences and encounters. In this way, the non-human being gains agency separate from its point of origin. The self and the other are at once the same and completely different. Similarly, in *Caprica*, self/other flows across bodies and media and at times co-exists in multiple forms. In a world with so much multiplicity undergirded by similarity, us and them relationships become very complicated.

Human, Machine, HumanMachine

In short, Zoe moves from human to code to machine. The human interacts with the code, as she develops and trains it, but the virtual Zoe must learn and grow apart from her human creator. The AI tries to duplicate the human at first. She realizes she is an agent rather than a replicated human, however, and she purposefully enters the centurion, creating a merged version of all the Zoes.

The show establishes a division between Zoe and the robot body by showing the actor, not the robot, during interactions between her and other characters. For example, when Daniel experiments on the centurion, he inflicts harm upon the robotic body, subjecting it to fire because of a traumatic experience from Zoe's youth. In this scene, however, viewers see him addressing the actor who portrays Zoe. Even though we know he sees the robot, the scene is chilling. Daniel suspects the AI version of his daughter inhabits the robotic body, and he seeks to torture her into divulging this by pulling triggers from his daughter's childhood trauma; showing the actor instead of the robot permits viewers to see her more expressive reaction to this horror. This division speaks more to mind/body than human/machine, however. She changes from Zoe in the machine, a virtual ghost, into Zoe as machine, a HumanMachine able to interact with the virtual. She merges human, machine, virtual, and cognisphere.

At first, *Caprica* privileges mind over body, dividing the two and even erasing the body in its visualization of the virtual version of Zoe. However, as Zoe multiples, the series collapses a tidy differentiation between mind/body, self/other, and human/machine, which presages the complications explored later in *BSG*. *Caprica* does demonstrate some of the advantages and limits proffered by the cognisphere, with the body serving as a trap, encumbrance, or advantage at various points. Because Zoe combines all these elements, however, she creates a cyborg that incorporates the cognisphere, imploding binaries along the way.

Playing Cyborgs in *Deus Ex*

Video games provide possibilities for interaction and customization not present in more static media. They create an embodied, (kin)aesthetic experience (Behrenshausen, 2007). Games tell stories using interactive (and often immersive) spaces. Furthermore, they have the capacity to advance claims via both story and game mechanics (Bogost, 2007, 2008). Sex and gender play a prominent role in gaming, and feminist game studies scholars have explored this area thoroughly (Chess 2018; Consalvo, 2013; Gray, 2014; Shaw, 2015b; Taylor, 2003).[3] Because they are a form of play, games draw in audiences; indeed, the ludological aspect of games helps to define them (Frasca, 2003; Raessens, 2006; Salen & Zimmerman, 2004; Sicart, 2011; Taylor, 2009; Yee, 2006). As a result, video games often engage players with a single text for tens to hundreds of hours, making them a particularly potent medium.

A player may see through the eyes of an avatar, like in a first-person shooter, or may see a third-person representation, like in many role-playing games (RPGs). Even a third-person avatar establishes an affective link between the player and the character (Black, 2017). Because the player actively cobbles augmentations together and trades experience for additional tools and abilities as s/he levels the character, the self becomes modular, with the capacity to interchange parts, rather than an unassailable unified whole. This modularity is amplified in the *Deus Ex* series of games, which features characters with extensive mechanical modification.

Contextualizing *Deus Ex*

The *Deus Ex* franchise includes six video games, beginning with the foundational *Deus Ex* (2000) and followed by *Deus Ex: Invisible War* (2003), *Deus Ex: Human Revolution* (2011), an iPhone puzzle game *Deus Ex: The Fall* (2013), a geolocation game *Deus Ex Go* (2016), and *Deus Ex: Mankind Divided* (2016). Except for the two mobile games, it merges the first-person shooter and RPG genres. Teams design and create most console games, including *Deus Ex*. Men occupied most of the production roles. However, the franchise has consistently involved women in prominent writing and supervisory roles, including on *Invisible War*, *Human Revolution*, *The Fall*, and *Mankind Divided*.

Critic and user ratings for all of the console games have been high.[4] *Deus Ex's* popularity is on par with triple-A series like *Halo*, *Mass Effect*, *Grand Theft Auto*, and *Assassin's Creed*. Across the franchise, the games have garnered numerous awards, nominations, and "best of" honors for design, innovation, visual effects, musical score, vocal performance, and storytelling. It has appeared in industry "best game of all time" lists, generated by gaming publications and critics, no fewer than 25 times. *Gamasutra* (2009) ranks it the second best game of the 2000s (behind only *World of Warcraft*), and their readers, comprised largely of game designers and dedicated gamers, rank it first for making the largest leap forward in game storytelling (Boyer & Cifaldi, 2006). This celebrated suite of games, spanning almost 20 years, provides a rich space to consider the re-working of mind/body, self/other, and human/machine, and they offer numerous dangerous dames with mechanical augmentation who both uphold and challenge postfeminist representations.

Multiplying Cyborgs in *Deus Ex*

Mechanically modified and augmented characters turn up frequently in science fiction video games. In the *Deus Ex* universe, such modification plays a significant role in the setting, gameplay, and narratives. Cyborgian alteration has become banal in this imagined society. These transhuman enhancements include a variety of prosthetics (usually arms or legs), forms of protection (armor, cloaking and stealth, health points, and healing aids), skill enhancers (reflex and speed boosters and increased abilities to focus, aim, track, navigate, or interact with other people socially), and improved abilities to attack (with electricity, weapons, and hacking). Some characters forego modifications; others sport extensive augmentation. The widespread integration of enhancements yields numerous examples of dangerous dames who have chosen to connect with the cognisphere or become cyborgs.

In all of the *Deus Ex* games, the player navigates a complex political landscape, employing stealth, attacks, and diplomacy to gather intelligence and try to maintain or effect peace among political groups in a volatile world. The games incorporate characters hailing from around the world, including the United States, Nigeria, Israel, the Czech Republic, China, Panama, Britain, and Russia. As a result, characters' races and ethnicities span a broad swath of humanity, with structural inequalities in the universe emerging primarily from differences in ability and political alliance.

Women work in many jobs in the games: as agents and spies, bartenders, executive assistants, hackers, pilots, merchants, actors, journalists, doctors, singers, and information brokers. The wide array prevents feminization of any industry. Some characters exhibit signs of serious mental illness such as dissociation or PTSD, but these are presented as characterizations rather than primary motives and do not affect women disproportionately. A few women function as victims or damsels, although the game tasks the player with rescue less frequently than other goals like gathering information. Some of the women are bosses (powerful villains) whom the player must assuage or defeat to proceed. The majority of the women act as allies, either as minor non-player characters (NPCs) who provide information, goods, or assistance to the player's character, or as colleagues who accompany the player's character on missions. Most characters are conflated with their jobs and the functions they can perform to challenge, defeat, or assist the player.

Across the franchise, the player both plays and encounters mechanically modified individuals. The attitudes expressed by NPCs toward people who have augmentations varies from fear to celebration to discrimination. As the *Human Revolution* character William Taggart puts it, "This enhancement technology threatens to change the course of human evolution, to redefine what it even means to be human." In most of the games, the protagonist's modifications are crucial to succeed, but augmentation often features prominently in the storyline, as well. In *The Fall*, for example, the protagonist searches for a cure for side effects caused by his modifications, and in *Mankind Divided*, the player enters a world in which augmented individuals have been hacked and forced to attack non-augmented people, leading to persecution and apartheid. *Deus Ex* does not shy away from exploring the political ramifications of differences in ability.

Transcending the Body; Sanctifying the Mind

In *Mankind Divided*, the player meets Allison Beatric Staněk. A military veteran, she disposed of bombs before being discharged for mental illness. After leaving the military, Allison, like Lacy in *Caprica*, becomes the "Mother" in an unofficial splinter cell of the Singularity Church of the MachineGod.[5] The Church believes that augmented people are chosen, and, like Clarice in *Caprica*, hopes humans can overcome the limits of the body and of death by communing with machines.

Driven by faith, Allison seeks to merge her consciousness with this deity via a machine (in the game, a "consciousness collector"), an act her Church refers to as "Ascension." Doing so entails physical suicide; submitting one's consciousness to the MachineGod kills the martyr's body and transfers the mind to the collection curated by the machine. Allison wishes to transcend the body to become all mind.

Allison's father asks the player to intercede. The quest requires infiltrating the Church and dodging guards, explosives, and other environmental hazards. Once the player reaches Allison, s/he can attempt to persuade her to forego the sacrifice. Depending on how persuasive the player is during this conversation, s/he may fail (leading to Allison's death), partially succeed (leading to her arrest), or fully succeed (leading to her arrest and a boon for the player).

Allison sanctifies augmentation. Her desire to leave her body behind is thwarted only if the player sufficiently critiques these choices. Allison focuses minimally on finding unity with others, expanding the capacity of the mind or body, empowering herself or others, or challenging limits. Instead, she views the body as a barrier preventing union with her deity. The deification of mind, managed by a computer, and the denigration of flesh expressed by Allison reinstantiates the mind/body binary and takes the valorization of transhuman augmentation to an extreme. Furthermore, given the historical gendering of the mind/body binary, Allison's disdain for her female body and celebration of the masculine mind reinforces the gendering of the binary.

Another character from *Mankind Divided*, Daria Myška, further reinforces this gendering of the mind/body binary. Both her mind and body have been enhanced, but, like Sarah Corvus in *Bionic Woman* (see Chapter 5), she is betrayed by the augmentations. Daria has strengthened her body significantly with enhancements to her defenses (shield), her stealth (cloaking), and her legs (jumping and dashing). Despite all of her bodily strength, Daria is socially uncertain and dedicated to her cats. She is a stereotypical cat lady. Indeed, her extreme anxiety, bordering on agoraphobia, initially led her to seek the augmentations, and she has an experimental neural personality implant to help her cope with these socioemotional challenges.

Daria's neural alteration overrides her entire personality. She transforms from a wilting wallflower into a manipulative serial killer because her experimental implant came from a male convicted serial killer. The strength of his mind overcomes hers; she even comes to prefer the foods he did. She has a very strong body, and, while her chip is active, she appears to have a strong mind as well. However, this strength comes from the implant's source. His mental strength overwhelms hers, leading her to misuse her physical strength committing atrocious crimes.

Daria reinforces the gendered mind/body divide, with the strength of mind coming from the implant's male source. In the end, Daria's strength is all physical—and artificial. She has not cultivated her body's strength. Instead, she technologically enhanced it. She cannot function in society until her neural implant, and a male mind, overrides her mousy personality. Although physically strong, Daria falls victim to the killer's mind, to the scientist's experimentation, and to the gendering of the mind/body binary.

Not Quite So Us Versus Them

The player's choices in *Deus Ex* change how NPCs react to the player, including conversational options and attitudes for future interactions and alliances. Although more commonplace in the second decade of the 21st century, this innovation changes gameplay and the story. The flexibility produces substantial variance from player to player. It also reinforces the illusion that the individual controls her/his destiny and alliances.

The player inherits organizational conflicts already in place among various factions. For example, UNATCO (United Nations Anti-Terrorism Coalition) has ties to the Majestic 12; the Juggernaut Collective and the Illuminati are at odds. NPCs from friendly organizations reward the player most, and these incentives encourage the player to accede to existing definitions of self, ally, and enemy. The firm sense of enemyship buttresses a rigid sense of one's political self (aligned with one's chosen allied organizations) and other (enemies).[6]

For example, the talented pilot Alejandra "Alex" Vega in *Mankind Divided* demonstrates great loyalty to the Juggernaut Collective. She recruits the player's character and rewards countering Illuminati moves. Similarly, Yelena Federova (who appears in *Human Revolution* and *The Fall*) is a senior member of the Tyrants. In *The Fall*, she is tasked with intercepting a senior member of the Juggernaut Collective. Such political machinations typify *Deus Ex* gameplay. Yelena proves one of the most challenging antagonists in *The Fall*. Her augmentations include enhanced health, armor, awareness, explosives, and prosthetic legs that amplify her speed, agility, and stealth; they also make her a dramatic 6'7" tall. Defeating Yelena reinforces the player's loyalty to the Juggernaut Collective, cementing a shared enemyship against the Tyrants.

Players can blur this strict division, though. For example, choosing to debilitate, rather than kill, adversaries can create allies among the "enemy." Turning to persuasive or stealthy means, rather than combative ones, can neutralize foes. For example, the player can prevent Daria from killing again by disabling her implant with a key phrase. Because of the political complexity of *Deus Ex*, the player engages in diplomacy and espionage as frequently as combat. Doing well in the game often entails sneaking, strategizing, and finding ways to avoid confrontation. Mike Orenich of LucasArts summarizes this well:

> It was the first game that I played which truly allowed you the freedom to complete the game/missions with multiple paths. The RPG elements (skills & augmentations) allowed you to customize as you progressed through the game, so you could blast your way killing everyone in sight or sneak through solving the game without killing anyone. The best part was how your actions influenced the story and the character's responses to you as the player. (*Gamasutra* design staff, 2009, para. 1)

The *Deus Ex* games require the player to think laterally and situationally, considering how best to adapt to an audience. In other words, these games reward rhetorical skills. The shifting political alliances and range of ways to engage with NPCs blurs the us/them binary, despite presenting a world where alienated political factions practice enemyship.

Balancing Human and Machine

With its plethora of transhuman cyborgs, *Deus Ex* demonstrates myriad responses to the human/machine binary, ranging from supporting to blurring to complicating to undermining it. One of the strongest female-bodied characters in the *Deus Ex* universe, Zhao Yun Ru, from *Human Revolution*, illustrates one lesson: the danger of abandoning balance in human/machine relations.

In her youth, Yun Ru was an Olympic-quality gymnast, but she suffered injuries in a car accident, preventing her from competing. As an adult, she turns her athletic skill to fencing. Like the women in *Kill Bill* (see Chapter 1), *Atomic Blond* and *Proud Mary* (see Chapter 3), and *Dark Matter* (see Chapter 5), Yun Ru has excelled in her career. She holds degrees in biology and nanotechnology, and, as the CEO of one of the largest firms producing the augmentations used throughout the games (Tai Yong Medical), Yun Ru is a tycoon and a power player. Unfortunately known by the racist moniker "Dragon Queen" (Kochiyama & Aguilar-San Juan, 1997; Omi & Winant, 2007) due to her race and power, she is smart, sophisticated, ruthless, and connected. Yun Ru seeks to monopolize the augmentation market on behalf of her political alliance: the Illuminati. Moreover, she wields her connections as weapons.

During her final battle with the player, Yun Ru employs guards, a panic room, and a signal broadcast to disable the player's augmentations. Her own modification interfaces her spine with a computer, connecting her to the cognisphere. Indeed, this creates a visual, material manifestation of how she accrues strength via connections. At the end of this battle, Yun Ru dies from an overload while interfaced with her computer, trying to direct all augmented people against the player. Her connections, integration of human with machine, and ambition to overpower humanity ultimately unmake her. She illustrates the danger of an implosion of the binary. She is neither human nor machine; she is both completely, endangering everyone.

Even in a world primarily populated by cyborgs, the divide between the human and the machine persists. At times, *Deus Ex* comes close to revealing the promise of removing this binary from our understanding of what it means to be human. In contrast, Yun Ru perishes because she tries to become more machine than human, reminding us that we need the human along with the machine, the cyborg with the cognisphere.

Postfeminism in Posthumanity

Together, the mind/body, us/them, and human/machine binaries intertwine, reinforcing and complicating one another in *Caprica* and the *Deus Ex* games. Modernity reinforced and advanced Enlightenment binaries like these, producing power relations through division. Feminisms have developed a range of tools to counter the resulting power relations, but, as we have seen, in posthumanity we are working to challenge the very bedrock founding these inequities by revealing the workings of these binaries and disrupting their power by exploring new ways to relate. The two texts we have examined in this chapter, *Caprica* and *Deus Ex*, and in Chapter 5 (*Bionic Woman* and *Dark Matter*) illuminate some of the possibilities that emerge from cyborgs and women who connect with the cognisphere.

At times, the texts reveal how the binary functions more than how it could be changed. *Deus Ex* reinforces the mind/body binary, for example. Allison seeks to upload her consciousness in order to become all mind and transcend the body, so she can unite with the divine. She subordinates body to mind. Daria's great physical strength is subsumed by the strength of the man's mind implanted in her own. Her physical strength and mental weakness together fortify the gendering of the binary. In sum, they simply illustrate the binary and its gendering.

In contrast, in *Caprica*, the mind/body binary expands. Zoe moves from an embodied subject as a teenage girl to all mind as the virtual Zoe exceeds the constraints of the human body to traverse the cognisphere. Her longing to enter the "real" world culminates in her appropriating the centurion, thereby constructing the consummate cyborg by connecting mind, body, human, machine, cyborg, and cognisphere. Furthermore, Zoe and Lacy (the Mother Superior of the Church of the One) together birth the monotheistic Cylons from female minds instead of bodies. They confound the traditional work and gendering of the mind/body binary.

Thus, we wonder: what gendered possibilities might emerge from reconceptualizing the body's intelligence as not subordinate to, or separate from, the mind's activities? Can transhuman modifications help us theorize this? In many ways, the virtual world already blurs the division between mind and body. Embracing this, and the concomitant challenges to us/them and human/machine, could provide new ways to think about the relationship between the mind and the body and the role gender plays in constituting subjectivity.

Both cases challenge us/them divisions. In *Deus Ex*, the player's choices lead to divergent experiences in the games' interactive, branching narratives. This reinforces the illusion that the player's decisions create the character and produce the self. Because games so frequently divide allies from enemies, the other frequently appears as an adversary. In some ways, this splits us dramatically from them, rending along existing political faction lines in the games, as shown by Alex and Yelena. However, players can resolve many encounters with the "enemy" by using nonviolent means of conflict resolution, sidestepping a quest or conflict, or allying with the adversary. Thus, the player can shift the world's political balance and undermine enemyship relations. Because the *Deus Ex* games emphasize rhetorical savvy and lateral thinking, the player also must learn to place a single interaction into a larger framework, consider the motives of others, and solve problems creatively. The player's options are constrained by structural factors, but the mechanics reward employing a broader and more inclusive range of criteria to identify members of "us" and discourage adhering to political alliances without reflection. All of this destabilizes traditional forms of political alliance, and it rewards nonviolent conflict resolution and systems thinking.

In *Caprica*, the self/other binary implodes completely. Zoe's various versions are all self and all other, intermingled in new forms, media, and bodies. She presages the complexity presented later in *BSG* by the Cylons, who similarly have multiple copies of the same self manifesting into multiple (and distinct) individuals. Although a sense of the unified subject persists in *Caprica*, and later in *BSG*, the firm boundaries around the self are unsettled by these multiplying, complicated selves.

This has important gendered implications. All of these characters demonstrate the ability to forge connections not grounded in biology or in traditional forms of organization and connection among subjects. The subject is not produced through (gendered) exclusions; defining I does not depend on identifying Not-I. If a series 6 Cylon meets another series 6 Cylon, are they an "I," a "we," or two "she"? The challenges to us/them divisions presented in these texts helps us envision what Young (2011) theorized: how we might find the other in the self and forge feminist connections grounded in facing similar problems rather than in similar essences.

The final binary we have discussed, human/machine, shifts in both *Caprica* and *Deus Ex*. Multiple people choose to become cyborgs, modified mechanically, or revel in their connection to the cognisphere. In the *Deus Ex* games, human and machine mingle so frequently that cyborgian identity has become ordinary. The games demonstrate that balance is necessary when hybridizing humans and machines, however. Yun Ru tries to become too much machine and the player is reminded that to aspire to become post-human is dangerous. Humanity has an important role to play in posthumanity, even if that role is not the lead. In *Caprica*, Zoe combines human, code, cognisphere, and machine. The flexibility she demonstrates in moving from flesh to computer to robot multiplies the options for subjectivities grounded in the human, machine, or HumanMachine.

This, too, has important gendered implications. Unlike the cases in the previous chapter, where a union with the machine is forced upon the women, the women in these two texts choose actively to become transhuman. As a result, they embrace the machine, and the promise of the cyborg and the cognisphere for feminist action. Their stories focus on striking an appropriate balance, rather than trying to recuperate humanity or falling victim to the machine. They expand gendered possibilities for women beyond victimage or apocalyptic motherhood. They do not resolve the relationship between human and machine in posthumanity, but they do not turn to outdated concepts like the nuclear family or tame the women through motherhood, like *Kill Bill* (see Chapter 1), the *Hunger Games* (see Chapter 2), *Proud Mary* (see Chapter 4), or *Bionic Woman* (see Chapter 5), either.

From these cases, we begin to see the importance of balance: siding not with mind or body, us or them, human or machine, but instead eliminating the false dichotomies. If we no longer center a unified self, would us/them matter as intensely? Does individual motive play as large a role when we begin to see the other within the self or collective? Are we most free as an embodied human subject, an AI navigating the cognisphere, or merged with a machine? What can we learn from these new possibilities to advance feminist politics? How can we confront postfeminist media representations of strong women? By unmaking, or at least challenging, these long-standing binaries, posthuman tales like these have the potential to equip us to move beyond the gendered discourses of Enlightenment thought to identify new ways for feminists to connect to one another and to resist the depoliticization that typifies postfeminist media.

Notes

1. The Ghost in the Machine, theorized by Ryle (1949), refers to Descartes's cogito. It indicates a consciousness distinct from the body it inhabits, and it has been used in tales ranging from manga to book chapters to an album by The Police.

2. Roxann Dawson directed one, and Kath Lingenfelter and Jane Espenson each wrote an episode.

3. Some of the key work in this conversation includes Apperley and Clemens (2017), Chess (2010, 2011, 2012, 2014, 2015, 2017), Chess and Maddox (2018), Cote (2016, 2017), Cunningham (2018), Evans and Janish (2015), Gray, Voorhees, and Vossen (2018), Lavigne (2015), Leonard (2006), Martey, Stromer-Galley, Banks, Wu, and Consalvo (2014), Murray (2017), Royse, Lee, Undrahbuyan, Hopson, and Consalvo (2007), Ruberg (2018), Shaw (2009, 2012a, 2012b, 2015a), Vossen (2018), Williams, Consalvo, Caplan, and Yee (2009), and Williams, Martins, Consalvo, and Ivory (2009). Feminist gaming scholars including Dietrich (2013), Gray (2012, 2014), Gray and Leonard (2018), Higgin (2009), Monson (2012), and Nakamura (2009) focus specifically on gaming and race. Others investigate gaming and sexuality, including Consalvo (2003), Nakamura (2012), and Shaw (2009, 2012a, 2015a, 2015b).

4. For example, for the 2000 *Deus Ex*: 8.2/10 *GameSpot* (Kasavin, 2000), 10/10 in *Eurogamer* (Fahey, 2000), 9.4/10 *IGN* (Blevins, 2000), and aggregate ratings from Metacritic (2018b): 90/100 across 28 critics and 9.2/10 across 1165 users. For the 2016 *Mankind Divided*: 8/10 *GameSpot* (Tran, 2016), 9.2/10 *IGN* (Ingenito, 2015), and aggregate ratings from Metacritic (2018c): 84/100 across 59 reviews and 7.6/10 across 743 user ratings.

5. Vinge (1993) coined "technological singularity" to describe the point at which superhuman artificial intelligence would lead to vastly accelerated technological innovation and growth, well beyond the capacity of humanity to create or to imagine. Popularized by Kurzweil (2005), the Singularity turns up in numerous discussions in transhuman and posthuman scholarship.

6. Engels (2010) provides an excellent overview of the concept of enemyship.

References

Apperley, T. H., & Clemens, J. (2017). Flipping out: Avatars and identity. In J. Gackenbach & J. Bown (Eds.), *Boundaries of self and reality online: Implications of digitally constructed realities* (pp. 41–56). Cambridge, MA: Elsevier.

Aubuchon, R., & Moore, R. D. (David Eick Productions and Universal Media Studios). (2009–2010). *Caprica* [Television series]. Los Angeles, CA: Universal Pictures Home Entertainment.

Behrenshausen, B. G. (2007). Toward a (kin)aesthetic of video gaming: The case of *Dance dance revolution. Games and Culture, 2,* 335–354.

Black, D. (2017). Why can I see my avatar? Embodied visual engagement in the third-person video game. *Games and Culture, 12*(2), 179–199.

Blevins, T. (2000, June 27). *Deus Ex.* What do you get when you mix *X-Files* with *Thief* and *The Matrix*? Futuristic finery, that's what. Retrieved from https://www.ign.com/articles/2000/06/28/deus-ex-3

Bogost, I. (2007). *Persuasive games: The expressive power of videogames.* Cambridge, MA: MIT University Press.

Bogost, I. (2008). *Unit operations: An approach to videogame criticism.* Cambridge, MA: MIT University Press.

Bostrom, N. (2005). A history of transhumanist thought. *Journal of Evolution and Technology 14*(1), 1–25.

Boyer, B., & Cifaldi, F. (2006, November 3). The *Gamasutra* quantum leap awards: Storytelling, #1. *Gamasutra.* Retrieved from http://www.gamasutra.com/view/feature/130205/the_gamasutra_quantum_leap_awards_.php?page=9

Chess, S. (2010). How to play a feminist. *thirdspace: A Journal of Feminist Theory & Culture, 9*(1), http://journals.sfu.ca/thirdspace/index.php/journal/article/view/273/273

Chess, S. (2011). A 36–24–36 cerebrum: Productivity, gender, and video game advertising. *Critical Studies in Media Communication, 28*(3), 230–252.

Chess, S. (2012). Going with the Flo: *Diner Dash* and feminism. *Feminist Media Studies, 12*(1), 83–99.

Chess, S. (2014). Strange bedfellows: Subjectivity, romance, and hidden object video games. *Games and Culture, 9*(6), 417–428.

Chess, S. (2015). Uncanny gaming: The *Ravenhearst* video games and gothic appropriation. *Feminist Media Studies, 15*(3), 382–396.

Chess, S. (2017). *Ready player two: Women gamers and designed identity.* Minneapolis: University of Minnesota Press.

Chess, S. (2018). A time for play: Interstitial time, invest/express games, and feminine leisure style. *New Media & Society, 20*(1), 105–121.

Chess, S., & Maddox, J. (2018). Kim Kardashian is my new BFF: Video games and the looking glass celebrity. *Popular Communication, 16*(3), 196–210.

Consalvo, M. (2003). Hot dates and fairy-tale romances: Studying sexuality in video games. In M. J. P. Wolf & B. Perron (Eds.), *The video game theory reader* (pp. 193–216). New York, NY: Routledge.

Consalvo, M. (2013). Women, sports, and videogames. In *Sports videogames* (pp. 95–120). New York, NY: Routledge.

Cote, A. C. (2016). *Changing the core: Redefining gaming culture from a female-centered perspective* (Doctoral dissertation). Retrieved from ProQuest Dissertations & Theses. (Order No. 10391553)

Cote, A. C. (2017). 'I can defend myself': Women's strategies for coping with harassment while gaming online. *Games and Culture, 12*(2), 136–155.

Cunningham, C. M. (2018). *Games girls play: Contexts of girls and video games.* Lanham, MD: Lexington Books.

Dietrich, D. R. (2013). Avatars of whiteness: Racial expression in video game characters. *Sociological Inquiry, 83*(1), 82–105.

Dvorsky, G. (2008). Better living through transhumanism. *Journal of Evolution & Technology 19*(1), 62–66.

Eidos Interactive. (2011). *Deus Ex: Human Revolution* [Video game]. Montréal, Canada: Square Enix.

Eidos Interactive. (2016). *Deus Ex Go* [Video game]. Montréal, Canada: Square Enix.

Eidos Interactive. (2016). *Deus Ex: Mankind Divided* [Video game]. Montréal, Canada: Square Enix.

Engels, J. (2010). *Enemyship: Democracy and counter-revolution in the early republic.* East Lansing: Michigan State University Press.

Evans, S. B., & Janish, E. (2015). #INeedDiverseGames: How the queer backlash to Gamergate enables nonbinary coalition. *QED: A Journal in GLBTQ Worldmaking, 2*(2), 125–150.

Fahey, R. (2000, August 1). *Deus Ex*: First person RPG reviewed. *Eurogamer.* Retrieved from https://www.eurogamer.net/articles/r_deusex

Frasca, G. (2003). Simulation vs. narrative: Introduction to ludology. In B. Perron & M. J. P. Wolf (Eds.), *The video game theory reader* (pp. 221–236). New York, NY: Routledge.

Fukuyama, F. (2002). *Our posthuman future: Consequences of the biotechnology revolution.* London, United Kingdom: Profile.

Gamasutra design staff. (2009, December 30). Gamasutra's top 12 games of the decade. *Gamasutra,* Retrieved from http://www.gamasutra.com/view/feature/4227/gamasutras_top_12_games_of_the_.php?page=7

Gray, K. L. (2012). Intersecting oppressions and online communities: Examining the experiences of women of color in Xbox Live. *Information, Communication & Society, 15*(3), 411–428.

Gray, K. L. (2014). *Race, gender, and deviance in Xbox live: Theoretical perspectives from the virtual margins.* New York, NY: Routledge.

Gray, K., & Leonard, D. (2018). *Woke gaming: Digital challenges to oppression and social injustice.* Seattle: University of Washington Press.

Gray, K. L., Voorhees, G., & Vossen, E. (Eds.). (2018). Introduction: Reframing hegemonic conceptions of women and feminism in gaming culture. In *Feminism in play* (pp. 1–17). New York, NY: Palgrave Macmillan.

Higgin, T. (2009). Blackless fantasy: The disappearance of race in massively multiplayer online role-playing games. *Games and Culture, 4*(1), 3–26.

IMDB. (2018). *Caprica*: User ratings. IMDB.com, Inc. Retrieved from https://www.imdb.com/title/tt0799862/ratings?ref_=ttexrv_sa_4

Ingenito, V. (2015, October 8). The smart evolution of *Deus Ex: Mankind Divided*. *IGN*. Retrieved from https://www.ign.com/articles/2015/10/08/the-smart-evolution-of-deus-ex-mankind-divided

Ion Storm. (2000). *Deus Ex* [Video game]. London, United Kingdom: Eidos Interactive.

Ion Storm. (2003). *Deus Ex: Invisible War* [Video game]. London, United Kingdom: Eidos Interactive.

Kasavin, G. (2000, June 27). *Deus Ex* review. *GameSpot*. Retrieved from https://www.gamespot.com/reviews/deus-ex-review/1900-2595408/

Kochiyama, Y., & Aguilar-San Juan, K. (1997). *Dragon ladies: Asian American feminists breathe fire*. Boston, MA: South End Press.

Kurzweil, R. (2005). *The singularity is near: When humans transcend biology*. New York, NY: Penguin.

Lavigne, C. (2015). 'She's a soldier, not a model': Feminism, FemShep and the *Mass Effect 3* vote. *Journal of Gaming & Virtual Worlds, 7*(3), 317–329.

Leonard, D. J. (2006). Not a hater, just keepin' it real: The importance of race- and gender-based game studies. *Games and Culture, 1*(1), 83–88.

Martey, R. M., Stromer-Galley, J., Banks, J., Wu, J., & Consalvo, M. (2014). The strategic female: Gender-switching and player behavior in online games. *Information, Communication & Society, 17*(3), 286–300.

Metacritic. (2018a). *Caprica*: Season 1. CBS Interactive, Inc. Retrieved from https://www.metacritic.com/tv/caprica

Metacritic. (2018b). *Deus Ex*. CBS Interactive, Inc. Retrieved from https://www.metacritic.com/game/pc/deus-ex

Metacritic. (2018c). *Deus Ex: Mankind Divided*. CBS Interactive, Inc. Retrieved from https://www.metacritic.com/game/playstation-4/deus-ex-mankind-divided

Monson, M. J. (2012). Race-based fantasy realm: Essentialism in the *World of Warcraft*. *Games and Culture, 7*(1), 48–71.

Murray, S. (2017). *On video games: The visual politics of race, gender and space*. London, United Kingdom: IB Tauris.

Nakamura, L. (2009). Don't hate the player, hate the game: The racialization of labor in *World of Warcraft*. *Critical Studies in Media Communication, 26*(2), 128–144.

Nakamura, L. (2012). Queer female of color: The highest difficulty setting there is? Gaming rhetoric as gender capital. *Ada: A Journal of Gender, New Media, and Technology, 1*, https://adanewmedia.org/2012/11/issue1-nakamura/

Newsom, V. A. (2004). Young females as super heroes: Super heroines in the animated *Sailor Moon*. *FEMSPEC, 5*(2), 57–81.

N-Fusion Interactive. (J. Parisi & C. Hong). (2013). *Deus ex: The fall* [Video game]. Shinjuku, Tokyo, Japan: Square Enix.

Omi, M., & Winant, H. (2007). Racial formations. In P. S. Rothenberg (Ed.), *Race, class, and gender in the United States* (pp. 13–22). New York, NY: Worth Publishers.

Raessens, J. (2006). Playful identities, or the ludification of culture. *Games and Culture*, *1*(1), 52–57.

Royse, P., Lee, J., Undrahbuyan, B., Hopson, M., & Consalvo, M. (2007). Women and games: Technologies of the gendered self. *New Media & Society*, 9(4), 555–576.

Ruberg, B. (2018). Representing sex workers in video games: Feminisms, fantasies of exceptionalism, and the value of erotic labor. *Feminist Media Studies*, doi:10.1080/14680777.2018.1477815

Ryle, G. (1949/2002). *The concept of mind*. Chicago: University of Chicago Press.

Salen, K., & Zimmerman, E. (2004). *Rules of play: Game design fundamentals*. Cambridge, MA: The MIT Press.

Shaw, A. (2009). Putting the gay in games: Cultural production and GLBT content in video games. *Games and Culture*, 4(3), 228–253.

Shaw, A. (2012a). Do you identify as a gamer? Gender, race, sexuality, and gamer identity. *New Media & Society*, 14(1), 28–44.

Shaw, A. (2012b). Talking to gaymers: Questioning identity, community and media representation. *Westminster Papers in Communication & Culture*, 9(1), 67–89.

Shaw, A. (2015a). Circles, charmed and magic: Queering game studies. *QED: A Journal in GLBTQ Worldmaking*, 2(2), 64–97.

Shaw, A. (2015b). *Gaming at the edge: Sexuality and gender at the margins of gamer culture*. Minneapolis: University of Minnesota Press.

Sicart, M. (2011). Against procedurality. *Game Studies 11*(3). Retrieved from http://gamestudies.org/1103/articles/sicart_ap

Taylor, T. L. (2003). Multiple pleasures: Women and online gaming. *Convergence*, 9(1), 21–46.

Taylor, T. L. (2009). The assemblage of play. *Games and Culture*, 4(4), 331–339.

Tran, E. (2016, August 19). Give me *Deus Ex*. GameSpot. Retrieved from https://www.gamespot.com/reviews/deus-ex-mankind-divided-review/1900-6416497/

Vinge, V. (1993). The coming technological singularity: How to survive in the post-human era. In G. A. Landis (Ed.), *Vision-21: Interdisciplinary science and engineering in the era of cyberspace* (pp. 11–22). NASA Publication CP-10129. Retrieved from https://ntrs.nasa.gov/archive/nasa/casi.ntrs.nasa.gov/19940022856.pdf

Vossen, E. (2018). *On the cultural inaccessibility of gaming: Invading, creating, and reclaiming the cultural clubhouse* (Doctoral dissertation, University of Waterloo). Retrieved from https://uwspace.uwaterloo.ca/bitstream/handle/10012/13649/Vossen_Emma.pdf

Williams, D., Consalvo, M., Caplan, S., & Yee, N. (2009). Looking for gender: Gender roles and behaviors among online gamers. *Journal of Communication*, 59(4), 700–725.

Williams, D., Martins, N., Consalvo, M., & Ivory, J. D. (2009). The virtual census: Representations of gender, race and age in video games. *New Media & Society*, 11(5), 815–834.

Yee, N. (2006). The labor of fun: How video games blur the boundaries of work and play. *Games and Culture*, 1(1), 68–71.

Young, I. M. (2011). *Justice and the politics of difference*. Princeton, NJ: Princeton University Press.

CONCLUSION:
ENVISIONING FEMINIST FUTURES

Media have material consequences, shaping our views of present realities and future possibilities. We began our inquiry with attention to gendered differences in access to power, noting that as U.S. women have made strides forward (e.g., the Equal Pay Act, Title VII, increased occupational power), postfeminist politics, backlash, and representations prevail. As feminist rhetoricians and critical media scholars, we have approached postfeminist representations of women's strength as pleasurable and powerful—but also concerning in their rhetorical consequences. As spaces where meaning is negotiated, media serve as "intensely political" sites of struggle where "patriarchal power may be both consolidated in its production and also rejected through feminism[s]" (Savigny & Warner, 2015, p. 2). The mediated texts examined in this book offer insights into social paradoxes including varied configurations of gendered ideals, roles, and relations.

In particular, we have explored how one specific type of woman, the strong female-bodied action hero, has been represented in film, television, and video games after the turn of the century. Dockterman (2019) identifies themes in female-bodied action heroes from the 1970s to the 2010s: The Icons (1970s), The Badasses (1980s), The Muses (1990s), The Avengers (2000s), The Team Players (2010s), and The Idols (summer 2018). Female-bodied action heroes began to frequent the film genre in the 1970s with icons such as Foxy Brown (1974), Ripley in *Aliens* (1979), and Princess Leia in *Star Wars* (1977) offering new models of women's power. In the 1980s, these heroes became even more badass, with tough women like Sarah Connor in *Terminator 2* (1991) typifying the female-bodied action hero in a decade brimming with action films. The 1990s' characters rocketed male directors (e.g., Luc Besson, Joss Whedon, Ridley Scott) to fame, and range from G.I. Jane (1992) to Buffy, the Vampire Slayer (1992). In the 2000s, when the characters discussed in this book first appear, fierce female-bodied action heroes continued to couple strength with sexuality. These "Avengers" included lead characters in adaptation films such as *Aeon Flux* (2005), *Catwoman* (2004), *Elektra* (2005); a number of roles played by Angelina Jolie in films like *Lara Croft* (2001), *Mr. and Mrs. Smith* (2005), *Wanted* (2008), and *Salt* (2010); and *Kill Bill* (2003, 2004, see Chapter 1). In the 2010s, more women working in teams appeared, such as those featured in larger ensembles including the Marvel and DC adaptations, young adult adaptations like *Divergent* (2014) and *The Hunger Games* (see Chapter 2), and a few headliners like *Mad Max: Fury Road* (2015) and *Rogue One: A Star Wars Story* (2016). She concludes her survey of strong female-bodied figures with films including *Wonder Woman* (see Chapter 3), stating, "Finally, we're getting different types of female heroes" (para. 16). Although we share some of her enthusiasm, we would like to see a media landscape in which diverse dangerous dames become the rule rather than the exception.

We posed a series of questions when we started our journey with the fierce female-bodied characters examined in this book, asking: What possibilities and constraints emerge from portrayals of dangerous dames with greater access to power? Do representations of women exhibiting kick-ass abilities provide new or unique equipment for living and feminist ways of being? And how do these mediated representations complicate or contradict meaningful feminist action? Across the chapters, we engaged a range of theories, including biopower, necropolitics, critical race theory and whiteness studies, gender performativity, and posthumanism, to help inform our readings as we sought to answer these questions.

We found that our specific strong action heroes, our dangerous dames, prove dangerous in multiple ways. First, they present a literal danger. These women wield weapons, and they frequently harm or kill others. Many suffer at the hands of others, as well, but domination features strongly in their characterization. They endanger others; they are dangerous. Simultaneously, they threaten to unsettle patriarchy. Their embodied strengths, and the progressive strides they make, provide new portrayals and new possibilities. They achieve success, demonstrate a range of capabilities, and brandish their access to power in ways that change the worlds around them. However, they also imperil feminisms. Although all function as positive role models at times, more frequently they reinforce troubling stories and structures. Some serve as inspiration more consistently than others; some never rise above a superficial presentation of "strong woman." They perpetuate the idea that, with the right training, women can be every bit as strong and kick-ass as men. In doing so, they portray gendered power as a matter of individual choice, in which women who "choose" to empower themselves through their attitudes and athleticism easily overcome all odds. Akin to Owen, Stein, and Vande Berg (2007), we find that these portrayals ignore structural constraints, including persistent patriarchal narratives, structural inequities, and intersecting oppressions that women face. This neoliberal representation of strong women hyperindividualizes, divides, and contains feminisms. These dangerous dames have the potential to expand gendered possibilities and offer audiences new equipment for living; however, they also reveal how the commodification of women's empowerment for popular audiences constrains these possibilities.

Overlapping Themes: Possibilities and Constraints

In reflecting upon our analyses, we find four overlapping themes in the representations of these dangerous dames. Like contemporary feminisms, they encompass contradictions, tensions, and differences, thus we recognize both the possibilities and constraints these characters offer audiences. Specifically, we determine that the fierce women examined in these texts simultaneously support and reject traditional gender scripts, enact sexual agency and are objectified sexually, display a broader but still limited range of racial diversity, and are embodied as both hero and victim. These disparities complicate the characters, demonstrate more dimension and depth, and allow for an increased range of audience interpretations (Hundley & Hayden, 2016). Nevertheless, because gendered representations function as political and ideological artifacts (Heywood & Drake, 1997; Owen, Stein, & Vande Berg, 2007), we identify continued regulation and disciplining of women's bodies (Bordo, 2004; Foucault, 1972; Grosz, 1995). Powerful women portrayed in postfeminist media serve as discursive formations training audiences to adhere to certain rules and roles, even as they bend and break others.

Gendered Scripts

Gendered scripts are both fortified and rebuked by these dangerous dames. Traditional and limited gender norms appear in the texts' presentations of heteronormativity, biological determinism, and gendered stereotypes. For example, the majority of the powerful women we studied are heterosexual, although a couple engage in same-sex relationships or have fluid sexualities. Likewise, half of these characters are driven by and rewarded for acting as, or aspiring to become, mothers and wives. That is, they fight to protect children (Brunsdon, 2013; Tasker, 1998), and they are compensated with children and/ or men (Dow, 2006).[1] This purports both heteronormativity and biological determinism.

Similarly, gendered stereotypes are both reinforced and challenged. Some of these women resist stereotypically feminine garb, whereas others embrace it. In certain cases, viewers witness the extensive work required to conform to these standardized notions of beauty. This is particularly obvious in *The Hunger Games* (see Chapter 2) and for the femmes fatales in *Atomic Blonde* and *Proud Mary* (see Chapter 4), where highlighting gender performance illuminates its artificiality and may even serve to parody such labor.[2] In this process, femininities and feminine performances are reconfigured as they are dislodged from essentialist portrayals.

At times, dangerous dames also challenge hegemonic masculinity, creating new embodied subjectivities and new forms of empowerment. A few characters occupy positions of power, which they use to help others (e.g., Mary in Chapter 4 and Two in Chapter 5) as well as to harm others (e.g., Beatrix in Chapter 1 and Yun Ru in Chapter 6). Even if they do not occupy positions of power, most of these women stand up for themselves and others, verbally or physically resist patriarchal authority, and address sexist or racist insults. At other times, gender stereotypes are exacerbated by characters upholding hegemonic masculinity or by acquiescing to men's directions, orders, and decisions. Hypermasculinity is confirmed when women mirror men's fighting styles, including their use of weaponry. Gilpatric (2010) finds that a gun is the number one weapon of choice (primarily among men), the second is the body (e.g., punching, kicking), and the third is blades. Our fierce female-bodied fighters demonstrate similar proclivities, again with a couple of exceptions (e.g., Katniss in Chapter 2, Zoe in Chapter 6, and Yun Ru in Chapter 6). Moreover, although most of the women are professionally successful, they enact plans or orders developed and dictated by men.

Our texts also illuminate challenges to false dichotomies, including mind/body, us/them, human/machine, and civilization/nature. For example, in several cases masculinity is aligned with mind and femininity with the body; in other cases, viewers can see a more flexible relationship in which women can be strong of mind and body in ways that dispel traditional gender stereotypes. These artifacts frequently reify the relation of femininity with nature, as Mother Nature or through a connection with animals, and masculinity with culture through civilization or technology. However, some of the artifacts we examined implode, blur, or transcend these dualisms and their false associations with gender.

Finally, most of these fierce female-bodied women fight as lone warriors, rather than as part of a team of compatriots. Although a few are afforded the opportunity to work with other powerful girls and women (e.g., Beatrix Kiddo and members of the DVAS in Chapter 1; Zoe and Lacy in Chapter 6; Two, Five, Nyx, and Android in Chapter 5), they more often than not literally kill each other. This invokes the petty, jealous, and catty "mean girl" stereotype (Behm-Morawitz & Mastro, 2008), and suggests that women are incapable of caring for one another. Consequently, rather than forming alliances, they remain divided, leaving men as their sole source of support. The more encouraging examples we analyzed show women joining forces with their opponents and undermining enemyship relations, which encourages viewers to contemplate the utility of unity and alliance.

Sexuality

Paradoxically, these powerful women simultaneously demonstrate sexual agency and are objectified sexually. Akin to Cocca (2016), we find that strong women are frequently sexualized and pose-oriented. She claims that these portrayals have decreased since 2000, yet our cases, particularly the femmes fatales, reiterate these objectifications and reassert the male gaze. The sexualization of women's strong bodies can fetishize our protagonists' dangerous abilities: "Almost all [femmes fatales] are the creation of imaginative male minds who believe their own sexual urges can't be controlled and, if things get out of hand, it's gotta [sic] be someone else's fault" (Guerrilla Girls, 2003, p. 20). Indeed, the gaze is alive and well in postfeminist media, continuing to position women's bodies as sexual objects and even sexualizing women's "sexual agency" (Gill, 2008, p. 35).[3]

These images reinforce the neoliberal rhetoric of "choice," including the "choice" to adhere to normative beauty standards and to deploy one's sexuality to increase access to power. Thornham (2007) notes that "the post-feminist heroine of the new women's genres … offers a new point of identification: a post-conventional subject position, characterized by freedom and choice" (p. 17). Portraying such choice as empowering obscures the historical and political consequences connected with the "body project" evident in consumer culture (Jacobs Brumberg, 1997; Owen, Stein, & Vande Berg, 2007). It also blithely disregards structural forms of oppression and presents politics as a form of personal accessory rather than a driving force for social justice and equality for persons of all sexes, genders, and sexualities.

The Multicultural, Depolitical Rainbow

Although Benshoff and Griffin (2009) hail the increasing racial diversity in film, we find that whiteness persists in the imagining of dangerous dames. The lead protagonist, in particular, is almost always white. This limited range or lack of racial and ethnic diversity perpetuates Eurocentrism and liberal and imperial feminist exclusions, in which gendered oppression is treated as primary or universal. Furthermore, considering the preponderance of white actors in our science fiction texts, we find that postfeminist media envisions a disappointingly white future. These dangerous dames hence do little to fight racist oppression or expand representation for women of color.

When characters of color do appear, they frequently serve as tokens or suggest a postracial multiculturalism, divorced from politics or from communities and cultures. By doing so, these texts depoliticize the quest for racial and ethnic diversity. We are encouraged that a couple of the characters we analyzed directly call out racism, which serves as anti-racist resistance. Nevertheless, such attempts fall significantly short of what society needs in order to address overlapping systems of power, persistent stereotypes, and lived inequities.

Embodiment

Contradictions appear in the representations of powerful women's embodiments, as well. The powerful women we studied operate as both heroes and victims; they are both penetrating and penetrated. Their bodies constrain them, and viewers watch many of these powerful women get raped, stabbed, beaten, shot, hacked, modified, burned, and killed. Thus, their bodies serve as Achilles heels, exposing them to threat at every turn. To thwart this weakness, they turn to a variety of weapons to extend and protect their bodies and bodily capacities. These include bracelets, high heels, magic lassos, knives, katana, bows, guns, and advanced technology. These augmentations fortify their female bodies with armor and assist them in achieving their quests. Like Superman's kryptonite, these heroes have weaknesses, too. We remain wary of the exploitation and eroticization of their bodies, which is not seen with most male action heroes.

The four overlapping themes reinforce, fracture, and/or transcend patriarchal ideologies. The portrayals of gender scripts, sexuality, race, and embodiment illustrate both feminist resistance and patriarchal compliance. Although we laud the feminist resistance, most of the texts demonstrate an appropriation of feminist ideals to discipline women and girls. Because "postfeminism is little more than a market-led phenomenon" (Gamble, 2000, p. 51), and because "the most powerful entities on earth are not governments, but the multi-national corporations that see women as their territory" (Greer, 1999, p. 336), the paradox comes as no surprise.

Resisting the Commodification of Feminisms

Capitalist logic governs media industries just like any other industry in late capitalism. Media conglomerates create films, television series, and video games, among other items, to make money. The control these massive companies can exert over representations, marketing, distribution, and circulation cannot be discounted; the success or failure of a given artifact depends as much on the production and ownership as its content. The vast majority of media mega-corporations are owned, directed, and operated primarily by men.

Indeed, feminists interested in media seek to place a broader spectrum of people in production, creation, and direction positions, in addition to diversifying representation in front of the camera, which has led to close scrutiny of media ownership and control, analysis of representation both on and off camera, and calls for inclusion riders (Belam & Levin, 2018). However, even placing women into positions of power within the industry may not suffice. Media created and controlled by women do not necessarily align with feminist progress. Many women in positions of power, like Marissa Mayer,[4] strike patriarchal bargains and lean in to the company, to the paycheck, to tokenism, and to perpetuating harmful myths and practices.

Media industries have taken note of the opportunity to increase their profits by adding new tales, drawn from feminist action in the public sphere, to their collection. Driven by a need to produce a return on their investments, these organizations have begun to feature, albeit slowly, more feminist representations. However, by appropriating and selling feminisms, they colonize and commodify feminist characters, agencies, and audiences for their own purposes: namely, profit. Although increased representation of an array of people should be welcomed and celebrated, we remain dubious about the potential for liberation, given the capitalist entanglements of these corporations and the lack of representation on the business side of media.

Despite these reservations, we have hope. We hope for a world in which feminists occupy positions of power in media production, without the pressure to strike a deal with patriarchy or to diminish other people along the way. We imagine these feminists issuing race-blind casting calls, diminishing discrimination in placing particular bodies in front of cameras by insisting on greater representation of size and ability, and awarding funding for blockbusters to people who have not had these opportunities afforded to them in the past. We aspire for all of these feminists, both behind the scenes and on screens, to be paid as much as their male counterparts and to be able to go to work without the threat of sexual harassment. We must remain vigilant, and we must continue to adapt feminisms in response to the ways they are co-opted and commodified by media. To this end, we wonder, how can we continue to conceptualize "women's power" in ways that are actually empowering?

Redefining and Rethinking "Women's Power"

Our hope is fueled by the presence of everyday heroes, including those in the classroom, courtroom, and Congressional offices. Courageous women in politics, from Anita Hill to Condoleezza Rice to Ruth Bader Ginsburg, have shattered glass ceilings and patriarchal norms, risking themselves and their reputations to advance social justice and women's rights. The 2018 midterm elections broke numerous records. Notably, 84 % of the women elected were women of color (Thompson, 2018). Making history, Ilhan Omar and Rashida Tlaib became the first Muslim women to join Congress, and Deb Haaland (Laguna Pueblo) and Sharice Davids (Ho-Chunk) became the first Native

American women to do so. The first openly bisexual senator, Kristen Sinema, was also the first woman elected to represent Arizona. Alexandria Ocasio-Cortez, a 29-year-old activist and democratic socialist, became the youngest woman ever elected to Congress. Women like these are heroes indeed.

We are inspired by women's digital and material activism. Young women played key roles in the 2011 anti-regime uprisings deemed the "Arab Spring," through both online networking and taking to the streets (see Johannson-Nogués, 2013; Newsom & Lengel, 2012). The #MeToo Movement, Take Back the Night marches, SlutWalks, and a range of other transnational movements continue to fight against gendered and sexual violence. The #BlackLivesMatter movement, launched in 2013 by radical black organizers Alicia Garza, Patrisse Cullors, and Opal Tometi, serves as an important "ideological and political intervention in a world where Black lives are systematically and intentionally targeted for demise" ("Herstory," 2018, para. 3). In 2016, the Standing Rock "Water Protectors" brought together over 300 members of federally recognized Native American tribes, along with over 3000 supporters, to resist the building of the Dakota Access Pipeline on the sacred lands of the Sioux. Protestors camped along the building site for six months, and although President Trump pushed the pipeline forward, the protests successfully garnered media attention, inspired grassroots movements, and facilitated solidarity among Indigenous tribes.[5] These acts and the people who enact them are certainly heroic, performing feminism in our everyday lives and serving as role models for people globally.

We find hope in mediated representations, as well. Despite our serious reservations about the dangerous dames we have examined, we have encountered places of potential and possibility in these representations. These heroes endanger gendered systems by demonstrating that femininity is not fixed and by destabilizing Enlightenment ontologies. Shifting representations of femininity and the media co-option of feminisms can repeat and naturalize patriarchal narratives and structures, but they can also alter them as they construct sources of power within systems of subordination. In this manner, even postfeminist representations, all too frequently apolitical, individualized, and sexualized, can proffer feminist subjectivities, embodiments, and spaces of political intervention. Knowing they are contained and controlled by patriarchal agents, we urge audiences to be wary of fully embracing the characters as liberated and liberatory heroes and role models. Instead, we urge them to remain mindful of the characters' postfeminist contexts and entanglements and to read with a critical eye.

Although this book has distinguished between feminism and postfeminisms—and we believe such a distinction remains conceptually useful and materially important—we must continue to extend our frameworks for thinking through relationships between women, gender, and empowerment. Much as "woman" needs to be unfixed as a universalizing category because gendered and sexed identities intersect with other social locations, including class, race, nation, sexuality, citizenship status, size, and ability, so too does "women's power" need to continue to be shaken loose from monolithic conceptions. The third wave's emphasis on choice, personal presentation and performance, and the individual ignores larger structural issues and discourages alliance and unity. Similarly, lingering elements of second wave feminisms continue to shape feminist theorizing, thinking, and teaching in ways that sometimes elide the nuances of both contemporary media environments and young women's lives. Among these outdated elements is a stance that suggests women's agency and their sexualization are always mutually exclusive. From this perspective, the woman who uses her sexuality to gain access to power is simply a dupe, a pawn in a deceptive system.

For example, in a recent meeting one of us attended, a colleague expressed disappointment that students consider a public figure like Beyoncé to be feminist. Although hooks (2016) agrees, and her critiques raise important points regarding the hypersexualization and commodification of black female bodies (also see Weidhase, 2015), one student, a woman of color, noted that she found the entire question of whether or not Beyoncé was a feminist to be asinine and anti-feminist. Beyoncé has achieved a level of celebrity and professional achievement few performers ever reach; she has frequently toured with a band comprised solely of women (a rarity in the pop music industry); she celebrates HBCUs and black culture; her songs address topics including women's independence, sexuality, health, and identity; she repeatedly has demonstrated solidarity with black activists; and "she has introduced feminism to new generations of young women" (Trier-Bieniek, 2016, p. 1). We find the question ridiculous, as well.

Why, then, this obsession with policing the boundaries of feminism and delineating who can or cannot be a feminist? Does a concern over feminism's "proper objects" (Butler, 1994) reinforce the constraints of second wave and liberal (white) feminisms and their elisions of difference? We believe it might. Feminisms, like femininity, are ongoing discursive constructions. Perhaps the question should not be which wave of feminism we are surfing or whether we are "post" feminism, but how to engage in scholarship, activism, and teaching that allows for complex understandings of diverse feminist frameworks and nuanced and changing fields of power and representation.

To the Future...and Beyond

Following in the steps of Owen et al. (2007), we have sought to explore the ambivalences of popular representations of women's power that "cannot be neatly categorized as either authentically 'feminist' or flippantly 'postfeminist'" (Carter, Steiner, & McLaughlin, 2014, p. 17). There are important differences between portraying women as one-dimensional (sexual) objects and multidimensional subjects, and we have addressed these differences throughout the book. However, we believe that our students can experience media portrayals of women differently than we do, and this does not mean they are not capable of critically understanding the reproduction of dominant ideologies. Actively listening to different students' takes on media texts requires following Carter et al.'s (2014) call to pay "careful attention to the speaking positions we adopt" and to be "aware of the forms of power we enjoy, with their specific claims to authority, and how others are disempowered" (p. 17; also see Lumby, 2014). It requires employing critical-rhetorical pedagogy (Ott & Burgchardt, 2013). As feminist media scholars, we have theories and tools to identify harmful representations, but we caution against becoming so attached to or limited by our theories that we miss how gender *is* reshaped in texts that contain both feminist and postfeminist impulses. By listening to our students and by attending to nuances in our objects of analysis, we can continue to advance theories and modes of critique that are capable of attending to our shifting media environments and changes in gendered configurations of, and access to, power.

For us, this book has not only been about media representations of dangerous dames: it is a book about social justice and about staying dangerous. Huffman (2014) argues that "conceptualizing social justice is considering what 'better' looks like" (p. 9). We envision a "better" range of stories. These stories involve women of color enmeshed in cultural communities, rather than plucked out, offered up as tokens, and depoliticized in a multicultural rainbow. These stories feature so many strong women, intersecting with so many other identities and ways of being, that modernist ways of thinking do not help audiences make sense of their tales. By engaging substantively with serious issues when they are raised, these stories hold the possibility for conducting, not just commodifying, feminist politics. These stories break free from aligning women with the body, creating spaces where "strong" can signify more than muscle or sex appeal and can account for strength of will, emotional maturity, and political efficacy.

Social justice can mean taking to the streets, but it can also mean helping students question dominant ideologies, develop media and information literacies, and engage critically with the messages they encounter. Our professors and mentors equipped us with tools that cracked open existing frames, enabling us to see in new ways. Offering students "courage, critical paradigms, generative vocabularies, contested theories, and impossible questions" enables them to transform their ways of thinking and being (Dempsey et al., 2011, p. 259). Critical frameworks prepare us, and our students, to intersect lived experiences, representations, and systems and structures of power. For this reason, "although a social justice approach is rooted in an understanding of how systems of oppression reproduce inequalities, and a rejection (hatred?) of those systems, it is an ultimately hopeful, and progressive vision" (p. 258). Thus, our vision for a "better" way is an optimistic one that we share with colleagues, students, and audiences.

We hope for a future where dangerous dames can break free from their current constraints, and where inspirational feminist role models continue to redefine and rethink what women's power looks like. We hope to see such role models placed in positions where they can affect media production and distribution. We hope for all types of stories, featuring and supporting feminist and progressive goals. Finally, we hope to motivate other feminists to join the cause, to fight as long and as hard as needed to see these hopes become realities.

Notes

1. In the case of Wonder Woman, she fights to protect women and children, simultaneously embodying the maternal logics of Republican Motherhood and the imperial logics of masculinist protection (see Chapter 3).

2. In her analysis of Lady Gaga's gender performance as a form of drag, Davisson (2013) points out that Gaga's hyperbolic gendered rituals are "exaggerated to the point where they appear awkward, perfunctory, and mechanized" (p. 64). In similar fashion, the femmes fatales figures we have analyzed as well as the hyperstylized performance of gender demonstrated by Effie Trinket and the residents of the Capitol in The Hunger Games can be seen to engage in forms of gender parody, in which "ritual behavior becomes so complete and

apparent that it turns 'an organic moment into something mechanical, and so reveals the mechanization underlying the original'" (p. 64; also see Hariman, 2008).

3. Gill (2008) describes how "sexual agency" becomes a form of regulation in media that mold feminine/ist subjectivities "to fit the current postfeminist, neoliberal moment in which young women should not only be beautiful but sexy, sexually knowledgeable/ practiced and always 'up for it'" (p. 35).

4. Mayer is former president and chief executive officer of Yahoo! and former executive and spokesperson for Google. As of 2019, she is co-founder of Lumi Labs, a Palo Alto, California technology company.

5. For more on Native American women's integral roles in the Standing Rock protests, see Latimer (2017) and Monet (2016).

References

Behm-Morawitz, E., & Mastro, D. E. (2008). Mean girls? The influence of gender portrayals in teen movie on emerging adults' gender-based attitudes and beliefs. *Journalism & Mass Communication Quarterly*, 85(1), 131–146. doi:10.1177.107769900808500109

Belam, M., & Levin, S. (2018, March 5). Woman behind 'inclusion rider' explains Frances McDormand's Oscar speech. *The Guardian*. Retrieved from https://www.theguardian.com/film/2018/mar/05/what-is-an-inclusion-rider-frances-mcdormand-oscars-2018

Benshoff, H. M., & Griffin, S. (2009). *America on film: Representing race, class, gender, and sexuality at the movies*. Malden, MA: Wiley-Blackwell.

Bordo, S. (2004). *Unbearable weight: Feminism, Western culture, and the body*. Berkeley: University of California Press.

Brunsdon, C. (2013). Television crime series, women police, and fuddy-duddy feminism. *Feminist Media Studies*, 13(3), 375–394.

Butler, J. (1994). Against proper objects. *differences: A Journal of Feminist Cultural Studies*, 6(2–3), 1–27.

Carter, C., Steiner, L., & McLaughlin, L. (Eds.). (2014). Introduction: Re-imagining media and gender. In *The Routledge Companion to Media and Gender* (pp. 1–20). New York, NY: Routledge.

Cocca, C. (2016). *Superwomen: Gender, power, and representation*. London, United Kingdom: Bloomsbury.

Davisson, A. L. (2013). *Lady Gaga and the remaking of celebrity culture*. Jefferson, NC: McFarland & Company.

Dempsey, S., Dutta, M., Frey, L. R., Goodall, H. L., Madison, D. S., Mercieca, J., Nakayama, T., & Miller, K. (2011). What is the role of the communication discipline in social justice, community engagement, and public scholarship? A visit to the CM *Café*. *Communication Monographs*, 78(2), 256–271. doi:10.1080/03637751.2011.565062

Dockterman, E. (2019). Evolution of the female action hero: From Ripley to Wonder Woman, these characters are fighting for the future. *Time*. Retrieved from http://time.com/female-action-heroes/

Dow, B. J. (2006). The traffic in men and the *Fatal Attraction* of postfeminist masculinity. *Women's Studies in Communication, 29*(1), 113–131. doi:10.1080/07491409.2006. 10757630

Foucault, M. (1972). *The archeology of knowledge.* New York, NY: Pantheon.

Gamble, S. (Ed.). (2000). *The Routledge critical dictionary of feminism and postfeminism.* New York, NY: Routledge.

Gill, R. (2008). Empowerment/sexism: Figuring female sexual agency in contemporary advertising. *Feminism & Psychology, 18*(1), 35–60. doi:10.1177/0959353507084950

Gilpatric, K. (2010). Violent female action characters in contemporary American cinema. *Sex Roles, 62,* 734–746. doi:10.1007/s11199-010-9757-7

Greer, G. (1999). *The whole woman.* London, United Kingdom: Doubleday.

Grosz, E. (1995). *Space, time and perversion: Essays on the politics of bodies.* New York, NY: Routledge.

Guerrilla Girls. (2003). *Bitches, bimbos and ballbreakers: The Guerrilla Girls' illustrated guide to female stereotypes.* New York, NY: Penguin Books.

Hariman, R. (2008). Political parody and public culture. *Quarterly Journal of Speech, 94*(3), 247–272. doi:10.1080/00335630802210369

Herstory, (2018). *Black lives matter.* Retrieved from https://blacklivesmatter.com/about/herstory/

Heywood, L., & Drake, J. (Eds.). (1997). *Third wave agenda: Being feminist, doing feminism.* Minneapolis: University of Minnesota Press.

hooks, b. (2016). Moving beyond pain. *bell hooks Institute.* Retrieved from http://www.bell hooksinstitute.com/blog/2016/5/9/moving-beyond-pain

Huffman, T. (2014). Imagining social justice within a communicative framework. *Journal of Social Justice, 4,* 1–14. Retrieved from http://transformativestudies.org/wp-content/uploads/Imagining-Social-Justice-within-a-Communicative-Framework.pdf

Hundley, H. L., & Hayden, S. E. (Eds.). (2016). *Mediated moms: Contemporary challenges to the motherhood myth.* New York, NY: Peter Lang.

Jacobs Brumberg, J. (1997). *The body project: An intimate history of American girls.* New York, NY: Random House.

Johannson-Nogués, E. (2013). Gendering the Arab Spring? Rights and (in)security of Tunisian, Egyptian and Libyan women. *Security Dialogue, 44*(5–6), 393–409. doi:10.1177/0967010613499784

Latimer, M. [Director] (2017). *RISE.* [Television Series]. New York, NY: Viceland.

Lumby, C. (2014). Post-postfeminism. In C. Carter, L. Steiner, & L. McLaughlin (Eds.), *The Routledge companion to media and gender* (pp. 600–609). New York, NY: Routledge.

Monet, J. (2016, December 13). The crucial roles women are playing at Standing Rock— In photos. *Refinery, 29.* Retrieved from https://www.refinery29.com/2016/12/132669/standing-rock-protest-womensphotos#slide-6

Newsom, V. A., & Lengel, L. (2012). Arab women, social media, and the Arab Spring: Applying the framework of digital reflexivity to analyze gender and online activism. *Journal of International Women's Studies, 13*(5), 31–45.

Ott, B. L., & Burgchardt, C. R. (2013). On critical-rhetorical pedagogy: Dialoging with *Schindler's List. Western Journal of Communication, 77*(1), 14–33.

Owen, A. S., Stein, S. R., & Vande Berg, L. R. (2007). *Bad girls: Cultural politics and media representations of transgressive women.* New York, NY: Peter Lang.

Savigny, H., & Warner, H. (2015). *The politics of being a woman: Feminism, media, and 21st century popular culture.* Basingstoke, United Kingdom: Palgrave MacMillan.

Tasker, Y. (1998). *Working girls: Gender and sexuality in popular cinema.* New York, NY: Routledge.

Thompson, D. (2018, November 7). 15 women of color who made history in the 2018 midterm elections. *Vibe.* Retrieved from https://www.vibe.com/2018/11/women-of-color-who-made-history-2018-midterm-elections-list

Thornham, S. (2007). *Women, feminism and media.* Edinburgh, United Kingdom: Edinburgh University Press.

Trier-Bieniek, A. (Ed.). (2016). Introduction. In *The Beyoncé effect: Essays on sexuality, race and feminism* (pp. 1–9). Jefferson, NC: McFarland & Company, Inc.

Weidhase, N. (2015). 'Beyoncé feminism' and the contestation of the black feminist body. *Celebrity Studies,* 6(1), 128–131. doi:10.1080/19392397.2015.1005389

INDEX

A

academia, women in 4
action heroes 5, 23, 36–37, 43, 46, 62, 78,
    94, 99–101, 153–154, 159
Adams, M. E. 75
Alias 33
Alien: Covenant 89
Alien series 25, 26, 33, 72, 154
*All the Women Are White, All the Blacks Are
    Men, But Some of Us Are Brave* 82
American Indian Movement 2
anti-blackness 102, 106
Aeon Flux 154
Arab Spring 161
Assassin's Creed 139
Atomic Blonde 27, 89, 90, 156
    dangerous dames in 91
    femme fatale in 93
    and framing women action heroes 96–97
    gender performativity in 92–94
    gender transgressions in 102–104
        sexual excess in 98–99
        violent femmes in 102–104
Aubuchon, R. 134
Avatar 43

B

Bad Girls 23, 24
Barthes, R. 7, 9, 10
Battlestar Galactica (BSG) 134–135, 137,
    138, 146
Baudrillard, J. 7, 31, 104
Benshoff, H. M. 158
binaries
    human/machine binary 17, 113, 119–
        120, 126–127, 138, 144–145, 147
    mind/body binary 17, 113, 114, 115,
        117, 122–126, 128, 141–143, 145, 157
    self/other binary 17, 136–138, 146
    us/them binary 17, 136–138, 143–144
biological determinism 16, 33, 49, 56,
    60–61, 62, 156

The Bionic Woman 112
  bionic speed 117
  feminine bionic bodies 117
  human/machine binary 119–120
  and intelligence 118–119
  mind/body binary 128, 142
  postfeminism in 128
  rebooted series 115–117
  and recuperation 118
  and senses 118
  and strength 117–118
biopower 53, 55, 60, 154
bisexual femme fatales 98
  See also femme fatales
bisexuality 11, 98, 161
#BlackLivesMatter movement 161
Black Panther 82, 89
black women 62, 82, 95, 99–102, 105, 125
blaxploitation films 29, 38, 94, 95, 96,
  100, 105
blonde bombshell characters 70,
  94–95, 105
  See also *Atomic Blonde*
Braidotti, R. 113, 114
Bridesmaids 43
Brown, J. A. 35, 38, 62
Brunsdon, C. 33
Burke, K. 15
Butler, J. 92

C

Cacho, L. M. 106
Calhoun, C. 99
Cameron, James 72, 73
capitalism, and media 4, 8, 9, 38, 39, 62,
  159, 160
Caprica 133
  and *Battlestar Galactica* (BSG) 134–135,
  137, 138, 146
  cognisphere 134, 135–136, 138, 145,
  146, 147
  creating cyborgs in 134
  HumanMachine 138

human/machine binary 138, 147
  mind and body integration in 135–136
  mind/body binary 141–143, 145
  postfeminism in posthumanity 145–148
  self/other binary 136–138, 146
  us/them binary 136–138
Carter, C. 163
Catwoman 43, 154
Chican@ Rights 2
Civil Rights movements 2
Civil Rights Act of 1964, Title VII 2
Clinton, Hillary 11–12, 82
Cocca, C. 157
cogito 114, 129, 148
cognisphere 15, 17, 112–113, 114
  Caprica 134, 135–136, 138, 145, 146, 147
  Dark Matter 121, 122, 125–126, 128
  Deus Ex 140, 145, 147
The Coldest City 95
contraception 2
controlling images of black
  womanhood 100
Corliss, J. 6
critical/cultural approaches 9, 164
critical race theory 10, 154
Cruel Intentions 98
Cullors, Patrisse 161
cyborgian/cyborgs 15, 16–17, 111–112, 114,
  120, 128, 140, 147
  See also *Bionic Woman*; *Dark Matter*

D

dangerous dames 43, 91–92, 154, 158
  and hegemonic masculinity 156
  overlapping themes in representations
  of 155–156
    embodiment 158–159
    gendered scripts 156–157
    multiculturalism 158
    sexuality 157–158
Dark Matter 112, 120–122, 129
  cognisphere 121, 122, 125–126, 128
  human/machine binary 126–127

hybridization 128
  mind/body binary 122–126, 128
  postfeminism in 129
Davids, Sharice 160
Davisson, A. L. 164
Delacroix, Eugène 76
Dench, Judi 25
depoliticization 3, 62, 98, 148, 158, 163
Descartes, René 129
Deus Ex 133, 139
  cognisphere 140, 145, 147
  contextualization of 139–140
  cyborgs multiplication 140–141
  franchise 139, 141–144
  human/machine binary 144–145, 147
  mind/body binary 142
  political landscape in 140
  postfeminism in posthumanity 145–148
  us/them binary 143–144
Divergent 43, 154
Dockterman, E. 153
Douglas, S. J. 38, 39
Dow, B. J. 59, 60

E

Earhart, Amelia 2
Eastwood, Clint 29, 39
ecofeminism 2, 10
Elektra 43, 154
embedded feminism 38
enlightened sexism 38
Enloe, C. 84
environmentalism 2
Equal Pay Act of 1963 2

F

The Fall 139, 141, 143
Farmworker's Movement 2
Farrimond, K. 98
Fast and Furious 6 43
female body, fetishizing of. See fetishization

feminisms 5, 11–12, 25, 161
  embedded feminism 38
  patriarchal appropriation of
    feminism 61–62
  and postfeminism 162
  resistance to commodification
    of 159–160
  second-wave feminisms 2, 10, 25, 162
  third-wave feminism 61, 162
femininity 5, 12, 24–25, 27, 37, 44, 47–49,
    56, 61, 68–70, 74, 77–78, 87, 89–106,
    114, 157, 161, 162
feminized masculinity 36, 48, 104
Femme Fatale 98
femme fatales 16, 27, 47, 90, 92–96, 98–
    100, 103, 104, 156, 157
fetishization 16, 90, 92, 96–99, 103, 105,
    125, 157
Food and Drug Administration 2
Foxy Brown 96, 154

G

Gadot, Gal 72–73
Gamasutra 140, 144
Garza, Alicia 161
gendered scripts 45, 48, 56, 62, 90, 92,
    156–157, 159
gendered stereotypes 5, 12, 34, 37, 48, 56–
    58, 61, 68, 78, 81, 90, 99, 103, 156
gender performativity 24, 90, 92–94,
    99, 154
gender transgressions 23–25, 90–92, 97, 99,
    102–104
Gentlemen Prefer Blondes 95
Ghost in the Shell 89
Gibson, K. L. 39
Gill, R. 165
Gilpatric, K. 30, 37, 156
Ginsburg, Ruth Bader 3
girl power 61–62, 136, 137
Grand Theft Auto 139
Greaghty, L. 63
Griffin, S. 158

Guardians of the Galaxy 43
Guardians of the Galaxy 2 89

H

Haaland, Deb 160
Halo 139
Hamilton, Linda 25
Haraway, D. 112
Hayles, N. K. 112, 113
hegemonic masculinity 10, 32, 33, 35, 37,
    61, 94, 121, 156
Henson, Tarji P. 89–90, 96, 102
Her 43
heteronormativity 1, 16, 156
    The Bionic Woman 127
    The Hunger Games 49, 56, 58–59, 60, 61
    Kill Bill films 34, 35
    Wonder Woman 69, 77, 78–79, 81
Heyse, A. L. 39
Hill Collins, P. 105
Hollywood 2–3, 67–68, 71–73, 81, 89–90,
    95, 101–102
hooks, bell 10, 105, 162
Huerta, Dolores 3
Huffman, T. 163
human/machine binary
    The Bionic Woman 115, 117, 119–120
    Caprica 138, 147
    Dark Matter 126–127
    Deus Ex 144–145, 147
The Hunger Games films 33, 43, 44, 45, 54,
    59, 100, 122, 154, 156, 164
    and hypercivilization 53–56
        exerting control through militant
            technology 53–54
        visual imagery and excess 54–56
    Katniss
        connections with fire 51–52
        metamorphosis into a mockingjay
            rising 50–51
        and the natural world 49–53
        as a postfeminist hero 46–49

uncivilized and untrainable
    nature 52–53
Mockingjay Part 2 58
naturalization of power structures 56–61
    biological determinism 60–61
    heteronormativity 58–59
    reaffirming traditional gender
        roles 56–58
patriarchal appropriation of
    feminism 61–62
patriarchal ideologies 49
and postfeminism 45–49
hypermasculinity 2, 16, 36, 156
    See also *Kill Bill* films
hypersexualization 75, 116, 162
hyperreality 7, 31–32, 36

I

images 6–7, 15, 29, 31, 35–36, 51, 54–56,
    71, 74, 76, 92, 94–97, 100, 103–104
Invisible War 139
Isley Brothers 31

J

Jameson, F. 15
Jenkins, Patty 3, 67, 73
Jolie, Angelina 25

K

Kagan, Elena 3
Kill Bill films 24, 94, 100, 117, 154
    excess and spectacle in 29
    femaleness of violence in 25
    heteronormativity 34, 35
    hyperreality 31–32, 36
    modern patriarchal ideologies 32–36
    multiculturalism 30
    New York Times report on 28

patriarchal ideologies 37–38
postmodern aesthetics in 25
postmodernism in 28–32, 30
superficial postfeminist ideals 25–28
visual elements in 25
King, C. R. 105
Knowles-Carter, Beyoncé Giselle 162
Kong: Skull Island 89
Kurzweil, R. 148

L

Lee, Bruce 29, 129
Leitch, David 91
Lepore, J. 68
Liberty Leading the People 76
lone warriors, female-bodied action
  heroes as 157

M

machines 114
  See also human/machine binary
Mad Max: Fury Road 154
Maleficent 43
male gaze 14, 16, 69, 73–75, 82, 90, 92, 93,
  98, 100, 124, 157
Mallozzi, J. 121
Marston, William Moulton 70, 71,
  72, 78, 83
masculinist protection 80
masculinity 1–2, 4, 10, 16, 27, 32–37,
  43, 46, 48–49, 56, 59, 61, 69, 72, 73,
  78–82, 82, 94–95, 99–105, 114, 121,
  125, 142, 156–157
Mass Effect 139
Mayer, Marissa 159, 165
McGee, M. C. 8
#MeToo movement 10, 14, 161
mind/body binary 157
  The Bionic Woman 114, 115, 117,
    128, 142

Caprica 141–143, 145
Dark Matter 122–126, 128
Deus Ex 142
Monroe, Marilyn 95
Moore, Demi 25
Moore, R. D. 134
Mr. and Mrs. Smith 154
Mullie, P. 121
multiculturalism 25, 30, 81, 158, 163
Mulvey, L. 73, 97

N

necropolitics 53, 54, 56, 114, 154
Nelson, Christopher 29
neoliberalism 5, 10, 155, 158
Newsom, V. A. 137
Nicholson, L. 17

O

Ocasio-Cortez, Alexandria 161
O'Connor, Sandra Day 3
O'Grady, L. 99
Omar, Ilhan 160
Orenich, Mike 144
Ott, B. L. 10
Owen, A. S. 23, 38, 92, 155, 163

P

Parillaud, Anne 25
Parks, Rosa 2
Peterson, Jordan B. 4
Petty, Lori 25
philosophical posthumanism 113–114
political economy 8, 9, 38, 39
Pollan, M. 6
postfeminism 3, 5, 8, 12, 27–28, 30, 32,
  153, 159, 163
  and feminism *see* feminism

in posthumanity 145–148
and postmodernism 25
postfeminist masculinity 59
postfeminist media 5, 13, 15, 17, 38, 45,
    46, 68, 90, 92, 102, 104, 111, 116, 134,
    148, 156, 157, 158
postfeminist representations 5, 13, 37, 38,
    62, 140, 153, 161
posthumanism 9, 10, 111, 113–114, 115,
    119, 121, 127, 129, 145–148, 154
    See also Caprica; Deus Ex
postracialism 30, 36, 158
Presley, Elvis 31
Pretty Persuasion 98
Proud Mary 27, 33, 89, 156
    controlling images of black womanhood
        in 99–102
    dangerous dames in 91–92
    femme fatale in 90, 92–96, 98–100,
        103, 104
    fetishization 90, 92, 96–99, 103, 105
    gender performativity in 92–94
    gender transgressions in 91–92, 97, 99,
        102–104, 102–104
    violent femmes in 102–104
    and women action heroes framing 96–97
Pulp Fiction 38

Q

queer 78, 98–99, 127–128

R

race 3, 9, 10, 15, 16, 27, 63, 67, 82, 89, 92,
    101–106, 135, 144, 154, 159, 162
Red Sparrow 89
representation 6–7, 10, 13–14, 15, 30–31,
    37–38, 45, 62, 89–90, 92, 97, 103, 104,
    111, 139, 140, 153, 154, 155, 158,
    159–161, 163, 164
Republican Motherhood 77–78

Reservoir Dogs 38
Roe v. Wade 2, 68
Rogue One: A Star Wars Story 154
role-playing games (RPGs) 139
    See also Deus Ex
Roth, B. 17
Rotten Tomatoes 72
Ryle, G. 148

S

Salt 43, 154
Saturday Night Fever 31
Saunders, C. C. 99, 106
second-wave feminisms 2, 10, 25, 162
self/other binary 17
    Caprica 136–138, 146
sexual agency 14, 100, 155, 157–158, 165
sexual assault 2, 10, 14
sexual harassment 2, 4, 10, 14, 160
sexuality 9, 16, 24, 72, 89, 90, 95, 98–100,
    102–105, 120, 124, 128, 154, 157–158,
    159, 162
sexualization 16, 27, 73–75, 90–91, 93, 97,
    99, 103–106, 125, 157, 161, 162
She: A History of Adventure 83
Simpson, A. 105
simulacra 7, 104
Sinema, Kristen 161
The Singularity 148
SlutWalks 161
social death 106
social justice 9, 158, 160, 163–164
Sotomayor, Sonia 3
spaghetti westerns 29, 39
Sperling, N. 67
Star Wars: The Last Jedi 89
Steele, V. 105
Stein, S. R. 23, 38, 155
Stuller, J. K. 94
superheroes 37, 67–69, 72, 74, 77–78,
    81–82, 89–90, 94–96
superwoman 94

T

Take Back the Night marches 161
Tarantino, Quentin 24, 28–29, 32, 36, 38, 39
Tasker, Y. 33
The Terminator 25, 72
Terminator 2: Judgment Day 33, 72, 154
Theron, Charlize 90, 95–96, 99
third-wave feminism 61, 162
Thornham, S. 92, 158
Thor: Ragnarok 89
Tierney, S. M. 36
Tlaib, Rashida 160
tokenism 158, 160, 163
Tomb Raider 89
Tometi, Opal 161
transhumanism 17, 113, 121, 133, 140, 142, 144, 146, 147
Trump, Donald 14, 161
Turner, Ike 106
Turner, Tina 95, 105, 106

U

Underworld: Awakening 33, 43
Underworld: Evolution 43
Underworld: Rise of the Lycans 43
us/them binary 17
    Caprica 136–138
    Deus Ex 143–144

V

Valerian and the City of a Thousand Planets 89

Vande Berg, L. R. 23, 38, 155
Vinge, V. 148

W

Wanted 154
Watercutter, A. 73, 74
Whalen, T. 113
whiteness 10, 36, 68–70, 80, 89, 95, 101–102, 154, 158
Wild Things 98
Wilhelm, H. 4
Winfrey, Oprah 3
womenandchildren 80, 81, 84
women's agency 9, 162
Women's Liberation 2
Wonder Woman 3, 67–69, 89, 102, 117, 154
    camera gaze 73
    and empowerment 91
    and feminism 71–75
    as historical (white) feminine/ist icon 69–71
    No Man's Land scene 75–81
        heteronormativity 77, 78–79
        Republican Motherhood 77–78
        saving womenandchildren 80–81
    resisting the male gaze 73–75

X

Xena: Warrior Princess 33

Y

Young, I. M. 80, 147

CULTURAL MEDIA STUDIES

Leandra H. Hernández and Amanda R. Martinez
Series Editors

In the past few years, our political, cultural, and media landscapes have cultivated a sharp, notable rise of media activism, more representations of diverse groups and characters, and the need for intersectional approaches to media studies. The #MeToo campaign, the 2017 and 2018 Women's Marches, Black Lives Matter marches, cross-border anti-feminicide activist marches, immigration marches, and increased representation of diverse sexual identities, racial/ethnic groups, and gender identities are evidence of the need for continued research on cultural media studies topics.

The Peter Lang Cultural Media Studies book series is accepting book proposals for both proposed book and fully developed manuscripts on a rolling basis for media studies books that explore media production, media consumption, media effects, and media representations of feminism(s), race/ethnicity, gender, sexuality, and related topics.

For additional information about this series or for the submission of manuscripts, please contact:

Peter Lang Publishing
Acquisitions Department
29 Broadway, 18th floor
New York, NY 10006

To order other books in this series, please contact our Customer Service Department:

peterlang@presswarehouse.com (within the U.S.)
order@peterlang.com (outside the U.S.)

Or browse online by series:

www.peterlang.com